teach®
yourself

humanism

D0533278

humanism
mark vernon

Launched in 1938, the **teach yourself** series
grew rapidly in response to the world's wartime
needs. Loved and trusted by over 50 million
readers, the series has continued to respond to
society's changing interests and passions and
now, 70 years on, includes over 500 titles,
from Arabic and Beekeeping to Yoga and Zulu.
What would you like to learn?

be where you want to be with **teach yourself**

For UK order enquiries: please contact Bookpoint Ltd, 130 Milton Park, Abingdon, Oxon OX14 4SB. Telephone: +44 (0) 1235 827720. Fax: +44 (0) 1235 400454. Lines are open 09.00–17.00, Monday to Saturday, with a 24-hour message answering service. Details about our titles and how to order are available at www.teachyourself.co.uk

For USA order enquiries: please contact McGraw-Hill Customer Services, PO Box 545, Blacklick, OH 43004-0545, USA. Telephone: 1-800-722-4726. Fax: 1-614-755-5645.

For Canada order enquiries: please contact McGraw-Hill Ryerson Ltd, 300 Water St, Whitby, Ontario L1N 9B6, Canada. Telephone: 905 430 5000. Fax: 905 430 5020.

Long renowned as the authoritative source for self-guided learning – with more than 50 million copies sold worldwide – the **teach yourself** series includes over 500 titles in the fields of languages, crafts, hobbies, business, computing and education.

British Library Cataloguing in Publication Data: a catalogue record for this title is available from the British Library.

Library of Congress Catalog Card Number: on file.

First published in UK 2008 by Hodder Education, part of Hachette Livre UK, 338 Euston Road, London, NW1 3BH.

First published in US 2008 by The McGraw-Hill Companies, Inc.

This edition published 2008.

The **teach yourself** name is a registered trade mark of Hodder Headline.

Copyright © 2008 Mark Vernon

Typeset by Transet Limited, Coventry, England.
Printed in Great Britain for Hodder Education, an Hachette Livre UK Company, 338 Euston Road, London NW1 3BH, by CPI Cox & Wyman, Reading, Berkshire RG1 8EX.

The publisher has used its best endeavours to ensure that the URLs for external websites referred to in this book are correct and active at the time of going to press. However, the publisher and the author have no responsibility for the websites and can make no guarantee that a site will remain live or that the content will remain relevant, decent or appropriate.

Hachette Livre UK's policy is to use papers that are natural, renewable and recyclable products and made from wood grown in sustainable forests. The logging and manufacturing processes are expected to conform to the environmental regulations of the country of origin.

Impression number   10 9 8 7 6 5 4 3 2 1
Year   2012 2011 2010 2009 2008

contents

acknowledgements		viii
foreword		ix
introduction: what is humanism?		xi
	some orientating principles	xii
	origins of the word	xv
	some indications of diversity	xviii
	a personal confession	xxii
	why humanism matters today	xxii
01	**classical antecedents**	**1**
	Prometheus unbound	2
	Milesian disputes	4
	man is the measure	7
	the Socratic revolution	9
	Aristotle and others	12
	going with the flow	16
	summary	18
02	**Renaissance humanism**	**19**
	the idea of the Renaissance	20
	antecedents of Renaissance philosophy	22
	origins of Renaissance philosophy	25
	anthropocentrism – a new philosophy	27
	language and education	34
	reading the 'book of nature'	37
	art and humanism	41
	the dignity of man	42
	the reformed mind	45
	Renaissance scepticism	50

the end of the Renaissance   52

summary   52

03   **Enlightenment humanism**   **54**

light dispelling darkness   55

deism and progress   59

human nature   62

empiricism examined   64

the ethics of sympathy   67

Godless morality   70

dare to know!   72

reason and responsibility   75

revolution   79

religion of humanity   81

summary   84

04   **contemporary humanisms 1: Marxism, utilitarianism and pragmatism**   **85**

Marxism   86

socialist humanism   90

the origins of utilitarianism   92

happiness and humanism   94

critics of utilitarianism   96

pragmatism   98

problems with 'what works'   101

pragmatism as a humanism   102

summary   104

05   **contemporary humanisms 2: existentialists and 'anti-humanists'**   **107**

radical freedom   108

problems with existential humanism   112

'anti-humanist' philosophy   115

Friedrich Nietzsche   115

the death of God   118

Michel Foucault   119

power-knowledge   120

summary   122

06	contemporary humanisms 3: Darwin, organized humanism and Christians	124
	the Darwinian revolution	125
	creationism and intelligent design	128
	evolution as a theory	129
	Darwinism and purpose	131
	organized humanism	135
	scientific humanism	141
	a new humanism?	145
	Christian humanism	146
	summary	149
07	ten pressing issues	151
	1 humanism after Auschwitz	152
	2 faith schools and religious education	156
	3 climate change	161
	4 good without God?	164
	5 gay rights and identity politics	169
	6 blasphemy	172
	7 progress	174
	8 mind-body problem	177
	9 namings, weddings and funerals	179
	10 mystery and wonderment	183
08	humanism as a way of life	187
	humanism in crisis?	188
	secular strength	190
	the search for meaning	192
	an old question revisited	194
glossary		199
taking it further		202
	further reading	202
	websites	206
index		208

acknowledgements

Mark Vernon would like to thank Mel Thompson, Lars Svendsen and Phil Star who kindly offered comments on all or parts of the manuscript, and Lisa Grey and others involved in the book's production at Hodder Education.

foreword

In the best tradition of the *Teach Yourself* series, this book assumes an open-mindedness and common sense in its readers, plus the willingness to engage with a few knotty concepts – which are presented in the clearest of terms. In fact, I have seldom read a clearer or fuller account of a complex subject in so short a space. And it's particularly welcome, too, because like many who find themselves called humanists, I remain unsure about what other people mean when they use the term.

Personally, I mean many things by it, and Mark Vernon's account of the history and the development of a humanistic view of the world, and his examination of the implications of such a view, is not only informative (I learned a lot from it) but also fair and balanced. A good test of fairness and balance comes, it seems to me, in the way any account of humanism deals with the persistence of religion in our world. I'm entirely with the author when he says that we should not distort or misrepresent what religion does in order to suit our convenience. One of Mark Vernon's 'Questions for atheistic humanists' is this:

'In your arguments against religion do you examine the best in religion? After all, you look to the best in humanity in your humanism and engage the most sophisticated sources when asking scientific and philosophical questions.'

Opponents of the humanist view – for the matter of that, diehard haters of religion – will not find any comfort in that advice. But it seems to me that there is little point in arguing with diehards in private: zealots are unmoveable by argument. The place to do that is in public, in an open forum, with an open-minded audience. This book is that sort of open forum, and like all books it offers most to a democratic reading – to the sort of questioning, considering, to-and-fro of mind to mind that characterises freedom of thought, and which is one of the great triumphs of the humanist spirit.

This is a time when supernaturalism, far from withering away under the bright light of scientific inquiry as some hopeful thinkers predicted, is resurgent and even, in some places, triumphant. It's also a time when the very survival of civilized life is under threat: our planet will not put up with abuse for much longer. We need a strong reminder that the best and most trustworthy measure of what human beings need is humanity itself, and that the work of the great humanist thinkers is the best place to discover the full reach of what that means. This book is an excellent and timely introduction to a subject that is more important now than it has ever been.

Philip Pullman, 2008

introduction: what is humanism?

What is humanism? At one level, it is possible to come up with a relatively straightforward definition. It is a movement that arose first with the thinkers of the Italian Renaissance in the fourteenth century. They looked at what it was to be human with fresh eyes and learned to value the human capacities for art, reason and science. To put it another way, they were anthropocentric, that is they had a tendency to focus on human beings as the most important feature of the universe. This was a theme that then developed over the subsequent centuries – in particular through the intellectual upheavals of the Reformation and the Enlightenment, two major episodes in human history that we will explore later.

Today, humanism can be said to be characteristic of any view that gives primacy to humans, and it is often used to contrast with a view that gives primacy to something else, such as God or the natural world or a political ideology. In the UK, the British Humanist Association (BHA) – one of the leading societies championing humanist causes – aligns being a humanist with being non-religious and so puts the number of humanists at between 15 to 30 per cent of the population. It is probably fair to say that more people live according to broadly humanist principles, especially if you don't link being a humanist with being non-religious, as in fact many don't. And as Claire Rayner, the BHA's vice-president puts it: 'I was a humanist without knowing it for many years.'

Now, you might look at this definition and come to the conclusion that there is a sense in which everyone is a humanist. After all, everyone is human. All people have a vested interest in the welfare of themselves and their fellow humans; all have cause to rejoice in human achievements.

Conversely, someone who did not celebrate the worth and dignity of human beings would, we might say, seem inhuman.

But humanism as a tradition of thought is a far more subtle and interesting notion than might first meet the eye. For as well as being an historical movement, it is a cluster of shifting and often conflicting ideas; it is a conversation and sometimes an argument between individuals about nothing less than how we should live.

So at another level, humanism could be defined by its diversity, a diversity born of the different ways in which humanists value the human, and the different ways in which they object to other systems of thought, be they religious, political or cultural. This spread of views partly explains why many dictionaries and encyclopedias of philosophy have no entry for humanism at all – or just a short one. Instead, they point you to a variety of entries that deal with the Renaissance, the Enlightenment, liberty, scientific discovery or atheism. Similarly, you will not find a reference to modern humanism in Bertrand Russell's *History of Western Philosophy*, though he would now be regarded as a leading humanist. In a sense, his whole *History* is about humanism.

So humanism is a rich subject but it can also seem elusive, which can make the study of it quite daunting. Just when you think you have a handle on it, you discover someone else claiming to be a humanist, and advocating a very different point of view.

However, its breadth is, in fact, a strength. After all, we are talking about what it is to be human. Why is that valuable? What should we make of our powers of discovery and reason? How do we understand our limitations and negotiate conflicting interests? Any simplistic answers to these questions will, in fact, be dehumanizing.

This book aims to introduce that diversity of opinion, to chart a path through that variety of thought, and to explore the practical ramifications of what it means to be a humanist.

Some orientating principles

Today, what counts as true humanism is contested, sometimes in acerbic language and with little goodwill – just as believers can argue about what it is to be Christian or politicians can argue about what it is to be a democrat. Within contemporary humanism, the divide is felt particularly over attitudes towards religion. It is not just that some humanists assert that atheism should be the defining characteristic of humanism. Many prominent voices argue that the scientific method is the only grounds for sure knowledge, or that a modern society should be one in which religion plays no part, say, in politics or education. Other humanists are pushing for widespread non-religious alternatives to ceremonies in life, such as funerals.

These are important issues to consider and we shall return to them several times during our exploration. Nevertheless, it is important to keep an eye on the bigger picture; that is the defining characteristic of the humanist tradition. We have already suggested a minimal definition of humanism: valuing what it is to be human. It is also clear that such a definition alone does not provide much of a grip on the subject. So is it possible to identify some orientating principles to be found within humanism that develop its nature and scope?

According to the *Oxford English Dictionary*, the philosophical meaning of humanism is:

> A belief or outlook emphasizing common human needs and seeking solely rational ways of solving human problems, and concerned with humankind as responsible and progressive intellectual beings.

This is a better starter for ten. It has introduced some new ideas – an emphasis on the value of rationality, a belief in human responsibility and that humankind can make progress. It can be expanded further to clarify distinctly humanist attitudes towards various areas of understanding. According to the philosopher Nicola Abbagnano, there are five areas which are particularly important to modern humanists, as he describes in an essay on humanism in the Macmillan *Encyclopedia of Philosophy*.

1 **Freedom** Humanists understand that there is always a risk that secular and religious institutions, such as governments and churches, can hold people captive when they should be promoting individual freedom. Thus, they consider human autonomy – that is the ability to determine your own actions and principles – to be of supreme value. Autonomy might manifest as freedom of choice or freedom from oppression. It might be thought to be guaranteed by God or right. There might still be a big debate among humanists about what it means to be free. But it is agreed that it is in freedom that human beings best flourish.

2 **Nature** Humanists believe that human beings are part of the natural world, and are something very special within the natural world. We are humans but also animals, and so our bodies, needs and senses should not be sidelined but are central. That contrasts with some views that have exclusively identified the most important thing about humans as being located, say, in our rational capacities or, for religious believers, in the possession of a soul. Such a view might suggest that human beings belong not so much in the natural world, as, say to the world of ideas or in heaven. But while not belittling reason, or the conviction that the human person is of supreme importance, the humanist conviction is that the natural realm is the one in which people are best understood.

3 **Personhood and history** We've said that humanists attach great importance to human personhood. This is a direct consequence of the Renaissance interest in history and the value that Renaissance humanists put on a scientific approach to history, by which they meant the goal of telling the truth as it happened and not, say, via the medium of myths or divine revelation. This led to a great scholarly effort to recover the details of particular times, people and events. That attitude, in turn, was a precursor to the modern idea of autonomous, rational personhood.

4 **Religion** All humanists have a questioning attitude towards religious traditions and authorities, even if they are believers. This leads some to reject religion outright. It leads others to seek to reform religious beliefs and institutions. Again, it was the Renaissance humanists who first identified the most important concerns. For example, they thought that the relationship between religion and civic life should be one in which religion supports political and secular goals, not the other way around. They also argued that there is a supreme need for religious tolerance to avoid wars and conflict.

5 **Science** Humanists value the advances made by modern science. This can be traced back to the Renaissance, too. It is then that mathematics was revived and came to be thought of as the language in which the natural world could be best described. It was also at that time that people thought to interrogate nature by repeatedly performing experiments. However, humanists differ on what they think is the legitimate scope of science, that is what limits there might be on the questions it can and cannot ask and answer – as well as the extent to which it can inform other kinds of knowledge, like ethics and philosophy.

Origins of the word

So we have identified some of the key issues around which humanism revolves – its close relationship with ideas of freedom, the natural world, human personhood, the critique of institutions like churches, and scientific progress. Further progress can be made on just what humanism is by considering the origins of the word.

Scholars believe that the word 'humanist' is derived from Italian slang. The first people to carry the label of humanist – or *umanista* – were fifteenth-century teachers in the schools and universities of Renaissance Italy. Their pupils called them *'umanista'* in the same way that students today might refer to their tutors as 'boffins' or 'dons'. These professors taught the *studia humanitatis* – or humanities, the collection of subjects that includes literature, philosophy and the arts. *Studia humanitatis* is a phrase that can in turn be traced back to the mid-fourteenth century. *Humanismus* is another related word. It was used to distinguish a curriculum based on classical Greek and Latin texts from one that focused on mathematics and science. So the students would have annoyed their teachers with the nickname they gave them: the slang *umanista* would have sounded distinctly coarse and unclassical!

However, all these references to humanism carried none of the specific associations that the word does today. The first appearance of 'humanism' in the modern sense, in print at least, was probably in 1808 when the German scholar Friedrich Immanuel Niethammer published *The Quarrel of Philanthropism and Humanism in the Theory of Educational Instruction of Our Time*. *Humanismus* was subsequently adopted and redefined by nineteenth-century historians to describe key aspects of the Renaissance. For example, in 1859 George Voigt published *The Revival of Classical Antiquity or The First Century of Humanism*, stressing the importance of the rediscovery of Ancient Greek and Roman texts to the fifteenth-century Italians.

By the twentieth century humanism had come to carry the explicitly contemporary associations of giving primacy to the human person in contrast with views that give primacy to something else. The history and implications of that change will be discussed later, not least in relation to the many meanings that have been attached to it throughout the course of the last century or so. Again, the diversities are important to remember when considering what is meant by modern humanism.

Pre-history and history at a glance

Another orientating perspective on what humanism is might be gained by surveying a few dates that are particularly important for humanists. They begin in the centuries long before the Renaissance, with the Ancient Greeks whom the Renaissance rediscovered. They then move through the Renaissance period, the Enlightenment period of the eighteenth century, and up to the modern day and the emergence of what might be called organized humanism, in the shape of humanist associations and societies.

6th century BCE – Alongside mythical explanations of the world, the Milesian philosophers Thales, Anaximander and Anaximenes first develop naturalistic understandings of things, that is an early science-like comprehension of the cosmos.

5th century BCE – The Sophist Protagoras writes: 'Of all things man is the measure.' Thucydides writes his *History of the Peloponnesian War*, the first political and moral analysis of a nation that is recognizably what we would call history.

399 BCE – The death of Socrates, having been charged with profaning the Athenian gods.

4th century BCE – The great Athenian philosophy schools – those of Plato, Aristotle, the Epicureans and the Stoics – thrive.

43 BCE – Cicero, a figure celebrated perhaps more than any other in Renaissance humanism, dies.

17 CE – Livy, whose *History of Rome* became a classic in his own lifetime, and was revived in the Renaissance, dies.

120 CE – Tacitus dies, the great Roman historian and Latin stylist who also became important to the first humanists.

1304 CE – Birth of Francis Petrarch, now widely recognized as the father of Renaissance humanism.

15th century – Teachers are called *umanisti* in Italy.

Late 15th century – Italic is invented as a humanist script and used in the printing presses of Aldo Manuzio.

1509 – In one week, Desiderius Erasmus writes *Praise of Folly,* his jibe against theologians and the Church.

1513 – Niccolo Machiavelli writes *The Prince*, his book on the thoroughly worldly nature of politics. It was published posthumously.

1572 – Michel de Montaigne retires from public life and begins writing his *Essays*, in part a re-evaluation of humanist motifs.

1616 – William Shakespeare dies – arguably the last great figure of the Renaissance.

1751 – Diderot and d'Alembert, as model 'freethinkers', begin publication of their *Encyclopédie* of human knowledge, widely regarded as a monument to the Enlightenment.

1770 – Baron d'Holbach publishes *The System of Nature*, arguably the first avowedly atheistic work.

1776 – The philosopher David Hume dies a model pagan death, at least according to his friend, the economist Adam Smith.

1784 – Kant publishes his article 'What Is Enlightenment?', and answers: 'Man's emergence from his self-imposed infancy.'

1808 – Probable first use of the word 'humanism' with contemporary associations in print.

1832 – Goethe dies – arguably the last 'Renaissance man', meant in the colloquial sense of a master of many things.

19th century – German historians invent the label 'Renaissance humanism' to describe that period of history.

1844 – Karl Marx works on his *Economic and Philosophical Manuscripts* in which he describes one of the first explicitly modern philosophies of humanism.

1869 – T. H. Huxley, a friend and defender of Charles Darwin, coins the neologism 'agnosticism'.

1902 – F. C. S. Schiller publishes *Humanism*, articulating an approach based upon pragmatism.

Early 20th century – The New Humanism movement in literary criticism emerges. The philosopher and writer Bertrand Russell popularizes what would come to be regarded as many distinctly humanist views.

1933 – Humanist Manifesto I signatories commit themselves to making what they called 'religious humanism' better understood, meaning an understanding of religion that promotes human worth.

1945 – Death of the theologian Dietrich Bonhoeffer at the hand of the Nazis, a key figure in Christian humanism.

1946 – The philosopher Jean-Paul Sartre gives a famous lecture entitled *Existentialism is a Humanism*.

1947 – The philosopher Martin Heidegger publishes his *Letter on Humanism*, a key critique of modern humanism.

1952 – International Humanist and Ethical Union (IHEU) founded, an umbrella organization for humanist associations and societies.

1960s – The 'Happy Human' logo of international humanism is first adopted by the British Humanist Association.

1973 – Humanist Manifesto II signed, responding to Nazism and now rejecting religion.

2002 – The fiftieth anniversary of the World Humanist Congress updates the Amsterdam Declaration, the document upon which the IHEU was founded in 1952.

Some indications of diversity

The humanist interests in freedom, nature, history, religion and science provide some fixed points around which humanist thought orbits. Its history offers another reference point. Now let us turn to the matter of its diversity and begin to develop a kind of conceptual map on which can be placed some of the elements over which humanists differ.

Historical diversity

The first way in which to be alert to diversity in humanism relates to one we have already flagged up, namely its development since the Renaissance. For although it makes sense to see the origins of modern humanism in Renaissance humanism, it is also important to be clear about how substantial differences have emerged.

For example, humanists up to the end of the nineteenth century would have seen humanism as nothing if not an educational programme founded upon the classical authors and concentrating on the study of grammar, rhetoric, history, poetry and moral philosophy.

This changed in the twentieth century. Certain aspects of humanism, such as human uniqueness, the scientific method, reason and autonomy were explored in relation to the philosophical systems that emerged in the twentieth century, notably existentialism, pragmatism and Marxism.

This led to the development, and in certain areas, eclipse of the beliefs of earlier humanists. For example, a greater emphasis on scientific method in the twentieth century, coupled to a firm belief in the intellectual progress that science can bring about, tended to reduce the emphasis that earlier humanists would have placed upon studying classical authors. Thus, today, it is perfectly reasonable to call yourself a humanist without ever having read a word of Cicero, something that would have seemed absurd to humanists up to and including the Victorian period.

Contemporary diversity

If humanism has diversified since the Renaissance, then modern humanism has itself diversified in a number of ways. For example, different contemporary humanist philosophical systems may stress different questions or claims. One approach may major on ontological issues, i.e. the question of what it is to be human; another on epistemological issues, i.e. how as human beings we can claim to know things. Another again, on educational issues, namely a broad conviction that human flourishing is best achieved by an education that values scholarship and criticism.

Then there are varieties of modern humanism that can highlight either ethical or political concerns. An ethical approach could stress perhaps that individual autonomy is key for human flourishing. A different political approach could stress that the social setting within which human beings find themselves substantially determines their character and powers.

There are also the humanists who believe that metaphysical questions are the determining issue, in particular relating to the role of religion. They say that to be a humanist is explicitly not to believe in God, or at least to be agnostic.

Diversity of 'schools'

Another way of getting to grips with the diversity within modern humanism is by labels. It is the method we will use most often in this book. Labels have their limits, of course. They can artificially force ideas into separate boxes. However, aside from clarity, the labels we shall use can be justified to the extent that they link different kinds of humanism to specific philosophical or theological ideas. Again, different 'humanisms' are not necessarily contradictory or mutually exclusive. And they all put human persons centre stage. However, in approach and details, different schools of humanism may disagree sharply, and in highlighting this, labels are also useful.

As a taster here are thumbnail sketches of five varieties of contemporary humanism:

1 Marxist humanism

Unsurprisingly, this is humanism that draws on the writings of Karl Marx. Marx himself used the word humanism mostly in his earlier work, notably the *Economic and Philosophical Manuscripts of 1844*. He associates communism with what he calls 'theoretical humanism', defined as out-growing belief in God, and with what he calls 'practical humanism', defined as out-growing the need for private property. The reason he believed we must outgrow religion and private property is that they cause division between human beings, so it is only with their suppression that what he calls 'positive humanism' can come into being. This might roughly be summed up as universal fellow-feeling.

2 Pragmatic humanism

This is the humanism that is associated with philosophical pragmatism, which can be defined in a nutshell as 'what works'. Pragmatists such as C. S. Peirce and William James argued that human reason can never achieve a total understand of things, so they opted instead for a *sufficient* understanding of things, which is often best gained by practical rather than theoretical means. F. C. S. Schiller, another pragmatist, published a collection of essays under the title of *Humanism*. He linked his pragmatism to the ancient aphorism of Protagoras who uttered: 'Man is the measure of all things.'

3 Existential humanism

In 1946, Jean-Paul Sartre gave a lecture entitled *Existentialism is a Humanism*. We will discuss the lecture fully later on, but for now note that existentialism affirms that our existence is the fundamental fact of what it is to be human; we are 'thrown' into being and that is what we have to cope with. This is the essence of freedom, according to Sartre, though learning how to be free is the greatest challenge to human beings because it is nothing if not frightening. Existentialism is a kind of humanism because it also believes that it is up to human beings to define who they are, take responsibility for themselves, and pursue an authentic existence. Sartre also describes the angst and despair that the humanist faces when they find themselves alone and without God.

4 Atheistic humanism

Whilst many varieties of humanism are agnostic about faith in God, and feel uneasy about religious authorities, there is a strong, even dominant, strand of contemporary humanism that explicitly identifies belief in a divinity as a block on human progress. Its most evangelical advocates would say that theology has as much intellectual respectability and empirical justification as belief in, say, tooth-fairies. Moreover, in a world facing new dangers from religious extremism, religion in all its forms must be resisted. It is this kind of humanism that tends to be organized in humanist associations and secular societies.

5 Christian humanism

Not all humanists are atheists or agnostics. Christian humanists call for a belief in God based upon reason as well as revelation. After all, if reason can make sense of nature then nature, for the believer, is itself a reflection of God. Christian humanists have different attitudes towards religious authorities. For example, the Protestant theologian and victim of the Nazi regime, Dietrich Bonhoeffer argued that Christians should be 'religionless' and worldly. Alternatively, Catholic theologians, particularly at the time of the Second Vatican Council, the great meeting of theologians in Rome in the sixties, developed an anthropocentric, secular style of theology.

To these five, for clarity let me add a sixth.

6 Renaissance humanism

As its label suggests, Renaissance humanism is today primarily of historical significance. And to recap, Renaissance humanists would not have called themselves so. Rather, though a diverse bunch, they saw themselves as students of the humanities, which in turn referred to an education based on Ancient Greek and Roman texts. Of all the humanisms it is arguably the least well defined; it was really a broad if defining cultural movement, often now simply referred to as the Renaissance. It is hard to overestimate the profound effect it had, particularly as a precursor to the Enlightenment.

A personal confession

Humanists value honesty. So in the interests of transparency I should perhaps say something briefly about where I see myself when set against these varieties of humanism. I used to be a priest, albeit a liberal sort, and whilst when I left the Church I was an atheist, I now call myself an agnostic. Moreover, my agnosticism is not of the shrug-of-the-shoulders variety. The reason I stopped being an atheist was because I sensed that the human imagination is a religious imagination, or at least it is in my case. While no longer feeling drawn by God, or a particular religious faith, I do feel drawn to the spiritual traditions that have evolved with human beings.

Also, I am conscious that both science and reason have their limits. In this, I take a lead from Socrates, who argued that the key to wisdom is not what you know, but rather understanding the limits of what you know.

And I follow T. H. Huxley, who coined the word agnostic, in thinking that there are some matters in life, notably the big matters, over which there are no final answers. Reason and science cannot decide. Indeed, they show that it can be hard even to know how to ask the right questions. People who force the issue, be that from a religious or scientific standpoint, do a disservice to humankind. What you might call an open, agnostic spirit matters – particularly in an age of extremes.

In this book we will cover all humanist positions with evenhandedness and thoroughness. Where there are differing positions I will clearly indicate when I am expressing a personal opinion and, it is, of course, up to readers to decide where they stand. That is, after all, part of what it is to be a humanist.

Why humanism matters today

Where all humanists agree is that humanism matters today. We live in a time of profound change. Nietzsche, who is often remembered for announcing the death of God, realized that his time and ours could be nothing less than turbulent. He thought it would take generations to come to terms properly with the momentous changes that have come about in the centuries since the Renaissance, notably in relation to modern science, and that is to say nothing of the specific challenges facing us today, such as climate change, global economic shifts, and the persistence of suffering and poverty.

Moreover, in those countries that are broadly secular, there is plenty of evidence that the process of secularization is not as many humanists had hoped or expected. The inexorable decline of religion, for example, has not materialized and if anything, has moved into reverse. This is, therefore, a moment of risk in human history. The things that humanists value – notably human freedom – are potentially under threat. So there is great value in humanists of all persuasions having a richer understanding of the tradition to which they belong. From such a position of confidence, they can value their differences with tolerance, engage fruitfully with all people of goodwill, and pursue the great humanist goals of flourishing and wisdom.

01

classical antecedents

In this chapter you will learn:
- about the Ancient Greek and Roman philosophers that are important in contemporary humanism
- how they caused a revolution in human thought
- why their ideas interest contemporary humanists.

We have noted that humanism properly got going, as it were, in the Renaissance period. And that what spurred those Renaissance thinkers to think differently – in this more anthropocentric way – was a rediscovery of Ancient Greek and Roman philosophers and historians. We will come to that rediscovery in the next chapter, but first, it is useful to turn to the Ancient Greeks and Romans themselves. In this chapter, then, let us retell the very earliest days of philosophy as it emerged in the West, with an eye to the themes that interested the humanists of the Renaissance and those that excite humanists to this day.

Prometheus unbound

We begin some time during the sixth century BCE, when one Thales of Miletus (*c.*585 BCE) – whom we now call the 'father of philosophy' – made a highly unusual claim: 'Water is the first principle of everything.' His thought seems strange to us now. After all water is not the first principle of everything – though if you live close to the Mediterranean, as Thales did, and depend in many respects on the sea, it was not an unwarranted observation. In the light of modern science, sub-atomic particles might be a better proposal, though even that is debatable.

But Thales is called the father of philosophy not because he was right about water but because he thought to identify a first principle of everything. He sought to *explain* the world as a way of living in it. He launched the project of philosophy, and science, which was known as natural philosophy then and until relatively recently.

Thales's approach was highly productive. He discovered how to inscribe a right-angled triangle in a circle and thereby measured the heights of the pyramids. He predicted an eclipse, showed the year has 365 days, and estimated the size of the moon. One year, he anticipated a bumper crop of olives from his understanding of the weather, invested in the olive industry, and made a fortune. He also had wit: when asked why he had no children, he said he was too fond of the darlings to have any.

Thales's philosophical entrepreneurialism, and his belief that the world could be understood – as opposed to being thought merely subject to the whims of the gods – makes him arguably the first humanist hero, too. However, it is also important to remember that he was far from being a humanist in any modern sense. For example, he believed in an enchanted world: 'All things are full of gods.' And when he performed his trick of placing a triangle in a circle it seemed to him only natural to sacrifice an ox in celebration.

This is why it is only in retrospect that the Ancient Greek and Roman philosophers can be linked to the humanist tradition, having been picked up and celebrated by the Renaissance humanists. Then, though, they inspired many of the thoughts that have become characteristic of humanism. So it makes sense to think of them as humanist antecedents.

The first philosophers (with approximate dates (BCE) of writing and a snapshot of teaching)

Thales (c.585) – who argued for a principle of everything.

Anaximander (c.550) – who wrote in prose and poetry.

Anaximenes (c.545) – who carried out experiments.

Pythagoras (c.530) – who inspired a 'religion' of mathematics.

Parmenides (c.500) – who pierced through 'seeming' to 'being'.

Heraclitus (c.500) – who sought to resolve apparent opposites.

Zeno (c.450) – who proposed logical conundrums.

Anaxagoras (c.450) – who believed in a multiverse.

Empedocles (c.445) – who proposed an evolutionary theory.

Protagoras (c.440) – who thought man the measure of things.

Democritus (c.420) – who invented the idea of the atom.

Gorgias (c.430) – who was a master of rhetoric.

Socrates (c.420) – who changed everything.

Plato (c.380) – who set the philosophical agenda ever since.

Aristotle (c.350) – who catalogued, analyzed and categorized.

Epicurus (c.300) – who taught people not to fear the gods.

Zeno of Citium (c.300) – who founded Stoicism.

Milesian disputes

So, Thales had launched philosophy. In the next generation, Anaximander of Miletus (*c.*550 BCE) wrote a book, *On Nature*. Moreover, he wrote it in prose not poetry – another innovation when it came to pondering what's what. He was an observer of human beings, noting that unlike the animals that seem quite capable of looking after themselves soon after birth, human offspring require years of care and attention. This was something of a conundrum since it could not always have been like this, otherwise the first human generation would have simply died out.

Anaximander is also striking because he disagreed with Thales. He refused to accept the teachings of his senior: elder no longer necessarily implied better. Thus, critical argument was born, the scepticism about authority that also chimes with later humanist sentiments. Moreover, Anaximander's rejection was profound. His cosmology entirely refutes the idea that there is a tangible first principle of everything, let alone that it is water. Instead, he proposed that the world is fundamentally made of the boundless and undefined – the 'Infinite', as he is sometimes translated.

Early experiment

Anaximander was followed by Anaximenes (*c.*545 BCE). At first, his investigations into nature might appear to be a step back: he proposed that the earth was flat and that it rested on air. However, he is also remembered for being an experimenter; a key element within any science. One of his experiments was to blow on your hand, first with your lips pursed, then with your mouth open. In the first instance, the air will feel cold; in the second, warm. Anaximenes drew a connection between density and temperature to explain the difference.

Having said that Anaximenes was an experimenter, his work is not fully scientific in the modern sense. He proposed no equations, made no measurements, and understood the world's physical properties as manifestations of their divine essence. So although these pre-Socratic philosophers, as they are called – all having lived before Socrates – speculated about explanations for phenomena, they knitted them tightly within the myths that also helped people to understand their world.

Maths and mysticism

After the Milesians, we reach the decades of perhaps the biggest hitters of the pre-Socratic philosophers – Pythagoras (*c.*530 BCE), Parmenides (*c.*500 BCE) and Heraclitus (*c.*500 BCE) – the individuals who made the greatest advances in thought for their times. They asked the abstract questions that, when you think them through, are utterly fascinating and often mysterious. For example, is it not amazing that creatures like ourselves can know things about the universe of which we are part, reflect upon our place in this order, and even see order within it – for at first glance it looks pretty chaotic, no more orderly than waves breaking on the sand of the beach?

Coming first to Pythagoras: the specifics of his life are mostly lost in legend. But his presumed discovery of the relationship between musical intervals and numerical ratios – that, for example, a stretched string can be made to sound an octave higher by halving its length – fed a rich mixture of mathematics and mysticism in his followers. For Pythagoreans, and indeed for anyone in the ancient world, the discovery did not suggest what it does to the modern scientist: that mathematics is a tool that can be used to tame the universe. Rather, they used maths to contemplate, to draw links between astronomy and harmony, to ponder the secrets of the heavens, to hear the music of the spheres. It was not until the end of the Renaissance, and the work of Galileo, that maths adopted its modern significance as an instrument of scientific advance. Even then, many of science's greatest, not least Newton, inherited the Pythagorean fascination with mysticism.

Gestures that reveal

After Pythagoras we can mention Heraclitus. He has had a tremendous impact on the history of philosophy, notably in the modern period through the work of two philosophers, Hegel and Heidegger. Heraclitus's work itself comes down to us in often enigmatic sayings. It seems that his aim was not so much to explain the world as to reveal it – 'neither speaking, nor concealing but gesturing', as he put it. By way of example, here are some of his thoughts:

'Everything flows and nothing stays.'

'You can't step twice into the same river.'

'A man's character is his fate.'

'The road up and the road down are one and the same.'

'The one thing that alone is truly wise is both unwilling and willing to be called by the name of Zeus.'

'The people must fight on behalf of the law as they would for the city wall.'

One way of looking at what Heraclitus was doing is to say that he had begun to think about thinking. So when he said, 'The road up and the road down are one and the same,' he might be pointing out that the same road will appear differently depending upon your point of view. Someone who is going to Oxford would say the road is taking them up to Oxford. Someone who is going to London from Oxford, would say the road is taking them down from Oxford. Put more generally, the lesson is that thought itself is relative to your perspective.

The science of being

Many philosophers today believe that the business of thinking about thinking achieved a critical moment in the life of our next pre-Socratic, namely Parmenides. Along with his disciple Zeno (c.450 BCE), he lived in the south of Italy. They can be thought of as mystics as much as philosophers, too, Parmenides being distinguished by leaving a poem that has survived in large chunks.

The poem is a riddle. It has variously been interpreted as a divine incantation or read as if it were a piece of logic. Whatever its original meaning, it introduces a distinction that has stuck, namely the difference between what Parmenides called the 'Way of Truth', that is understanding things as they are in themselves, and what he called the 'Way of Seeming', that is understanding things as they appear to us. For Parmenides, the Way of Truth is more important, and what it reveals is quite startling. Parmenides believed that all being is the same, undifferentiated and everlasting. This contrasts dramatically with the Way of Seeming – the way we see things every day – which tells us that the world is shifting, fragmented and mortal. The effort to pierce the humdrum Way of Seeming to glimpse the transcendental Way of Truth – transcendental meaning independent of direct human experience – is the goal of the science of being, or ontology. Ever since, ontology has been part of philosophy, and often one of the most difficult at that.

Paradoxical jolts

Some of Parmenides's ideas were illustrated by his disciple Zeno, famous now for his paradoxes. For example, he asked what happens when you move from A to B. First, you travel half the distance between the two points. Then you travel the next half, and so are now three-quarters of the way there. You move again and halve the distance to B once more. And so on, and so on. And yet, if you can only halve the distance you have to go each time, you will never quite reach B, your destination: there will always be another half to go. Hence even an everyday occurrence, like moving from A to B, conceals something of a paradox.

Why does this matter to humanists? Well, in fact they have been annoyed and delighted by Zeno's paradoxes in turn. Bertrand Russell loved them for inspiring new mathematical insights. Rationalists have dismissed them as ingenious but unprofitable puzzles. Another interpretation of Zeno understands them as connected to Parmenides's struggle to pierce the Way of Seeming to the Way of Truth: the paradoxes quite deliberately set up logical impasses that in their very irresolution urge the perplexed to move beyond the world of things, where the conundrums are never resolved, to the world of Being itself.

Man is the measure

Very much more could be said about these pre-Socratics, and others. However, let us move on now and consider a philosopher who came a generation later, and who no humanist would consider annoying. That man was Protagoras (c.440 BCE). Protagoras was an ambassador to Athens and seems to have been something of a devious man, though he won great favour in the hearts of the new democrats – democracy forming in his time. Not much of his teaching survives apart from two fragments. They have, however, resonated throughout the history of humanism.

One year, in the house of the playwright Euripides, Protagoras read out a treatise he had written called *On the Gods*. Its opening words were unforgettable:

> About the gods, I cannot be sure whether they exist or not, or what they are like to see; for many things stand in the way of the knowledge of them, both the opacity of the subject and the shortness of human life.

Protagoras was an agnostic. He did not know whether God existed or not, and believed it was not possible to know in principle. Having said that, he almost lost his life when he was accused of atheism – a confusion of the two stances on the question of divinity that has proved remarkably persistent. But if Protagoras expressed a form of scepticism in relation to our knowledge of the gods, he was not backward in coming forwards about the possibility of knowledge in other spheres of life, for the other saying for which he is remembered is this: 'Man is the measure of all things, of the reality of those which are, and of the unreality of those which are not.'

This is an important phrase and has been interpreted in various ways:

• It has led to Protagoras being called the father of relativism, on the assumption that what he meant was, if man is the measure of all things then there is nothing outside of man by which his measure can itself be measured: knowledge is self-reflexive, or relative.

• On the other hand, the phrase might be merely an expression of the limitations of human knowledge, again, commensurate with his belief about the unknowability of the gods. If humans only have the measurements they can make to go by, there may be all sorts of things about which we know little or nothing, simply because they are beyond our measuring.

• Then again, Protagoras might be thought to have captured the essence of another aspect of humanism, namely that the only relationship which matters to human beings is our relationship with ourselves.

Protagoras was just one of a group of philosophers together known as the sophists. Other sophists included Gorgias, Antiphon, Prodicus and Thrasymachus. The group had diverse thoughts but it is particularly remembered for providing the emerging democracy of Athens with a quasi-system of philosophical education. Interest in the sophists in relation to humanism was revived in the modern period by the philosopher Hegel. He argued that the sophists represented a contrasting tradition to the pre-Socratics such as Thales. If those pre-Socratic philosophers were primarily interested in natural philosophy, then the sophists were primarily interested in humanity itself and, in particular, how we can know things and defend our beliefs.

Having said that, the sophists have often had a bad write-up in Western philosophy because Plato thought them the inferior philosophical cousins to his hero, Socrates – the individual to whom we now turn.

The Socratic revolution

Socrates (470–399 BCE) and Plato (c.428–347 BCE) are so important to our investigation because more than any other single event, it was the rediscovery of Plato's writings, and the image of Socrates that they carried, which fired the imagination of the Renaissance humanists. As Cicero put it, Socrates 'called philosophy down from heaven to earth'. That was a crucial condition for humanism ever to get off the ground.

Possibly all of Plato's written work survives, leaving us with a body of astonishingly brilliant philosophy, up to 29 dialogues and at least one letter. Indeed, as it was famously said by the philosopher A. N. Whitehead at the beginning of the twentieth century, all subsequent philosophy has been called a footnote to Plato, since his work is so rich. Plato himself is often remembered for various doctrines, like the Theory of Forms, the idea that this world is just a reflection of a perfect world that exists elsewhere. But another part of Plato's genius was that he was also his own best critic, suggesting that philosophy for him was not ultimately about proofs or even truth – though he certainly aspired to correct knowledge – but exploration and personal change.

He must have gained this focus from Socrates, the individual under whose influence Plato fell. Socrates himself wrote nothing: 'Socrates's life,' Kierkegaard said, 'is like a magnificent pause in the course of history: we do not hear him at all; profound stillness prevails – until it is broken by the noisy attempts of the many and different schools of followers to trace their origin in this hidden and cryptic source.' So it is mostly through Plato that we know of him.

However, we can be sure about some of the details of his life. Socrates's father, Sophroniscus, was a stone mason; his mother, Phainarete, a midwife. He appears on the historical scene aged about 35 when he was noted for his military service in the Peloponnesian War. Within a few years he was well enough known as a philosopher to be the butt of the jokes of the satirist Aristophanes. He also met fierce opposition that culminated in dying for his beliefs at the hand of the state by drinking hemlock.

Though known as a philosopher martyr now – and so an inspiration for many humanists – during his life he was as well known for less earth-shattering qualities, such as being a man who didn't wear shoes and who had declined the advances of the most desirable individual in Athens, Alcibiades. However, he gathered around himself an inner circle of disciples who subsequently transmitted his teaching to the wider world. He had an unconventional attitude towards women for his time, apparently attributing his most profound insights to a priestess called Diotima. And as we've said, he did not write anything – a fact that carries great significance, if Plato is right: he worried that words on pages frequently come to be quibbled over for their own sake when they should serve a far greater purpose, namely changing lives. He saw that the letter kills while the spirit gives life.

Socrates's teaching and death

Other teachings of Socrates inspired subsequent humanists. He endorsed a version of the so-called Golden Rule – to do to others as you would have done to you, be they friend or foe. He rebuked the authorities of his day, the politicians and the poets, for confusing their clever words with real wisdom. He adopted the Delphic imperative as his mantra: 'Know yourself!' – which meant a profound intellectual and psychological examination of yourself, conducted with friends with whom it was vital to speak as honestly and generously as possible. 'The unexamined life is not worth living,' he is famously remembered for saying, because it would be one that was both deluded and failed to be transformed.

Another element of his teaching was a profound sense of uncertainty. As a result of this, Socrates became famous for rubbing people up the wrong way by questioning what they thought they knew. The early dialogues of Plato – the ones that are taken to be closest to the historical Socrates – are distinguished by the fact that they end in so-called *aporia*. These are intellectual impasses when the interlocutors realize that the original question they asked – what is friendship, courage, virtue or goodness – simply does not admit of an easy answer. Socrates confessed to being very conscious of not being wise at all. What he seems to have meant was that the key to wisdom is not how much you know but understanding the limits of what you know.

Religious calling

Socrates became a philosopher in a striking way. He had a word from an oracle. The oracle was that of Apollo at Delphi: 'No one is wiser than Socrates,' the Pythia had said. Socrates came to interpret the oracle as meaning that no one was wiser than he because no one else comprehended the depth of human ignorance about things as he did. Thereafter, he devoted his life to exploring the limits of human knowledge.

He thought it a valuable thing to do, partly because Athens in its 'Golden Age' was at severe risk of being undone by hubristic foreign policies and over-confidence in technology, and partly because he had in effect been told who he was by a god. At his trial he defended himself, saying, 'I have been ordered by the god to do this, both in oracles and dreams, and in every other way that a divine manifestation has ever ordered a man to do anything.' Philosophy was for him a calling and a mission.

So a religious attitude towards life was integral to his philosophy. In Plato's dialogues and elsewhere he is depicted as making sacrifices, attending feasts, pouring libations, offering prayers and pursuing oracles. He seems to have believed that religious practice was invaluable since it is an exercise in humility: if the divine realm represents the place where all things are complete and understood, then for humans, to be religious is to inculcate a way of life that embodies a state of 'learned ignorance'. This was picked up by the individual who is sometimes called the first Renaissance humanist philosopher, Nicholas of Cusa, a great admirer of Socrates.

Humanist reception

Today, Socrates receives a mixed reception amongst humanists, because on a number of counts it is hard to pin him down:

- His method of teaching – referred to as Socratic dialogue because he taught by asking people increasingly penetrating questions – can either be presented as a democratic exchange among equals in search of truth, or a nitpicking confrontation in which a clever individual undermines the beliefs of others. If you look at it in the first way, Socrates is a hero; if you see if in the second way, he is not so worthy of merit.

- There is a debate to be had as to whether Socrates (and Plato for that matter) was a rationalist or religious, or a mixture of both. In favour of the former view is Socrates's search for 'inductive arguments and general definitions' as Aristotle subsequently defined his key aims. In favour of the latter are the religious practices that Socrates engaged in, as well as the metaphysics of Plato who, in his theory of Forms, saw the universe as divinely ordered and ultimately only revealed in a mystical, beatific vision.

- It also seems that Socrates had a suspicion of science. It was not that he thought science worthless; it was that he believed science could not answer the most important questions about how to live. He began his career as a natural philosopher, like many of the pre-Socratics, but turned to moral philosophy when he recognized its limits in this respect.

- Another question is whether Socrates is politically open-minded or a quasi-totalitarian? The issue here is perhaps the most famous work of Plato, *The Republic*, in which Socrates is portrayed as endorsing a society in which everything is held in common, poets are banned, and the city is ruled by an elite.

- Finally is he a martyr because he was a freethinker or because he was a religious innovator? He seems like a freethinker for encouraging his followers to think for themselves; because of that he was charged at his trial with corrupting youth. He seems like a religious innovator because he often spoke about his own divine voice, was likened to a god by Plato, and was also charged at his trial with bringing new gods to the city.

Aristotle and others

One thing is for sure. In 399 BCE Socrates died, executed by drinking hemlock. After his death, Plato, and Plato's pupil, Aristotle (384–322 BCE), set up schools of philosophy to continue the philosophical movement to which he had so singularly contributed. We've said something about Plato, but Aristotle is another key figure to mention in this pre-history of humanism. Not only a pupil of Plato, he was another genius from these extraordinary decades of human history, a teacher of Alexander the Great and a hugely influential philosopher with very wide interests, including logic, ethics, metaphysics, science, rhetoric, politics and aesthetics.

He is important in the history of ideas not only for his work – which, in the areas just listed, set an agenda for centuries after him – but also for his style of doing philosophy. Aristotle weighs arguments, unpacks insight, prefers the plausible, seeks to classify, and asks about the nature and goals of philosophy itself. His work comes down to us in 30 surviving books representing about 2000 modern pages, though ancient sources say he wrote 150 books in total.

Like Socrates and Plato before him, the way Aristotle has been regarded by humanists has varied. (This disagreement amongst humanists can now be regarded as a permanent feature of our discussion, the cause and product of humanism's diversity!) For example, the Renaissance humanists tended to be wary of Aristotle. The reason for this is that in the Middle Ages that came before them, and which in a way they reacted against, Aristotle was thought so important that he was known simply as 'The Philosopher'. Inasmuch as the Renaissance rejected the Middle Ages, they also rejected him, at least in part. Today, things might be said to have shifted. In fact, now humanist philosophers may well prefer Aristotle to Plato, because they see Aristotle as having espoused an empirical approach to knowledge, whereas Plato preferred the high speculations of the metaphysical. This difference was memorably captured in the Renaissance artist Raphael's famous picture, 'The School of Athens'. It shows Plato pointing to the heavens and Aristotle to the ground – though so neat a distinction between the two thinkers can easily be contested.

Plato and Aristotle were not the only individuals to carry on developing the philosophical tradition. Another group of philosophers was known as the sceptics. In the third century BCE, some time after Socrates's death, they attempted to revive what they saw as the authentic teaching of Socrates, based upon his profession of ignorance. Taking a lead from Pyrrho of Elis (c.360–c.270 BCE), they injected life into a way of doing philosophy that later inspired many humanists, including Montaigne, Hume and others. It is called scepticism. As a philosophy it comes in various 'degrees' depending on how strongly you take the central tenet of ignorance that nothing can be known, or at least nothing of absolute certainty can be known for sure. However, scepticism should not be confused with relativism, since a sceptic may still believe in truth – just that it is unknowable. Nor is it to be confused with cynicism which was another ancient way of life focused on showing contempt for property and wealth. Cicero is the key source for our understanding of ancient scepticism, many ancient sceptics not committing their thoughts to paper/papyrus/tablets on principle – again following their hero Socrates.

Don't fear god

About the same time, there emerged another school of philosophy that plays a strong part in contemporary humanism. It was led by Epicurus (c.341–270 BCE) and so is known as Epicureanism. He began life as something of a traveller but settled in Athens in 306 BCE, aged 35, and stayed there until his death. The school he founded he called the Garden. It was set up outside the city, Epicurus believing that nothing was more antithetical to the life of tranquility he sought than the turbulent and competitive atmosphere of the *polis*. Remarkably for the time, his students included women and slaves.

Ancient sources say that Epicurus wrote 300 books, though all that survives are two short collections of sayings and three letters. However, several of his followers in subsequent generations, notably Ancient Rome, preserved the Epicurean philosophy that he inspired in their own writing. Probably the most important later Epicurean was Lucretius (c.95–52 BCE), the Roman poet, remembered for writing *De rerum natura* – 'On the Nature of Things'. He argued that nothing can compromise your own autonomy in the search for your happiness. For example, it is irrational to worry about your postmortem non-existence. He also argued that human beings are fundamentally material creatures that cannot survive death. He thought that any religion which suggests otherwise is damaging superstition.

Another fascinating piece of Epicurean philosophy came to light when a papyrus was found in Herculaneum, the city that alongside Pompeii was destroyed by the famous eruption of Vesuvius. It included a 'four-part cure' that popularizes and sums up Epicurus's approach to life:

> Don't fear god,
> Don't worry about death;
> What is good is easy to get, and
> What is terrible is easy to endure.

To put it another way, Epicurus advocated a very practical philosophy of life. It achieved a genuinely popular following for centuries, lasting well into the Christian era. He diagnosed that the fundamental obstacle to happiness is anxiety. The philosophical life was one which aimed at removing all those anxieties. Hence, he said, don't fear the gods, because there are no divine beings that can threaten us. Second, don't worry about death, because there is no life after death, and so we won't be around to mourn the loss. Third, what is good in life is easy to get for the simple reason that, actually, we need very little in life to make it good – sustenance and friendship, being about the only essential things on Epicurus's list. Fourth, don't worry about suffering because it is usually not so bad, and is more fearful in the prospect than in the actuality.

Incidentally, Epicurus demonstrated his teaching in his own life, when he died. He suffered a hideously painful death from kidney stones. And throughout the agony he insisted that remembering pleasurable times with friends was enough to transcend the pain.

Ancient hedonism

It is worth dwelling a little longer on Epicureanism because today Epicurus's name has become synonymous with hedonism; the philosophical belief that pleasure is what counts in life. For example, it was an idea that was later picked up by the Utilitarians, a key modern humanist theory of ethics that we shall come to. However, ancient hedonism is often misunderstood; in particular, it can be mistaken as a philosophy of perpetual consumption. Indeed, Epicurus was misunderstood in his own time, being himself accused of gluttony and sexual debauchery. However, he meant something rather different: be satisfied with what you have. He said that if all he had was some bread and water, he would be as happy as the gods.

This philosophy of hedonism might be excused by thinking it was suited to periods of history when resources were scarce; even the relatively prosperous in Epicurus's day often lacked basics – or had them removed as a result of war – and so found themselves to be anxious. Today, though, everything is pretty much plentiful, at least in the West, and so another ancient maxim might be more appropriate: eat, drink, for tomorrow we die. However, Epicurus said that this attitude would equally lead to unhappiness since it inculcates a habit of always wanting more. It results in the covetous character who is never satisfied no matter how much they have.

For the same reason, Epicurus was rather suspicious of philosophy, too, for all that he was a philosopher. He thought it encouraged people to seek more knowledge than was really available to mere human beings, thereby creating intellectual anxiety.

Another way in which Epicurus can be misunderstood is in relation to his saying about not fearing the gods. It seems to imply he was an atheist. But was he? Well, not quite. Rather, he commended not fearing the gods because he believed there is no life after death – and because anything the gods might throw at you in life is easy to endure. In other words, he argued there is no need to *worry* about the gods, not that gods did not exist. Moreover, the good Epicurean might actually consider contemplating the life of the gods. After all, the gods are happy, live in a state of bliss, are unconcerned with anything, and are invulnerable to harm. In short, they are model Epicureans.

Another interesting ramification of Epicurean theology is his materialist understanding of nature. For example, he was challenged to explain how the world is so good for human habitation if the gods, who presumably created it, do not care about us; as people say to this day, the 'design' of the world just seems too fortuitous to dismiss as mere chance. Epicurus answered that the world happened by accident, and having just happened was governed by material laws of nature. He followed the teaching of another pre-Socratic philosopher, Democritus, in this respect, who believed that the fundamental component of matter is atomic and that atoms move, coalesce and disperse according to natural laws, not according to the hand of God. You can see that many modern arguments about religion, the world, natural laws and God have a very long pedigree indeed.

Alongside thinking philosophically, Epicurus also argued that friendship is an excellent way to find and live the happy life. 'Friendship dances around the world, announcing to all of us that we must wake up to blessedness,' he wrote. Many Epicureans lived in small communities as a result.

Going with the flow

Finally, in this chapter, let us refer to one more school of thought, and one more philosopher – this time a Roman – both of which will reappear later as we progress.

The school of thought is Stoicism. Another hugely influential school of ancient philosophy, it was contemporary to Epicureanism and takes its name from the *stoa,* or marketplace porches, where its advocates taught. The key insight of the Stoics was that human behaviour is at its happiest when it falls in line with the divinely ordered cosmos. In this sense, all that is important in life is trying to do the right thing. Goodness is moral virtue; wickedness is the only evil. The modern phrase 'being stoical' that derives from this philosophy reflects this thought to a degree. It means accepting what happens to you. The original Stoics talked about 'going with the flow', the task of philosophy being to shape your life so that you can do so. Incidentally, Stoicism has not only influenced some humanists but it made a profound impact upon the early Christians. In the Bible, Saint Paul quotes a hymn to Zeus written by the Stoic Cleanthes.

The best texts of the Stoics that survive are a few fragments by Chrysippus (*c.*280–207 BCE), *The Meditations* of the Roman emperor Marcus Aurelius (121–180 CE), *The Discourses* of Epictetus (*c.*55–*c.*135 CE) – the philosopher who began life as a slave – and the works of Cicero that combine Stoic and Epicurean thought. And Cicero (106–43 BCE) is the last philosopher for us to note from this period.

A Roman statesman from the turbulent period of the end of the Roman Republic and the rise of Julius Caesar, Cicero was an orator and writer whose elegant Latin inspired the Renaissance humanists to high standards of rhetoric. He is not usually thought to have been philosophically innovative but he was intellectually eclectic, being sceptical in his epistemology and Stoical in ethics, and drawing on the Epicureans, too. His philosophical works include: *Consolatio* on death; *Hortensius* on studying philosophy; *De Finibus* and *Tusculan Disputations* on virtue and happiness; *On the Nature of the Gods* and *On Fate* about theology and determinism; and *On Duties* which contrasts the nature of animals with human nature. In the modern period this last book was taken as a key text in the study of how to be a gentleman. A keen republican, Cicero was killed on the orders of Marc Anthony in the terror that followed the death of Julius Caesar.

Summary

We began this chapter at the very origins of Western philosophy, with its 'father', Thales, and his efforts to explain the universe by the principle that all is water. This aquatic vision was rejected by those who followed him, though they picked up on his general motivation – to seek to explain things by a natural understanding of the world, as one that ran quite happily for them alongside the mythical.

The pre-Socratic philosophers Pythagoras, Heraclitus and Parmenides came next – all majoring on another key area of philosophy, the attempt to think about thinking itself. And then came Protagoras, the agnostic sophist who uttered a phrase that has echoed down the centuries: 'Man is the measure of all things.'

The stage was set for the birth of Socrates, a man whose life and death shaped our civilization. Humanists have disagreed on what they make of him. Was he a model freethinker or a religious innovator, a champion of reason or a critic of science, a martyr or actually rather anti-democratic? What is certainly the case is that no account of humanism escapes his influence.

After Socrates came other controversial figures – Plato, beloved by the Renaissance for his vision, and Aristotle, perhaps more loved by humanists today for his empiricism. Then there was Epicurus who believed that you should not fear the gods, and that what matters in living a good life is how you relate to pleasure. And finally, we came to the Stoics and Cicero, the Roman writer who thrilled the Renaissance humanists with his fine writing and powerful oratory.

Our prehistory is complete. We can now make something of a historical leap, though one that is justified, because with it we come to the first real humanists, those inspiring figures of the Renaissance.

02

Renaissance humanism

In this chapter you will learn:
- what inspired the Renaissance humanists
- about the famous and diverse figures of the period
- how to assess the lasting contribution they have made to the humanist tradition.

Many Ancient Greek and Roman philosophers were interested in questions which focused on what it is to be human. Socrates, in particular, 'called philosophy down from heaven to earth', as Cicero put it. In the following centuries of Christianity, through the Middle Ages, that anthropocentric tradition of thinking can be seen as a thread running through many great philosophers' thoughts. However, when we reach the fourteenth century – and the birth of the Renaissance – instead of being part of philosophy, anthropocentric concerns become a major theme in their own right – arguably *the* major theme. Humanism proper was born.

In this chapter, we will look at the thinkers of the Renaissance, how humanism proper emerged, what issues it brought to the fore, how it related to other currents of cultural change, what legacy it left for the centuries that followed and how they link with humanism today. But first, let us turn to the idea of the Renaissance itself because, paradoxical though it may seem, the Renaissance humanists neither called themselves 'Renaissance' nor 'humanist'. It was only later that this period of intellectual and artistic innovation was clearly recognized as such, when historians of the nineteenth century looked back and sought to analyze and label the early days of what we now call the modern period. In other words, just what the Renaissance is as an idea is an important first question in its own right.

The idea of the Renaissance

The scholarly demarcation of a period called the Renaissance, out of which humanism grew, can be pinpointed to a date – and one long after the Renaissance ended. In 1860, the great Swiss historian Jakob Burkhardt (1818–97) published his seminal cultural history, *The Civilization of the Renaissance in Italy*. It sold rather slowly at first, but in retrospect Burkhardt almost single handedly ensured that, henceforth, the Renaissance would have its own chapter whenever the Western history of humanity is told.

His book is an important document when considering the philosophy of humanism because in it he describes the Renaissance as a period with its own artistic, political, social and psychological characteristics, and he tells a story about the period still popular amongst humanists that goes something like this:

For centuries, even a millennium, Europe had been sunk in a dark age, precipitated by the collapse of the Roman Empire in the fifth century CE. Barbarism swept in to fill the vacuum left by the departure of classical culture. The Church played an ambivalent role in these bleak times. It sustained some of the ancient learning but mostly for a clerical elite, and simultaneously fed superstition to the servile masses. Human beings were subject to a misanthropic religion managed by an authoritarian church.

Then, the story continues, came the fourteenth-century Italian Renaissance, the subject of Burkhardt's study. A revival of urban life in towns and cities led to the rediscovery of the literature of antiquity, coupled with a distinctly modern philosophy focused on secular values, science and the glories of humankind. Burkhardt wrote:

> In the Middle Ages ... man was conscious of himself only as a member of a race, people, party, family, or corporation ... In Italy this veil first melted into air ... man became a spiritual *individual*, and recognized himself as such.

This idea was the heart of Renaissance humanism. It is anthropocentric and ended the Middle Ages by breaking the power of the Church and ushered in a cultural dynamism that we still value and enjoy today.

But is this story right? In short, not quite. To be fair to Burkhardt, this summary is a gross simplification of his work. But it is also the case that since his book's publication, historians have painted an ever-more complicated picture of what really happened. They have incorporated subtle economic factors into a richer account of the period and shown that Renaissance Italians would barely have seen themselves as modern, let alone humanist, in the way we might do: there is still much scholarly debate about the origins, the causes, the culture and the impact of the Renaissance. Having said that, Burkhardt was right in defining a period of history in which something startling did happen, something that resonates powerfully with those who call themselves humanists today. That is why it is absolutely central to our question of what humanism is. So to begin to build up a more nuanced understanding of the Renaissance, let us first take a step back, and consider some of its philosophical antecedents in the Middle Ages.

Antecedents of Renaissance philosophy

The reason we must do this is that for all that it is easy to assume that the Renaissance marked a radical break with the medieval period before it, as the simplistic reading of Burkhardt implies, the roots of Renaissance philosophy were buried deep in the medieval period. In other words, if it were a love of Ancient Greek and Roman writers that powered the 'new learning', medieval scholars had access to many of the same classical texts too. Moreover, the Middle Ages included periods during which interest in authors such as Cicero surged as well. The so-called Carolingian Renaissance, under Charlemagne (747–814 CE), was one. It anticipated what was to come. Libraries were built for expanding manuscript collections and educational reforms were introduced, based on the methods of Alcuin at York, teaching classical texts to secular as well as monastic clergy.

Alternatively, you can consider figures like Boethius (c.480–525 CE) the author of the sublime *The Consolations of Philosophy*, that was much admired during the Renaissance, once it got going. His key thought was that eternity can be defined as the possession of everything at the same time, and he wrote commentaries on Cicero and Aristotle, and essays on logic, theology and mathematics, too. Though imprisoned, tortured and executed – during which period he wrote the *Consolations* and when he sought solace not in religion but philosophy – he argued that bad fortune can be a blessing since it reveals 'friends who are true friends'.

It is also worth remembering that the Middle Ages produced such genius laymen and poets as Dante Alighieri (1265–1321). His famous *Divine Comedy* looks forward to the Renaissance inasmuch as it is concerned with practical moral and political issues, not the metaphysical and speculative ones for which the philosopher-theologians of his own time are often remembered – the 'scholastic' philosopher-theologians as they are called.

Then there is the fact that from the mid-twelfth century, Aristotle in particular was so well known and regarded that he was referred to simply as 'The Philosopher' and has been called the 'oracle' of the medieval university. Thomas Aquinas (1224–74), one of the greatest philosophical minds of all time, lived in the mid-thirteenth century. He wrote several definitive commentaries on Aristotle and in his greatest work, the *Summa*

Theologiae (which he was still writing when he died), he knitted Aristotelian thought with Christian theology more completely than anyone else before or since.

In fact – and this is a sign that it is right to talk of the Renaissance for all that it continued as much as broke with the past – the very dominance of Aristotle in some ways hindered a wider reading of other Greek and Roman texts during the Middle Ages. For example, when European Christians conquered Constantinople during the Fourth Crusade of the thirteenth century, a window several decades long opened up in which Plato and Homer might have been reintroduced into the West. But it was Aristotle's philosophy that shaped the education of priests and, when coupled to the dictates of canon law, other texts simply did not get a look in. This explains why medieval scholasticism came to be regarded by some Renaissance humanists as the antithesis of their own ideals, though in truth it was not. It was also humanists who invented derisive myths that scholastics liked nothing better than to waste time calculating the number of angels who could dance on the head of a pin.

So it is wrong simply to imagine that the medieval writers were somehow primitive when compared with their humanist successors; far from it. In fact, in terms of pure philosophical sophistication and weight, figures like Aquinas eclipse any of the Renaissance writers that followed him.

Islamic humanism

If the roots of Renaissance humanism were firmly planted in the Middle Ages, it is also important to draw attention to another cultural flowering on which the later humanist revival depended. That is the period which might be called Islamic humanism that began in the late-ninth century and extended into the twelfth.

It is fair to describe it as a humanistic movement since it is characterized by a love of learning, the betterment of humankind, and many of the philosophical problems that were to occupy the Renaissance thinkers – including the relationship between Aristotelian and Platonic philosophy, and the relationship of the two with religion.

Much of the best intellectual activity of this period centred on Baghdad in modern-day Iraq and the so-called 'House of Wisdom' built during the Abbasid dynasty. Throughout the ninth century, Arabs translated many works of Aristotle and some of Plato. The medical works of the ancient world also attracted much attention, including those by Galen and Hippocrates. From India came scientific and mathematic texts, such as those of Archimedes and Euclid, and with them came the Arabic numerals that are familiar to us today and without which it is impossible to conceive of modern mathematics developing. Algebra was invented in Baghdad, too.

The father of Muslim philosophy in the ninth century was Al-Kindi (died c. 870) who wanted to reconcile the ideas of neo-Platonism with Islamic theology. He also wrote a book in which an individual facing death seeks solace not in a religion but wisdom. After, Al-Kindi a number of subsequent philosophers took up the challenge of thinking through fundamental problems in philosophy. The way in which they posed those problems is still recognizably the same today.

'The Commentator'

At the start of the eleventh century another great scholar exploded onto the scene, Ibn Sina or Avicenna (980–1037), when he published the first of what was to become five encyclopedias. He was well known for his knowledge of medicine and substantially developed the metaphysics of Aristotle. It is notable that in the most important parts of his *Metaphysics* he makes no appeal to the revealed truth of the Qur'an but bases his conclusions on rational principles. It was this that made his work accessible to Christian scholars, carrying the influence of Islamic humanism to the West.

Another great name to recall is that of the twelfth-century Averroes (1126–1198). He produced a masterful commentary on the works of Aristotle that was held in such esteem in the West that Averroes was known simply as 'The Commentator', mirroring the title given to Aristotle. Again, he anticipated themes of the later humanists because for much of his life he was involved in battles against his conservative fellows and defended the right of reason to investigate matters of theology. To this end he wrote treatises such as *The Harmony of Philosophy and Religion*. He believed that revelation and reason gave access to the same ultimate truths but simply at different levels. In a sense he argued that religion was philosophy for the masses.

Then there was the Jewish physician and philosopher Moses Maimonides (1135–1204) who was also a major contributor to this period of humanist-like learning. His most lasting book,

The Guide for the Perplexed, was written in Arabic. It contains perennial themes not only because of its concern to reconcile Jewish religion and Aristotelian philosophy, but also because of the agnostic line of argument he developed: in short, God is entirely unknown and unknowable because divinity is so radically different from humanity. The only way theology can proceed is by saying what God is not. This is difficult, Maimonides continues, since most people seek positive knowledge of God, and if they cannot find this, it will lead them to dismiss the divine. Thus people perpetuate stories such as that God answers prayers and punishes sin.

Origins of Renaissance philosophy

So in the Christian and Muslim worlds of the Middle Ages, there were plenty of big hitters thinking in ways that the Renaissance humanists were to make their own. Perhaps as always in history, no movement has ever emerged without its antecedents, without earlier stirrings that have sown the seeds for what was to follow. But what did happen to give the Renaissance that Burkhardt identified as its particular shape?

First, there were political events, and perhaps the most important of these was the Council of Florence in 1439. The Council was called because the Ottoman Turks were seriously threatening the security of the Byzantine Empire – that being the inheritor of the Roman Empire after it had become Christian, though instead of being centred in the western city of Rome it was centred in the eastern city of Constantinople. The Christians of the East sought assistance from Christians in the West in the shape of a crusade to defeat the Muslims.

The Pope, who controlled things in the West, agreed but he set a condition on his help. Ever since the eleventh century, the churches of the East and West had been divided. Now the Pope wanted them to be reunited. This unity is what the Council proclaimed. The reconciliation did not last, but it did bring Byzantine scholars to Florence, which substantially boosted an already established interest in the Greek language in the city. Intellectually something new could begin.

For example, a leading theologian, George Gemistos Plethon, gave lectures during the Council, arguing that Aristotle – the key philosopher for theologians of the Middle Ages – was over-valued. Plethon preferred Plato as, unlike Aristotle, Plato

believed in a creator God and the immortality of the soul,
matters that were central to Christianity and over which
Aristotle seemed ambivalent at best.

This sparked a fierce debate between the advocates of each side.
Champions of Aristotle accused the Platonists of heresies like
the transmigration of souls into animals and of 'disgusting'
practices like pederasty and exercising in the nude, for both
sexes – things that were celebrated in Plato's dialogues. Others
tried to forge a middle ground. Nicholas of Cusa (1401–64) –
arguably the first Renaissance philosopher, also a cardinal,
mathematician and scientist – argued that the philosophy of
both Plato and Aristotle was limited. In a way, that was
inevitable, he said, because knowledge of God was ultimately
beyond any human conception.

New manuscripts recovered

If the Council of Florence failed to bring a lasting reconciliation
between the Christians of the East and West, it failed in its
political goals too, inasmuch as Constantinople fell to the Turks
in 1453. However, this represented another boon for
scholarship. Greek refugees flooded into Rome and Florence,
bringing with them their precious collections of manuscripts.
Libraries were revived or opened in both places to collect and
house them.

This surge in the discovery and recovery of Greek and Roman
manuscripts can be placed alongside the political events of the
time as the cultural events that gave rise to the Renaissance. The
histories of Tacitus, the poems of Catullus, the Epicurean
philosophy of Lucretius, the architecture of Vitruvius and the
cookbook of Apicius (all in Latin) are texts that are still read
today, and they might have all been lost were it not for the
Renaissance. When it came to Ancient Greek works, the early
Renaissance humanists assembled what is essentially the canon
for such texts, a list including works of Plato, Aristotle,
Demosthenes, Plutarch and Plotinus. The so-called Church
Fathers from the first five centuries of Christianity and the Bible
itself also became new matters for deep and profound study, as
indeed were manuscripts from various mystical and occult
traditions.

Economic drivers

Finally, alongside political and cultural events, it is important to remember the economic factors that played an important part in the birth of the Renaissance, particularly in its spread from Italy northwards through Europe. After all, if scholars read the new manuscripts and then presented themselves as the natural inheritors of the culture of Ancient Greece and Rome – as they did – it was their original training as notaries, the bureaucrats of a thriving economy, that gave them a taste for literature in the first place.

Further, the fruits of the new scholars' intellectual labours also represented substantial commercial opportunities to enterprising merchants and bankers. Equipped with printing presses, knowledge could be distributed along the same channels as other goods. Places like Venice became centres of Renaissance learning because they were already centres for traders and financiers.

These economic factors led to another understanding of the Renaissance that later historians developed, namely that of civic humanism. Like the idea of the Renaissance itself, civic humanism was only later applied to the period, though it has become an important concept in terms of understanding what happened in Renaissance Florence and, indeed, for articulating the significance of these events for the modern day. Civic humanism is an idealization of republican life – inspired by that of Ancient Rome – in which economically independent and politically active individuals uphold a collective way of life in defense of their liberty, notably in the Renaissance against medieval-style monarchical tyranny. The term was invented by the historian Hans Baron, in his *The Crisis of the Early Italian Renaissance: Civic Humanism and Republican Liberty in an Age of Classicism and Tyranny* (1955).

Anthropocentrism – a new philosophy

So, the Renaissance can be said to have taken shape because of various political, cultural and economic factors. Politics brought disparate people together. Then, as they tried to sort out their political differences, they shared their cultural inheritance. Those manuscripts and ideas spread further along the trading roots of Europe, the economic element. Now let us ask another question and develop this picture of the Renaissance further: how did its philosophy – its humanism – come to separate itself from its past?

What marked it out was a particular boldness of engagement with the philosophers of Ancient Greece and Rome. The Renaissance humanists became fascinated by different things from their medieval forebears. For example, they grew more interested in the historical context of ancient texts and wondered how their insights and wisdom might be applied to themselves in their day. The elegance of the Latin of writers like Cicero and the corresponding philosophical uses of rhetoric also engaged them. Many came to regard the Stoical attitudes or sceptical advice of these authors as almost personal sources of wisdom. That was all pretty new.

This is where we can see something of the new Renaissance individualism that Burkhardt identified. The ancient texts were no longer just read as illumination of the old divinely sanctioned social hierarchies, but began to resonate with emerging secular political and personal ideals – secular here meaning not the radical separation of Church and state, something that only occurred centuries later, but treating the human world as the primary sphere of reference, for all that this was a world in which divinity was still seen as pervasive. In other words, Renaissance humanism was at least as much a personal practice as a theological philosophy. Alongside the old theocentrism was emerging a new anthropocentrism.

A new enthusiasm

If the Renaissance can be identified as the time when 'man became a spiritual *individual*, and recognized himself as such', to recall Burkhardt's phrase, let us have a look at some of the key players from the first 100 years or so of the movement.

Consider first Francesco Petrarca (1304–74) – or Petrarch as he is usually known – the individual who is thought of as the 'father of Renaissance humanism'. His own father wanted him to pursue a legal education, but from an early age he developed a love of Cicero and, hence, rhetoric and style; and a love of Virgil and, hence, poetry. The life of the notary could not contain him. He became gripped by the idea that the Ancient Greek and Roman authorities had much to teach him, and the world in which he lived. He would devote his life to them.

His enthusiasm for literature, and the energies he devoted to recovering lost manuscripts, became one of the hallmarks of the Renaissance humanist. One of his earliest projects was reassembling a complete copy of Livy's *History of Rome*. That involved not only collating various fragments but improving the manuscripts with notes and corrections.

Petrarch is remembered today for his sonnets in Italian, the *Canzoniere*, but his importance for Renaissance humanism lies more in his Latin works like *De viris illustribus* or 'On Famous Men', in which he retold the lives of famous Romans. He also wrote and collected his own letters to friends, having been inspired to do so by finding a manuscript of Cicero's letters to his friend Atticus. Once published, they formed the first humanist letter collection, and had a great impact upon subsequent generations of humanists, not only for the way Petrarch cultivated a certain image of himself but also because of the way he discussed the Renaissance obsession with the imitation of Cicero and Seneca – as son does father, 'with likeness but not identically'.

Living the truth

Having said that, it is generally reckoned that Petrarch only achieved a genuine renewal of ancient philosophy – as opposed merely to its repetition or imitation – in one work, namely *On His Own Ignorance*. Here he makes a case for appealing to the emotions and the imagination in ethics by the use of rhetoric. This is in opposition to the medieval scholastics, the moral philosophy of which deployed logic and natural theology. His point was that to live the truth you have to *love* it, as well as know it. This is why, he continued, humanist studies not only make someone knowledgeable but good in their character and deeds as well as their minds.

For all of his substantial philological and historical scholarship, Petrarch's love of all things classical, and his attempts to establish a continuity between ancient and contemporary times, did show him up as naïve on occasion. For example, in 1347 he supported the efforts of Cola di Rienzo to restore the ancient republic of Rome. This revival culminated in Cola being ritually bathed in the font of Constantine and declared 'Tribunus Augustus' on the Capitoline Hill. Perhaps Petrarch excused Cola's excesses since he had himself been crowned with laurels in 1341 on the same mount before publicly extolling the virtues of poetry.

Learned ignorance

After Petrarch perhaps the next really big figure of the Renaissance was someone we have already mentioned, Nicholas of Cusa. He was a student of the late-medieval confraternity called 'The Brotherhood of the Common Life', that also educated and influenced other key figures who were to follow, such as Erasmus and Luther. This community was noted for its anti-intellectualism, regarding the philosophy of medieval scholasticism as worthless sophistry. Aged 31, Nicholas was a delegate at the Council of Basel (1431) which objected strongly to the ecclesiastical supremacy of the Papacy. He subsequently switched to the Pope's side and was made a cardinal in 1448. Throughout, though, he was a committed reformer of the Church and sought reconciliation between opposing parties, perhaps because of his own eclectic intellectual interests. He warrants the description 'humanist' because of that mix of commitment to, and critique of, religion.

De Docta Ignorantia or 'On Learned Ignorance' is probably Nicholas's best known philosophical work. In it he argues that the wisest of individuals, from Solomon to Socrates, all realized one central fact: the most interesting things in the world are also the most difficult to explain. They therefore came to the conclusion that they knew nothing of the most profound matters at all. So the great challenge of intellectual life is to learn of and understand this human ignorance. 'The more [a man] knows that he is unknowing, the more learned he will be,' Nicholas writes. Nicholas can be called an agnostic humanist.

He put human ignorance down to the Platonic doctrine that truth is simple and unitary whereas people are complex and multiple. Thus, when it comes to trying to understand the truth, we are like someone trying to draw a perfect circle by constructing a polygon with an ever-increasing number of sides: no matter how many sides are added, the polygon will only approximate to the perfection of the circle. Human beings similarly always come up against contradictions in their philosophy. Only in God are these contradictions reconciled, what Nicholas called the *coincidentia oppositorum* – the realm in which all opposites meet.

Plato on love

After Nicholas, we come to Marsilio Ficino (1433–99), the man who played the biggest part in bringing Plato to the

Renaissance. By 1469, as the court philosopher of Cosimo de' Medici of Florence, he had translated the complete works of the student of Socrates. Though the debate about the place of Aristotle continued, the net result was that over the course of a single generation, Plato became a perfectly respectable philosopher for study in the West and his dialogues were being incorporated into the education of scholars and clerics.

Ficino translated a number of other Greek works, notably Plotinus' *Enneads* that drew on Plato and had nearly been lost in the West. He was not only a translator, he wrote commentaries on four of the most important Platonic dialogues, most famously the *Symposium*. His spiritualized interpretation of Plato's discourse on love was enormously influential.

This in turn showed how Christian theology can be based upon Platonic doctrines. Ficino's idea was that love is an attraction that moves from the physical to the spiritual so that the true lover is automatically led to God. Indeed, against those who favoured Aristotle, he argued that Plato provides a more robust basis for Christianity and so must have been divinely inspired. Thus, when Plato discusses the Form of the Good in *The Republic*, Ficino equates Plato's transcendent conception of goodness itself with the Christian beatific vision of God.

Occultism

Ficino was also responsible for the revival of Hermeticism in the Renaissance. Hermeticism is a tradition of mystical and magical writings closely related to occult interests. It came in the shape of a body of esoteric ideas that was a mix of astrology, alchemy and speculations on the origins of human beings and the universe. Ficino translated the *Corpus Hermeticum*, the treatise supposedly written by an Egyptian priest and contemporary of Moses, Hermes Trismegistus, after whom the tradition is named – though it was subsequently shown to have been composed by a Greek in around 200 CE. In fact, when Ficino first set eyes on the *Corpus Hermeticum*, he delayed his work on Plato to finish the *Hermeticum* first.

Now, to humanists today, an interest in hermeticism and alchemy seems like an extraordinary confusion of intellectual priorities. However, it must be remembered that during the Renaissance there was no easy division between religious faith, occult traditions, philosophical learning and practical ethics. So, occultism can be seen in some ways as bridging the gap between the Ancient Greek conception of science, with its close links to mythical understandings of the world, and a modern conception of science that is essentially instrumental: hermeticism mirrors the approach of the ancients inasmuch as it is embedded in a speculative contemplation of the cosmos, expressed in secrets and wonder; but it is also like modern science because it is about manipulating materials in order to achieve certain practical ends, most famously of course in the pursuit of the philosopher's stone and the elixir of life. Occultism can be thought of as a quite natural humanist occupation, at least during the Renaissance. It was another manifestation of the new individualism.

Similarly, there was a surge in work on Kabbalah, the Jewish mystical tradition that Christians in the Renaissance took up as a tool for interpreting the Bible. And this leads us to another key figure in the first Renaissance century, Pico della Mirandola (1463–94).

Eclectic schools of thought

Alongside great classical learning, Pico, as he is known, learnt Hebrew and the kabbalistic devices of *gematria*, which assigns numerical values to letter, and *natorikon*, which reads words as abbreviations. He did this because he believed that all systems of thought and belief should be integrated together. From this syncretism shared truths would emerge, and thus ultimate Truth. He was also a great believer in debate. At the age of 23, he published 900 theses that dealt with matters from various, often conflicting, strands of Christian, Muslim and Jewish thought. One thesis read: 'No science can better convince us of the divinity of Christ than magic and the Kabbalah.'

His contribution led to Papal condemnation and he was imprisoned for a short time. A more orthodox project – at least to the contemporary humanist mind – was a mammoth undertaking to reconcile Aristotelian and Platonic philosophy, though his early death, aged only 31 – some say having been murdered with poison – cut it short. He is remembered today particularly for his *Oration on the Dignity of Man* (see below) – the speech with which he planned to introduce the discussion of his theses.

Professional heresy

By way of contrast to Nicolas of Cusa, Ficino and Pico alike, consider another life, that of Lorenzo Valla (1407–57), another classical scholar with great philological skills.

Valla was a Roman who, having received a humanist education, hoped to work at the Papal court. He could not secure employment, he assumed because of factions that worked against him, and it appears to have filled him with resentment. So in 1435 he moved to Naples and became secretary to the King, Alfonso I. There he deployed his considerable scholarly abilities to become what has been called a self-styled 'professional heretic'.

He is the author of several treatises that were influential throughout the fifteenth century including *On the Profession of the Religious Life* in which he homed in on the hypocrisy of friars who supposedly led lives of poverty, and criticized the medieval conviction that monastic life was superior to that of lay people.

A champion of classical Latin, he was at the forefront of those humanists who disliked what they regarded as turgid medieval Latin and the dry scholastic approach to philosophy that came with it. His philological skills led to a breathtakingly audacious result when, in his thirties, he showed that a purportedly ancient document, which 'proved' that the Roman Emperor Constantine the Great had bequeathed substantial lands and powers to the Papacy, was a forgery. As if that was not provocative enough, he then went on to question whether the Apostles' Creed – a central statement of belief in the Church – could ever have been written by the Apostles. He was found guilty of heresy and was only saved by the intervention of his patron, Alfonso. Perhaps this was why Martin Luther, the later Protestant reformer, had a very high opinion of Valla and his writings.

In spite of all this, Valla was able to return to Rome for the last decade of his life because in 1448 the pro-humanist Pope Nicholas V appointed him Papal secretary.

Language and education

We have examined the antecedents to Renaissance thought in the medieval period, and the political, cultural and economic events that led to its inception. We have also looked at some of the key players in its first generation – the great lover of all things classical, Petrarch; the agnostic cardinal and scholar, Nicholas of Cusa; the great translator and interpreter of Plato, Ficino; the man with eclectic interests and a desire to debate, Pico; and lastly the rebel Valla.

We will continue to meet new characters as we move through the Renaissance centuries. But it is now perhaps helpful to identify some more of the big themes that contribute to what humanism has become today. One of the most important was the stress on language and education.

The eyes of Niccolò Machiavelli (1469–1527) are good ones to look through as we consider this issue. His name has become synonymous with some of the darker aspects of Renaissance life, namely political shenanigans: he asked how the state can use its power to maintain law and control, and concluded that it is necessary for leaders to know that it is not always rational to act virtuously. However, as well as being an influential and effective Italian statesman and founder of political science, he was also a player in the development of ideals about language and education that the humanists valued.

Consider this extract from a letter written by Machiavelli to his friend Vettori. In it he describes what he does after his political 'day job':

> Evenings I return home and enter my study; and at its entrance I take off my everyday clothes, full of mud and dust, and don royal and courtly garments; decorously reattired, I enter into the ancient sessions of ancient men. Received amicably by them, I partake of such food as is mine only and for which I was born. There, without shame, I speak with them and ask them about the reason for their actions; and they in their humanity respond to me.

In Machiavelli's description of his evening habits, we catch a glimpse of the almost religious devotion that the humanists had for the ancient authors. They searched for and grappled with these Latin and Greek texts not just as a hobby or interest but for the personal and social education that they might find in them.

It is for this reason that if any one thing can be said to characterize humanists it was their desire to master the rhetoric they saw exemplified in 'the ancient sessions of ancient men'. Language was the beginning and the end of their understanding of a humanist education – though, as ever with the humanists, there were dissenters. For example, Pico wrote the following to an author who apologized for his poor Latin: 'The philosopher has one duty and aim: to unlock the truth. Whether he does so with a wooden or a golden key is of no concern to me, and it is certainly preferable to unlock it with a wooden key than lock it with a golden one.' Also, it is comforting to learn that although the humanist ideal required mastery in Greek as well as Latin, most fell short when it came to the Greek.

Inventing neoclassical prose in the composition of Latin poetry, orations, letters, plays and histories can be thought of as a first key product of Renaissance learning. The humanists strove for ever-higher standards of eloquence – no doubt another expression of the interest in the personal – and Latin itself developed substantially over the period between the fourteenth century, when Petrarch first drew attention to the limitations of medieval Latin, and the sixteenth century when medieval Latin grammars stopped being printed. More negatively, some of the most vociferous verbal confrontations during the Reformation at the end of the Renaissance, for example, between Thomas More and Martin Luther, were undoubtedly exacerbated by the highly rhetorical Latin the opponents had learnt as a result of their humanist education.

Printing and errors

We have briefly alluded to printing, though it is an issue most certainly worth covering in its own right. The printing press first appeared in Italy in the late 1460s. It meant that manuscripts could be reproduced almost without limit. However, it also exacerbated a problem with which the medieval copyists were familiar: the corruption of texts by the introduction and then reproduction of textual errors.

The solution the Renaissance humanists developed was to identify and correct mistakes before manuscripts got anywhere near the press. So the humanists had to become master editors and philologists. Of course, establishing the authoritative version was often not a straightforward matter: one person's correction might well be another's corruption. Arguments were common. But with that emerged the basic principles of textual criticism: working from what had been identified as the oldest manuscripts, understanding the linguistic characteristics of particular authors and developing theories of redaction.

The results of this enterprise were not always purely academic. For example, secular law in medieval universities had been based upon the Byzantine Emperor Justinian's *Corpus Juris Civilis* or 'Body of Civil Law'. Medieval theologians had used it to justify unlimited Papal power, reading Byzantine authoritarianism directly into their own times. The humanists were able to set the text in its historical context and thereby make an argument – if not always winning the day – for authority to rest within city-states rather than with the Pope in Rome.

A note on italics

The italic typeface was invented probably sometime before 1500 by the humanists. They wanted to encourage a sense of informal intimacy in relation to their newly-recovered and newly-printed classical texts; the new cursive script also looked antique to the Renaissance mind. The first significant use of it was for an edition of Virgil's *Opera*, printed by Aldus Manutius in Venice that appeared in 1501. Italic was also handy since more letters could be printed per page in small volumes.

Extolling the vernacular

It was not only classical languages that humanists wanted to master. The vernacular came to be equally important. Machiavelli wrote his most famous book, *The Prince,* in powerful Italian prose. Another striking case in point is that of Michel de Montaigne (1533–92), the late Renaissance philosopher who has been called the French Socrates. Latin was his first language, since his father would only have Latin spoken in front of him at home. Nevertheless, the young Montaigne was to become arguably the greatest writer in French of the sixteenth century. The legacy of this aspect of Renaissance education continued when the revolutions in science of the sixteenth century were revealed to the world in what might anachronistically be called 'creative non-fiction': the astronomer Galileo (1564–1642) wrote dialogues and the philosopher Descartes (1596–1650) in first-person French. It was as if, for any good humanist, style was not an optional extra. It was central to the successful communication of their work.

As the Renaissance progressed, the earlier link between humanists and the profession of the notary, quintessentially so in the case of Petrarch, loosened too. The new humanist occupation became teaching, their interest education not the law. However, it also became characteristic of humanists not to work in universities but to seek wealthy patrons or run their own businesses. Not least of the significant results of this shift was the formation, in the sixteenth century, of secondary schools based upon the humanist curriculum. These schools were both Catholic and Protestant and provided pupils with a pre-university education that became very popular because, unsurprisingly, with it students did much better at university.

Reading the 'book of nature'

With the linguist and educational interests of the mature, later years of the Renaissance emerged another key theme that shapes humanism to this day, namely a determining interest in the development of science. In the fifteenth century, the work of the astronomers and physicists of antiquity, who had long remained dormant, was revived. The Pythagorean belief that the sun is the centre of the universe is one obvious example of this, as is the Platonic conviction that nature could be understood by geometry. According to tradition, Plato had the following written above the entrance to his ancient school, the Academy: 'Let no one ignorant of geometry come under my roof.' When that was coupled to the stress on education, it generated scientific possibilities that were nothing short of revolutionary.

Francis Bacon (1561–1626) was arguably the first really important Renaissance figure in this respect. He was a lawyer and parliamentarian who, as a client of the Earl of Essex, rose through the Elizabethan court. Under the reign of James I, he reached the pinnacle of his political career when he was appointed Lord Chancellor in 1618. He benefited from a humanist education and held opinions typical of many humanists such as being antipathetic to Aristotle. In 1606, he published *The Advancement of Learning*, in which he sought to establish a systematic basis for scientific enquiry.

He has been called the founder of modern experimentation and lends his name to the Baconian understanding of science. This is composed of several parts. For example, Bacon realized that science would progress best if it were regarded as a collective activity. He wanted to set up specialist research facilities and though these did not materialize in his own lifetime, he inspired the founders of the Royal Society in the seventeenth century. He argued that care needed to be taken with induction – the scientific principle by which general laws can be inferred from particular cases. In order to avoid rash generalizations, Bacon believed that scientists needed to proceed on the basis of thoroughgoing and transparent procedures.

Dominion theology

More darkly, Bacon also adopted metaphors of violence when explaining his experimental method. 'The secrets of nature are better revealed under the torture of experiments than when they follow their natural course,' he wrote. He believed that humankind had God-given rights over nature, following the words God spoke to Adam and Eve in Genesis: 'Grow and multiply, and fill the earth, and dominate it.' It is a view of science that is instrumental; science should serve the interests of humankind – in other words, it was another manifestation of the new anthropocentrism. This so-called 'dominion theology' has been strongly criticized in the face of contemporary environmental concerns. On the other hand, Bacon acknowledged the limits of science, arguing that the wise scientist does not confuse the study of natural things with those that he took to be divine.

He is also remembered for his *Essays* (1625), though they are essays in a different sense from those of Montaigne. If Montaigne 'assayed' himself in a search for wisdom and self-understanding, Bacon's essays read as summaries of know-how in various matters, gleaned from his life of high achievement. For example, his essay on friendship is advice to a monarch on the necessity of having friends that are not beholden to the Crown. Alternatively, in 'Of Studies', he argues that Renaissance-style literary study is valuable but needs to be kept in its place. It must be tempered by experience. He wrote:

> To spend too much time in studies is sloth; to use them too much for ornament is affectation; to make judgement wholly by their rules is the humour of a scholar. They perfect nature, and are perfected by experience ... for studies themselves do give forth directions too much at large, except they be bounded in by experience.

The story goes that Bacon died from a chill that he caught while stuffing a chicken with snow to see if the cooling effect would preserve the meat. Aside from his written contributions, he has in this way been presented as a martyr to science.

Early naturalism

Having discussed Bacon, it is worth remembering that there are striking differences between science as understood by the Renaissance humanists and as understood by humanists today. Consider the philosophical doctrine of naturalism. Today naturalism carries an exclusive sense: it means the belief that the material world – nature – is all that there is. In particular, it excludes the supernatural. To the Renaissance humanist, though, naturalism was meant inclusively, implying that human beings live in the natural realm alongside others. The supernatural may still have a part to play, even a defining part.

The distinction is well illustrated by the work of Lorenzo Valla. In his book *De Voluptate*, 'On Pleasure', he argued for a Christian version of Epicureanism. Epicurus, the Greek philosopher, had been an advocate of a kind of hedonism, the theory that pleasure is the key question in life. But it was not a theory of excess, as hedonism is often taken to mean today. Rather, he argued that people should learn to take pleasure in what they have – a nuanced position that many medieval theologians apparently missed, too, since Epicurus was regarded by them as impious. A naturalistic Epicureanism, in the sense that many humanists use the former word today, would imply the need to take pleasure in material things. For Valla, though, Renaissance naturalism did not prohibit what he took to be the highest pleasure of all: the pleasure the soul enjoys in the afterlife.

Valla's Epicureanism was inspired by another distinctive aspect of Renaissance naturalism. If human beings were part of this world, he argued, then their social and political lives mattered as much as the religious and speculative. His target here was the medieval scholastics again, who tended to ascribe a higher value to metaphysics and contemplation.

However, this thought carries a corollary that is perhaps again surprising when set alongside the modern meaning of naturalism. The Renaissance humanists worried that too much of an interest in nature, that is in science, might neglect the study of humanity's social and political natures. Thus, Leonardo Bruni could write in *Isagogicon Moralis Disciplinae*, or 'Introduction to Moral Philosophy':

> Moral philosophy is, so to speak, our territory. Those who betray it, and give themselves over to physics, seem in a way to occupy themselves with foreign affairs and to neglect their own.

He did not mean that 'physics' should not be studied, but that it should not be studied to the neglect or detriment of moral philosophy.

Heliocentrism and persecution

There is another way in which the years of the Renaissance, and those that followed, made the pursuit of science rather different from what it is today. It was at times a risky subject for humanists to pursue. Many were persecuted and some were killed for beliefs linked to the new discipline. The person who has become a symbol of this clash between the new learning and the old Church is Galileo Galilei (1564–1642).

Galileo might have been remembered for his fundamental contributions to the study of motion, and his powerful advocacy of the notion that the book of nature was written in the language of mathematics and thus could be explored by experimentation. After all, when he showed that the speed at which a ball drops is not proportional to its weight – by dropping two balls from the top of Pisa's famous leaning tower – he caused quite a stir. Science had presumed weight determines fall, as Aristotle had.

Galileo also had an interest in telescopes. At first, he became known for the improvements he made to this new technology. When he turned his more powerful telescope to the heavens and discovered the moons of Jupiter and many more stars than could be seen with the naked eye, even greater financial rewards followed. But things started to go wrong when he showed that Venus had phases like the moon, Saturn had rings and the sun sunspots. This suggested to him that the heavens were not perfect and confirmed his belief in the Copernican theory that the sun was the centre of the universe, not the earth. In 1615, the Inquisition declared that heliocentrism was heretical. Galileo was admonished by Robert Cardinal Bellarmine not to teach it.

Then, in 1630, Galileo completed another book, *Dialogue Concerning the Two Chief World Systems, Ptolemaic and*

Copernican, in which he discussed heliocentrism but only as a hypothesis. The dialogue is a witty read, featuring a character named Simplicio as an old-fashioned Aristotelian. The Florentine censors did not object to it. However, Pope Urban III advocated a position that was remarkably similar to that of Simplicio. In 1633 the Inquisition noticed the similarities and Galileo was summoned to Rome. The trial that ensued reached an impasse and it was a kind of plea bargain that led to Galileo renouncing his heresy in exchange for a life of house arrest.

Persecution and hermeticism

In many ways Galileo got off lightly; a few years earlier the Italian philosopher Lucilio Vanini had been burnt at the stake for proposing that natural explanations might account for miracles. However, that it took 350 years for the Vatican to pardon Galileo has become infamous in the annals of contemporary humanism, and Galileo has become a symbol of the conflict between science and religion. His conviction did have a pernicious effect at the time. For example, it deterred Descartes from publishing his own revolutionary scientific work a few years later.

What is often forgotten now, though, is that at the time heliocentrism was not so much associated with new science as with old occultism. It reflected the mystical, ancient Egyptian view of the universe propagated in hermeticism and it was this that many in the Church objected to. For example, such occultism was the crime that took Giordano Bruno (1548–1600) to the stake. In modern times Bruno has been transformed into a martyr of free philosophical enquiry, notably in the nineteenth century when his statue was set up in Rome's Campo dei Fiori. But it was only with his occultism obscured that he could be celebrated as such.

Art and humanism

Another theme that it is worth considering is that of the relationship between the arts and Renaissance humanism. If Burkhardt's book, *The Civilization of the Renaissance in Italy*, established the link between the Renaissance and humanism, Giorgio Vasari's sixteenth-century book, *Lives of the Artists*, suggested that there had been a parallel development in the visual arts, too. Might this, then, be another expression of humanism that we should consider? After all, twentieth-century humanism was to become closely associated with the arts. Vasari himself had argued that the thirteenth and fourteenth centuries witnessed art in an infancy that grew into the fifteenth- and sixteenth-century period of sublime perfection. And yet, any straightforward link between Renaissance art and Renaissance humanism is in fact hard to establish.

One possible point of contact was the humanists' interest in antiquities, including sculpture and architecture. For example, it is surely no coincidence that Nero's famous palace in Rome, the *Domus Aurea*, which had been buried for centuries, was rediscovered towards the end of the fifteenth century when visitors were lowered in their hundreds into the rooms or 'grottoes' that remained underground. Artists were amongst them, including Filippino Lippi and later Raphael – whose signature can still be seen on a wall. They copied what they saw and variously incorporated it into their work, notably in the Vatican.

However, it is one thing to share a belief that Ancient Roman civilization represented an excellence that was worth imitating, as both the artists and the humanists did. It is another thing to suggest that the development of Renaissance art was itself an expression of humanism. There was a handful of humanists who wrote about art, notably Leon Battista Alberti (1404–1472), who produced treatises on painting, sculpture and architecture. What is questionable, though, is the use they might have been to any actual painter, sculptor or architect. Scholars today have suggested perhaps very little.

The most important synergy between Renaissance humanists and artists seems to have been in terms of the former helping to create an environment in which rich patrons would commission works by the latter featuring secular history and classical mythology. For it seems likely that most Renaissance humanists had the same attitude towards art as medieval churchmen: art should be didactic – its function was to instruct the masses. The written word alone was the proper medium for the pursuit of ideas.

The dignity of man

Perhaps the single most important theme for which the Renaissance humanists are remembered by humanists today – putting even science in second place – is their championing of the freedom and dignity of humankind: man became an object of wonder. During the Renaissance, man's maker, God, shared in the glory, but it was a substantial shift to suggest that the Creator's special creature was worth contemplating too. Once again, a new anthropocentrism was rubbing up against medieval theocentrism. Let us now address the theme head on.

The Renaissance celebration of humankind can be set against a tendency to be pessimistic about human nature in the medieval period. That reached a peak at the end of the twelfth century when Lothar of Trasimund, later to become Pope Innocent III, wrote a treatise entitled *On the Misery of the Human Condition*. The treatise did what it said on the cover and was very popular for so doing.

Things started to change when, in 1452, the humanist Giannozzo Manetti wrote a counterblast praising humankind, *On the Dignity of Man*. Drawing on Saint Augustine as well as Cicero, Manetti argued that a Stoical suppression of the passions was unnatural. He contrasted the old Pope's picture of the human body as putrefaction with one of harmony, reflecting God's nature. Like God, no more powerfully do human beings reveal their true dignity than in creative acts.

This was a theme that gained momentum over the Renaissance years, arguably culminating in the 1496 treatise of Pico della Mirandola, the *Oration on the Dignity of Man*. Typical of Pico's syncretistic approach is his knitting together of the book of Genesis and Plato's *Timaeus*, both again dealing with creation. He imagines God speaking to humanity, saying: 'We have set thee at the world's centre that thou mayest from thence more easily observe whatever is in the world.' Or, a little further on: 'Thou shalt have the power, out of thy soul's judgement, to be reborn into higher forms, which are divine.'

Philosophically, perhaps the most profound innovation in Pico's *Oration* was his departure from Aristotle. In Aristotelianism, the nature of something determines its limits. A flower must grow into a flower; even a person's potential is limited by their human nature. Pico abandoned this theory. He argued that man was made in freedom rather than according to nature. Thus, human beings can choose for themselves what they become by being endowed with tremendous powers of self-creation, the wise adopting a spiritual path. This is, in fact, what it means to be a person, an almost limitless quality that human beings share with the truly limitless God.

Many contemporary humanists continue to celebrate Pico because he draws attention to the freedom of humankind in a particular sense, that of being able to make choices. They follow Burkhardt in regarding Pico as a pioneer of individualism and modernity.

Man as magus

However, other recent scholarship has called this interpretation of the *Oration* into question – and this reflects back on the issue with which we first came across Pico, namely his interest in hermeticism and Kabbalah. The new scholarship argues that when Pico was talking about human freedom he meant it in a very different sense from the contemporary humanist. Pico's freedom was that of the magician – the *magus* – the person who could control matter through secret knowledge. Alternatively, when Pico declares that humanity has the power 'to be reborn into higher forms, which are divine,' he is saying people can have access to divine, as in occult, knowledge. This is rather different from the idea that humankind might itself be divine and so in some sense be equal to, or perhaps eventually do away with, God.

Similarly, it used to be thought that his 12 books against astrology were objecting to the astrological assumption that the heavens controlled humankind, and thus curtailed human freedom. Rather, it seems that he objected to the astrologer's belief that the heavens could influence the mind as well as matter. For Pico, the mind is rather on a par with the heavens in being able to influence matter along with the stars.

Taming the herd

Another figure to remember when considering the complex nature of the Renaissance humanist attitudes towards human dignity is Machiavelli. As part of his work in politics he studied Roman history, and many of the incidents he read about convinced him that people need to be ruled by power lest they become unruly like a herd. 'Men are corrupted and make themselves become of a contrary nature, even though good and well educated,' he argued in his *Discourses*. Ill-fortune is the enemy. He believed that it is only by struggling daily to attain virtue that human beings can train themselves and thereby gain dignity.

Machiavelli is in some ways an anomalous figure to include amongst the Renaissance humanists since he often criticized his fellows. In his *Discourses*, he complains that while the celebration of antiquity is common in his day, few people get beyond mere celebration. However, many argue that it is right to think of him as a humanist, if only to highlight that the humanists taken as a whole rarely agreed about anything.

Machiavelli studied with humanist teachers, loved Latin – though he wrote in Italian – and was drawn particularly to the philosophy of Epicurus. Indeed, a manuscript in Machiavelli's hand of the great Epicurean poem by Lucretius, *On the Nature of Things*, survives to this day. He had an ambivalent attitude towards Christianity, believing it exalted weakness. However, he did not want to do away with the Church, an aim he regarded as futile. Rather, he thought the Church should be used to increase the power of the state.

Machiavelli's best known work, *The Prince*, was written in 1513–14 in order to secure employment from Lorenzo de' Medici the Younger. He failed in that respect, though his work is now thought of as a canonical text in political science. In it he articulates how a state can most effectively maintain law and order – leading to the necessity sometimes of doing things that are themselves immoral but, when considered in the round, prevent greater evils.

The reformed mind

We have looked at a number of key figures in the emergence of the Renaissance, and also at some of the key themes that they adopted as their own – language and education, science, the dignity of humankind. We must now adopt a slightly more historical perspective once again, for as the Renaissance summer moved towards its autumn, another major religious and political change began to make its presence felt. It was the Reformation.

The *Encyclopedia Britannica* defines the Reformation as a 'religious revolution that took place in the Western Church in the sixteenth century; its greatest leaders undoubtedly were Martin Luther and John Calvin. Having far-reaching political, economic, and social effects, the Reformation became the basis for the founding of Protestantism, one of the three major branches of Christianity.'

It is hard to overestimate the impact that humanist scholarship had on the Reformation. Many historians argue that the Reformation would not have happened without it and that the events which shattered Europe can be called that rare thing: a genuine and literal battle of ideas. The Reformation was also important in securing a future for many of the nascent developments in the Renaissance, not least those that centered on the interest in humankind. However, most pre-Reformation humanists did not see their work as subversive but rather as helpful to the Church as the guardian of truth, as well as being commensurate with their own Christian faith.

After all, new translations of the New Testament and Psalms had been published during the fifteenth century, decades before Martin Luther (1483–1546) pinned his Ninety-Five Theses to the door of a church in Wittenberg in 1517, the first symbolic act of the Reformation. From these translations, the first attempts at what can be called modern Biblical criticism had begun to emerge. For example, in 1516, Desiderius Erasmus (1466–1536), in a Latin translation of the New Testament, had doubted Saint Paul's authorship of the Epistle to the Hebrews and Saint John the Evangelist's writing of Revelation.

It is also worth remembering that although the Greek New Testament that Erasmus published with his Latin translation subsequently became the cornerstone of Protestant theology, he remained a Catholic. Nevertheless, there were enough sticklers for tradition, particularly in the universities, who regarded the new learning as amateur or immature. Thus the humanists and the reformers often found they had common enemies. So it would be truer to say that mostly there was a coincidence of interests between them rather than that they were fighting from a common cause.

Tolerance and truth

The Reformation can be seen as the end of the Renaissance period, and it was a time blighted by the wars of religion that followed in the sixteenth and seventeenth centuries. Subsequent reactions to the horrors committed during this time played no small part in the cultivation of the secular ideals of religious tolerance, another humanist theme. This is based upon the belief that it is vital for peace and prosperity that religions be allowed to co-exist in mutual freedom and tolerance. No one should be able to repress another.

However, unlike the humanists today who would advocate the necessity of a separation of Church and state in a secular setting, the original humanist conception of things was different in this respect. Most of them were of the opinion that all human beliefs shared a fundamental unity because, however discovered, they were all a reflection of ultimate Truth. One of the most optimistic individuals in this regard was Pico. He thought that universal peace would ensue when the common origins of all the traditions that interested him were recognized. And Erasmus and Thomas More, in the sixteenth century, defended religious toleration on the basis that the details of people's convictions were often ambiguous and difficult to ascertain precisely. Dissenters should therefore always be allowed and debate encouraged.

However, by the mid-part of the sixteenth century, the Catholic Council of Trent and Protestant Calvinism became suspicious of the virtues of tolerance. For if in liberal minds diversity can be seen as manifesting an underlying unity, in conservative minds diversity can also be interpreted as undermining unity. There is a fine line between the two, and it is easy to slip from one to the other. Erasmus's own books became subject to the censor, and with the brutal course of events that followed, toleration almost died.

Renaissance friendship

Our brief discussion of the Reformation has brought to mind the figure of Erasmus. So on a happier note let us consider his friendship with another key player of the time, Thomas Moore (1477–1535).

Erasmus was a priest who published books concerned with piety as well as philosophy that sold well across Europe. He was born in Rotterdam to a poor family, attended university in Paris, and lectured at Cambridge during the reign of Henry VIII. Thomas More, Henry VIII's chancellor and author of *Utopia*, was a close friend of Erasmus. More lost his head when he refused to accept his King as the head of the Church of England, but in the twentieth century was made a saint by the Catholic Church. Though he believed he did not have a vocation to the priesthood, and trained in law, he remained a pious man throughout his life.

The intimacy of the two friends inspired them both to greater things. More's *Utopia* – meaning 'no place', a word that he coined himself – pays homage to Plato who had written about another theoretical state in *The Republic*. More advocated the mitigation of human evils rather than the search for a universal cure because he believed human fallibility would always undo them. *Utopia* can be thought of as a response to Erasmus's earlier *Praise of Folly* in which he had written: 'No state has been so plagued by its rulers as when power has fallen into the hands of some dabbler in philosophy.'

The Bible in translation

More was a great supporter of Erasmus's translation into Latin of the New Testament. In return, Erasmus presented More as a model intellectual to other European humanists, not least because of his Stoical commitment to learning. For example, in his translation of the Bible, he strove hard to be faithful to the Greek version, even to the extent of changing some of the gospels' most famous lines: the first words of John's gospel were not translated as 'In the beginning was the Word' but 'In the beginning was the speech [or discussion].'

As a Catholic, Erasmus was unsuccessful in trying to get Martin Luther to moderate his language after Luther was condemned by the Pope in 1520. He shared many of the emerging Protestant concerns about the Church, though he did not follow Luther when the reformer ditched five of Catholicism's seven sacraments and taught that salvation could be achieved by faith in Christ and faith alone. The most lengthy philosophical dispute between Erasmus and Luther concerned free will. It is a topic that has become increasingly important in philosophy since the Reformation, arguably because of the Reformation. Luther thought there was no such thing, so corrupted were human beings by sin. Erasmus believed that people did have free will, though he argued not so much by expanding on subtle points of philosophy – much of which he despised as scholastic verbiage – as by asking why, if there was no such thing, the Bible was so full of encouragement to take care when choosing between good and evil.

Thomas More, Erasmus's friend, had a parallel argument with another reformer, this time the English Bible translator William Tyndale (1490–1536). More argued that if the actions of people were all determined – i.e. there is no such thing as free will – then all of their actions would also be excusable since they could not be held accountable for them. In short, morality would cease to exist – a charge faced by all deterministic accounts of human behaviour.

More fell out with Henry VIII when the king wanted to create a Church of England independent of Rome. He was duly executed – an act that shocked even Protestant Europe. Erasmus described More as 'a man for all seasons', and his genius as 'such that England never had and never again will have its like'.

Humanism's greatest son?

If Erasmus was arguably the Renaissance's greatest scholar, then someone else will undoubtedly be remembered as its greatest son, the literary genius William Shakespeare (1564–1616) – a genius who was as profoundly shaped by the Reformation as the Renaissance.

Shakespeare was the son of a lowly citizen from a provincial town and received a modest grammar school education. That he should become, through the writing of plays and poems, not only successful in his own lifetime but subsequently be recognized as one of the greats of world literature, is no small indication of the success of Renaissance humanism.

Shakespeare shows his debt to humanism at a number of levels. Ben Jonson famously thought it was remarkable that although Shakespeare had 'small Latin and less Greek', his work shone alongside the greatest of the Greeks and Romans. That he is at ease with ancient sources meant he must have relied on the translations of the humanists. He also wrote in blank verse as well as rhyme, following the humanists who thought rhyme unclassical.

Alternatively, Shakespeare was a playwright who used dramatic literature to think, and in particular to think about, what it is to be human. Thus, inasmuch as the scholastics of the medieval period loved to systematize, Shakespeare seems close to the humanist aspiration of finding not abstract answers to the fundamental questions of life but practical ones. As Aristotle says in the *Poetics* – a text that became increasingly important in the late Renaissance – poetry is philosophical because it expresses the universal, though not by seeking systems of unified thought but by exploring the kinds of things that might happen, not least in the lives of real people.

The dangers of rhetoric

At another level, Shakespeare shows his indebtedness to humanism in his central interest: human beings. Pico's *Oration* on *the Dignity of Man* must have influenced him, when in *Hamlet* he has the prince contemplate, 'What a piece of work is a man ...' However, as befits the later humanist period, Shakespeare is ambivalent about many of the themes celebrated by earlier humanists, too. Take rhetoric. *Julius Caesar* contains a brilliant demonstration of its double-edged power in the speech delivered by Mark Antony over the still-warm body of Caesar. Antony deploys rhetoric to deadly effect when he whips up the crowd and sparks more bloodshed. Perhaps Shakespeare had read Plato's worry about this art when the philosopher – another master of it – wrote in his dialogue, the *Phaedrus,* that rhetoric can make 'the likely be held in higher honour than the true'.

Alternatively, Shakespeare can be read as interrogating one of the favourite moral philosophies of the humanists, namely Stoicism. Consider another passage from *Julius Caesar,* the soliloquy of Brutus when he persuades himself that to murder Caesar, his friend, is an honourable action when done for the sake of the Republic. Stoicism is a philosophy that believes moral distress can be solved through rational argument. In Brutus's soliloquy, Shakespeare weaves in a strand that leaves the audience feeling something is not quite right with the logic Brutus has deployed to resolve his dilemma. It is as if Shakespeare is saying that reason can be used as a way of avoiding the pain of difficult choices, but only under the guise of an inhuman detachment.

Renaissance scepticism

We have seen now, several times, that Renaissance humanists argued about many things – the goodness of human nature, the virtues of Plato and Aristotle, the freedom of humankind. However, they also debated the nature of truth itself. For some, such as Pico, truth was out there, waiting to be discovered. For others, truth was far less certain. So as we come towards the end of our examination of Renaissance humanism, let us look at how the sceptical tradition of ancient philosophy was reinvigorated at the time.

Montaigne is the key figure here. The works of the Ancient Greek radical sceptic Sextus Empiricus were unknown in the Middle Ages. They were rediscovered in the mid-sixteenth century and popularized by Montaigne. Montaigne lived in France during a period of its history marked by sectarian strife and war. At a more personal level, in mid-life, he fell into a period of profound melancholy, following the deaths of a child and a very close friend. His essays were a kind of therapy, and scepticism suited his mood. 'All that is certain is that nothing is certain,' Sextus had written – and he meant nothing.

This philosophy puts Montaigne somewhat at odds with the optimism of some humanists who came before him. They knew of more moderate forms of scepticism, but not the sort that called all judgements made by humankind into question, whether based on the senses or reason.

For example, in his longest and one of the most famous of his essays, 'Apology for Raimond Sebond', Montaigne displays his classical learning with copious quotes from Greek and Roman authors. However, many of them serve to deflate not praise human nature – sometimes by contrasting the extraordinary abilities of animals with the pedestrian capabilities of humankind; sometimes by arguing that even humanity's greatest faculties, like reason, are strictly limited. Following Cicero, he wrote: 'It is impossible to say anything so absurd that it has not been said already by some philosopher or other.'

Questioning ancient authority

Alternatively, in his essay, 'On Experience', he undermined one of the implicit assumptions of many Renaissance thinkers, namely that because a text originated in antiquity it came with a kind of natural authority. Montaigne complained that the trouble with a high regard for antiquity is that contemporary times differ so radically. Roman and Greek authorities must be ripped out of their historic period and so can only roughly be reapplied to later times and places.

Montaigne also argued that the pretensions of human knowledge were exposed by the faith of the religious believer who received insights not by the clumsy processes of reason but the bright lights of revelation. This opinion contrasts directly with what many humanists today take as humanism's defining characteristic: it relies on human capacities alone. Having said that, Montaigne's argument is a more subtle one than that of the believer who simply falls into the arms of their church. Montaigne is following Socrates in suggesting that the key to wisdom is not the accumulation of knowledge but an understanding of the limits of knowledge. In this, he is still widely read as an exemplar of the sceptical strand within humanism.

The end of the Renaissance

The Renaissance period ended with the strife of the Reformation. But even so, by the end of the sixteenth century, humanism as a movement could claim to have become the dominant culture of the establishment across Europe. It even straddled both sides of the, by then, deeply entrenched Protestant/Catholic divide. Translations and popularizers, like Shakespeare, carried the humanist mentality from the elite who could afford an education to the people. Humanists had transformed Latin and broadened the curriculum, though those that wanted to had not ousted Aristotle who remained at the centre of any education until the scientific discoveries of the seventeenth century.

Summary

So how can we sum up Renaissance humanism? First, by again stressing its diversity. Humanists were both optimist and pessimistic about human capabilities. They submitted to classical authorities and were sceptical about the same authorities. Temperamentally, some were quietist, others were firebrands. However, Renaissance humanists shared several common attitudes, in particular, they exhibited the anthropocentrism that Burkhardt spotted as a new, defining kind of self-referential individualism. They did not all champion the dignity and freedom of humankind without qualification. But even those who critiqued it implicitly concurred with the notion that humankind was a worthwhile object of study for humankind.

They can also be said to some degree to have been liberal, for all that the term itself is anachronistic when applied to the period: many humanists advocated tolerance, had a sense of cultural relativism and believed in an individual's free will. Having said that, there was also a strong strand of conservatism in Renaissance humanism, stemming from its respect for the past.

They were usually religious men, some deeply pious, who saw the integration of reason and religion as central to the humanist task, again unlike many who would call themselves humanist now. However, they were not systematic thinkers like the giants of scholastic theology before them, or the greats of the Enlightenment who were to follow, and to whom we shall soon turn. Philosophy in the Renaissance was a way of life as much as a framework for thought.

The greatest of the Renaissance humanists became gadflies like Socrates, and voices of conscience like Cicero. The legacy of the Ancient Greek and Roman texts that they left is invaluable and they reinvigorated debates that still do not suggest easy resolution. Some struggled with the limits of human knowledge; others rejoiced in its great insights; and some opened the way for sceptical philosophy. Others were fired by the dream of human cultural, social and intellectual progress. But in this mix of opinion and passionate debate lie the connections that humanists today can still feel with their Renaissance forebears.

03

Enlightenment humanism

In this chapter you will learn:

- about the key themes of Enlightenment philosophy
- how some of its greatest figures conspired with and against one another
- that the arguments about religion within humanism are centuries old.

We have examined Renaissance humanism, with its powerful but complicated re-evaluation of language, education, science and the dignity of humankind. We have also seen how the period did not so much come to an end as become dispersed throughout the intellectual and cultural life of sixteenth- and then seventeenth-century Europe. Its distinctive impact became absorbed in the wider religious and political turmoil of the Reformation.

Progress in science also picked up in the seventeenth century. And then another force came to the fore, one with particular significance for contemporary humanism. It was called the Enlightenment. It marked another distinctive shift in attitudes towards the humanist themes of humankind, knowledge, religion and ethics that shaped the tradition as it comes to us today – though again, it should be remembered that no one at the time would have thought of themselves as a humanist. So to explore the arguments, personalities and impact of the philosophy of the eighteenth century and following years, first let us ask just what the Enlightenment was, and how it began.

Light dispelling darkness

In the first half of the eighteenth century, the title pages of several German philosophy books appeared to share a common design. The sun was shown shining through departing clouds. To ensure the message was not missed a caption might spell it out, reading something along the lines of 'light dispelling darkness'. In short, these books carried a philosophy that saw itself as enlightening – or as of a period of Enlightenment, or *Aufklärung* as it is in German. The power behind this enlightenment was reason. And, depending on whose book you were reading, the darkness the enlightenment was dispelling was that of ignorant beliefs, repressive governments, oppressive priests and/or unscientific opinions.

The leitmotif of the Enlightenment had probably originated elsewhere. In England, historians have pushed its inception all the way back to the Glorious Revolution of 1688 when many of the issues that became non-negotiable to Enlightenment thinkers, and subsequently contemporary humanism, were written into English law: freedom of the individual, *habeas corpus*, religious toleration, parliamentary rule and, of course, the rule of law itself. There was a marked intellectual flourishing in England at this time, too, that found a variety of expressions in the publication of pamphlets and newspapers, the opening of public libraries and a widespread interest in the theatre. These developments were heralded as symptomatic of an enlightened age.

Alternatively, in 1704, Isaac Newton (1642–1727) – the genius of the Enlightenment whose earlier book *Principia Mathematica* invented calculus, overturned Aristotelian science by making the laws of motion fundamental, and explained gravity as action at a distance – published his second great treatise, this time on light, entitled *Optiks*. A few years later, it led Alexander Pope to pen his brilliant lines: 'Nature, and Nature's Laws lay hid in Night: God said, *Let Newton Be! and All was Light*.' And about the same time, the Frenchman César de Saussure had written a letter back home, remarking how 'wonderfully well lighted' London was. He meant it literally and yet his comment worked metaphorically too.

In Scotland another Enlightenment was underway, this time revolving around a group of intellectuals including the economists Adam Smith (1723–90) and Adam Ferguson (1723–1816), and the philosophers David Hume (1711–76) and Thomas Reid (1710–96). They pursued their interests across a variety of fields but were committed to a scientific outlook, even when they found it problematic. They felt sure that the new prosperity Scotland was enjoying was kindling a superior, if not flawless, new way of life.

France, too, had a claim to be the birthplace and home of the Enlightenment. Since the turn of the seventeenth century, French *philosophes,* or 'freethinkers', had been developing the themes for which the Enlightenment as a philosophical movement became known. They revolved around questions about God, human nature and the possibility of a scientific understanding of social and political institutions. Religious toleration was advocated. The relationship between belief and morality was probed. The proofs for the existence of God were investigated. Historical and empirical studies explored the goods and ills of the human condition.

The sum of knowledge

If there was one date on which all this enterprise came together, it could be in 1751. In that year the slow but steady publication of the famous *Encyclopédie* edited by Denis Diderot (1713–84) and Jean d'Alembert (1717–83), subtitled 'A Rational

Dictionary of Arts and Sciences' began. The project had started out relatively modestly but soon the two editors massively expanded their ambition. They searched out and found a collection of writers, scientists and clergymen – many at the time unknown – that, like Rousseau and Voltaire, were to become famous. They were committed to the cause of furthering knowledge by collating in one place the essentials of every art and science.

The *Encyclopédie* has assumed a central place in the history of humanism because of what it stood for and what it contained. A flavour of it can be gained by considering two short extracts – the first taken from the entry entitled 'Humanity':

> [Humanity] is a feeling of good will toward all men. Ordinarily only great and sensitive souls are consumed by it. This noble and sublime enthusiasm is tortured by the sufferings of others and tormented by the need to relieve such suffering; it fills men with the desire to traverse the world in order to do away with slavery, superstition, vice, and misfortune ... I have discovered this virtue, which is the source of so many others, in many heads but in very few hearts.

Then there is this from the entry 'Religion':

> [It has been said that the] diversity of religions, that is to say, the various manners of honoring God, are agreeable to Him because they all have the same object, they all tend to the same purpose, whatever their various means ... [This is] a false principle since God has declared that he was rejecting one cult or another as insufficient or imperfect, and that he was adopting another one as more pure and more reasonable.

Goodwill towards human beings; artistic sensitivities; a horror at suffering and a desire to spread justice; a sharp critique of popular theology and the Church – in short, the *Encyclopédie* propagated a philosophy of rationalism, confident in the power of reason, and exemplified an optimistic if nuanced account of the possibility of human progress. Coupled to its celebration of the 'mechanical arts' – the machines that were transforming the world in the Industrial Revolution – it became nothing short of an Enlightenment manifesto.

But the *Encyclopédie* can be thought of as representing something else about the Enlightenment, too, namely that characteristic of humanism with which we are already familiar: its diversity. For the contributions from the principle players in this great work showed nothing if not a substantial spread of opinion. Let us now turn to some of them, their lives and beliefs.

The atheist wing

Consider the philosophy of the two editors, d'Alembert and Diderot. D'Alembert was originally a scientist, having contributed to advances in Newtonian physics, and believed that once scientific explanations had been found for all things, which they would, knowledge itself would come to be seen as unified. He was also a passionate advocate of the need for the public to be educated about science. In this way humankind would continue to progress. This is no doubt why he became involved with the *Encyclopédie*. However, though a theological sceptic and hostile to Christianity, he refrained from becoming overtly anti-religious. For example, when the Jesuits were expelled from France in the mid-1760s – a triumph for their religious not rationalist opponents – d'Alembert wrote a pamphlet arguing that though the Jesuits had been compromised by their love of power, they were nevertheless excellent scholars and educators.

The other editor, Diderot, was different. He was a self-confessed atheist. In fact, in 1749, he spent three months in prison because of his *Letter on the Blind*. Though a minor document in terms of the history of ideas, it can be thought of as a model piece of writing from the kind of atheistic humanism he typifies. On the one hand, the *Letter* advocates supremely humane goals, in this case teaching the blind to read by exploiting their sense of touch. It took another century for Louis Braille to put the idea into practice. On the other hand, Diderot allows himself to be led by the new discoveries in science. In the *Letter*, he ponders what looks like a nascent theory of evolution as a result of advantageous adaptation and the survival of the fittest. And then behind these two apparently disparate speculations lies a materialist atheism that not only gives priority to the senses, as the way human beings interact with the world, but also questions the evidence for any indications of design in the universe. It was for challenging this long-assumed 'proof' of God's existence that he was imprisoned.

Another prominent atheist of the period was the Baron d'Holbach (1723–89). He enjoyed substantial inherited wealth and deployed it by funding an infamous philosophical salon. Though a genteel man, some of the opinions expressed at these gatherings were so shocking that otherwise robust *philosophes* withdrew, including it seems d'Alembert. D'Holbach contributed hundreds of articles to the *Encyclopédie*, on scientific themes. Perhaps his wealth provided him with a sense of security since he also published, if under pseudonyms, explicitly anti-Christian diatribes with titles such as *Christianity Unveiled*. He also championed the life of a Catholic priest, Jean Meslier, who had died in 1729 and left behind a kind of confession in which he expressed regret for having spent a lifetime teaching the 'errors' of Christianity, having privately preferred social reform and atheistic materialism all along.

Another book of d'Holbach, *The System of Nature*, not only celebrated atheism and derided religion, but propounded the view that human beings were machines devoid of free will: 'We are no more in charge of events than colliding balls are able to determine the directions in which they bounce.' Having said that, he also did not hesitate to open up his home to offer sanctuary to the fleeing Jesuits in the 1760s.

Deism and progress

D'Alembert, Diderot and d'Holbach represent one wing of the Enlightenment, that of overt even aggressive atheism. But others occupied more central, if also passionately felt, ground.

François-Marie Arouet de Voltaire (1694–1778) was one of these. Voltaire was a deist, someone who believes that the existence of God is amply displayed by reason and in nature, though differing from orthodox believers inasmuch as deists argue that any revealed knowledge of God – derived say from holy books – is mistaken. One practical outcome of this position is that deists hold that God does not answer prayer. So whilst not an atheist, deism nonetheless put Voltaire at odds with the Catholic Church and, indeed, the French king. He was jailed twice, had books banned and was eventually banished. His personal life exhibited the liberties not uncharacteristic of freethinkers. He never married but had two long-term affairs with women.

Voltaire seems to have been stirred to outright confrontation with the Church after a particularly ugly incident in Toulouse. Toulouse was a fiercely Catholic city in southern France where the clergy enjoyed effective sovereignty. In 1761, Voltaire took into his home the Toulousain family of Jean Calas. As head of the family, Jean himself had been brutally executed by the Church as a result of a rumour that he had murdered his son for becoming a Catholic. Voltaire felt great sympathy at this story of what he interpreted as medieval, hideously backward persecution. It helped persuade him of the need to be a man of action as well as of letters. Soon after the incident he adopted his motto, *Écrasez l'infâme!* – Crush the infamy! – and became a campaigner as well as a writer.

Having said that, Voltaire always remained hard to pin down. For example, he was not afraid to pick a fight with atheists too. Consider this section from his *Philosophical Dictionary*, a book that became his own personal alternative to the *Encyclopédie*:

> Atheism is a monstrous evil in those who govern; and also in learned men even if their lives are innocent, because from their studies they can affect those who hold office; and that, even if not as baleful as fanaticism, it is nearly always fatal to virtue ... as a well-known author has said, a catechism announces God to children, and Newton demonstrates him to wise men.

This excerpt exemplifies a number of principles Voltaire held dear, including that atheism undermines the foundations of morality, and hence is 'fatal to virtue', particularly among the uneducated. As he put it elsewhere, 'If God did not exist, it would be necessary to invent him' – though for Voltaire there was no need to do so since evidence in nature abounded all around.

The Lisbon earthquake

Moreover, Voltaire argued that the universe was a direct consequence of God's existence: be it for good or ill, God had no choice but to create the world in which we live, for creativity is part and parcel of the divine nature. This inevitability was how he came to understand the existence of evil in the world, and in particular the catastrophic earthquake of 1755 in Lisbon – an event that killed 30,000 people and shook the faith of many to the core.

Voltaire tried to come to terms with this event in a number of ways. Probably the most famous resulted in his philosophical fantasy *Candide*. Candide is a young man and disciple of one Doctor Pangloss who, because of the misfortunes that befall him, cannot believe that the world in which he lives is 'the best of all possible worlds'. He retires and finds happiness in cultivating a garden, a practical way of life that avoids needless speculation about why some things happen.

In another similarly pessimistic work, *Poème sur le désastre de Lisbonne*, Voltaire makes a different point. He rages: 'Evil is upon the earth, You foolish philosophers who cried: "All is well".' It is a rebuke both to the optimistic atheists who championed scientific progress and the complacent believers who opined that all rests secure in the hands of God. In the poem, Voltaire admits his own ignorance about the implications and meaning of terrible events. But he prefers to wrestle with that uncertainty than seek consolation in the hope that things will get better, whether through divine grace or human endeavour.

Mistakes in materialism

Voltaire also charged atheists with making a mistake about their philosophy of materialism. Materialism is the view that everything is made of physical matter and physical matter alone, excluding the possibility of spirits, say, or disembodied forms. Voltaire noted that the scientist proceeds as if matter is all there is because matter is all science can work on. However, this *practical* materialism – implicit in the experimental methods of science – is not the same as making a commitment to a *doctrine* of materialism as if matter really is all that exists, an affirmation which an atheist might make. Voltaire thought that these different kinds of materialism are what can be erroneously confused. He unpicked the difference in a direct riposte to d'Holbach, *God, a Reply to the System of Nature*.

In this Voltaire followed the ideas of the most important English philosopher of the early modern period, John Locke (1632–1704). In a number of works, including *Letter Concerning Toleration* (1689), *Treatises of Government* (1690), *Essay Concerning Human Understanding* (1690), Locke argued for popular consent in politics and religious toleration. He also thought of philosophers as 'under-labourers' – in his case to Newton – their task being conceptually to prepare the ground for a proper scientific understanding of things. This is an idea of philosophy that is still common, particularly in Anglo-American universities.

Locke also had an interesting tripartite model of what it was to be human. For Locke, human beings are at once men and women (that is human animals), spirits (that is souls) and persons (that is individuals who are conscious of themselves as individuals). It was a complicated system that Locke himself knew faced many difficulties that were not easily resolved. For example, how do these different parts link to one another to form the seamless human whole that we experience in our everyday lives? But what is significant about Locke's model is that it opposes strict materialism, highlighting how that philosophy flounders at certain points also. How, for example, can materialists explain why free will feels like such an intimate and indispensable part of what it is to be human if, as d'Holbach had suggested, it is nothing more than a sophisticated delusion? This is another debate that continues to this day.

Turning back to Voltaire, and considering the matter of human progress – another tenet of the humanism of Diderot and d'Alembert – the French deist was also agnostic. Publicly, he could certainly present himself as a champion of the advancing capabilities of humankind and the triumph of reason through Enlightenment. But perhaps this was more for rhetorical effect than private convictions. In 1762, he wrote: 'I rather share the opinion of the Englishman who said that all origins, all laws, all institutions, are like a plum pudding: the first person put in the flour, the next added the eggs, the third the sugar, a fourth raisins; and so we have plum pudding.' In other words, if it exists at all, progress is perhaps more a process of chance than design. A better way of defining his humanism is simply to say that it stems from the fact that his chief interest is in human beings – something he once confessed to the famous Enlightenment sovereign Frederick the Great. It is a simple, uncluttered definition of humanism that still appeals to some.

Human nature

In the characters of d'Alembert, Diderot and d'Holbach we have considered the phenomenon of Enlightenment atheism. In the philosophies of Voltaire and Locke we have seen something of a critique of that position, and the themes of deism and ambivalence about progress that existed during the Enlightenment too. We will turn now to a third and arguably defining theme of humanism, one that dominated the Renaissance too, namely that of the nature of what it is to be human.

To do so, let's consider another person who moved in the circles of the *philosophes* and was different again: Jean-Jacques Rousseau (1712–78). Best remembered as the author of *The Social Contract* (1762), *Émile* (1762) and *Confessions* (1770), he also contributed to the *Encyclopédie* – this time with pieces on music. He was a friend of Diderot and friendly with Voltaire and d'Alembert, although to put it more accurately, he was friendly with them until 1750, when he shocked them all, not with another version of deism or attack on atheism but with an altogether different kind of heresy. He declared himself to be not just a sceptic about human progress but an out-and-out denier.

For some contemporary humanists, this would be enough to exclude him from the fold. However, Rousseau can rightly be called a humanist because, like Voltaire, his chief interest was human beings. He would also agree with Diderot's rhetorical question, 'Why not make man the central focus?' In fact Rousseau had a particularly strong doctrine of humankind – or 'Man' as he put it. Nowhere is this clearer than in his 1762 masterpiece, *The Social Contract*, that begins with the famous line, 'Man is born free, but is everywhere in chains.' It is a summary of his doctrine of human nature.

Consider the use of the word 'Man' in that sentence. It is an abstract noun, referring not to men – even less women – amidst the toils and tribulations of actual lives. Rather, it refers to a universal conception of the essence of humanity. The first line of the book could be rewritten as, '*Man* is born free, but everywhere *men* are in chains.' In other words, Rousseau subscribes to what is called essentialism: in spite of what you see of the *men* enslaved around you, there is an underlying essence of *Man* within them that is free. This is the truest part of them, though it may be deeply concealed.

Civil liberties

For Rousseau the thing that enslaves individuals, that denies them their essentially free natures, is the social order into when they are unavoidably born. He contrasts this harsh reality with an imaginary 'state of nature' in which someone might freely follow their animal desires for food, sleep and companionship. There are ills in this natural state, notably of pain and hunger. However, nothing in the state of nature induces anything like the competitive desire for power that is characteristic of a developed society and that, thereby, enslaves us.

In this state – the state of the real world – men and women are forced to seek protection from economic and technological forces that oppress them, while at the same time they strive to thrive by aligning themselves with the very same things. This is what entails the loss of freedom. As a result, people are forced into co-operation which is nothing if not a curtailing of individual choices in the effort to accommodate those of others. Rousseau devises his social contract to mitigate this loss – to loosen the chains. It is one in which sovereignty is shared with each citizen, in return for which each citizen agrees to obey the laws laid down by that sovereign power. *Man* loses his natural liberty. *Men* gain their civil liberties.

The same essentialism is found in the earlier publication of 1750 that so shocked his fellow *philosophes*. This piece was in the form of an essay that he subsequently worked up into a book, *Discourse on the Origin of Inequality*. In the *Discourse* he describes how the ideal human is a 'noble savage', embodying a goodness that is uncorrupted by the institutions and advances of society. This is what caught the breath of the *philosophes*: Rousseau was explicitly saying that he didn't believe in social progress! Voltaire, who as we have seen was privately unsure about such things, summed up his confrères' feelings when he described the *Discourse* as a 'book against the human race'.

Even when he developed the theory in full in *The Social Contract*, and implied that human betterment was possible if the right kind of society could be constructed, the contract read like a necessary restriction on what the likes of Diderot and Voltaire took to be human beings' natural freedom. The split between Voltaire and Rousseau became complete when Rousseau later revealed that Voltaire was the anonymous author of various incendiary and potentially treasonable tracts. Voltaire replied by revealing that Rousseau was the father of five illegitimate children whom he had unceremoniously abandoned in a foundling hospital. This was a serious mark against his character, even in the eighteenth century.

Empiricism examined

Rousseau's idea of what it was to be human – that we are essentially free, though enslaved by society unless that society has the right kind of contractual politics – is just one model of human nature. The issue is important for humanism, so let us turn to another and again very different perspective on this question. We can do so by picking up on the story of the Enlightenment as it was unfolding in Scotland.

David Hume is the key figure here – not least because at the same time that Rousseau was splitting with Voltaire, Rousseau feared for his security in France, and so fled to London with Hume. Hume went out of his way to help Rousseau. Nevertheless, after only a year, a very public quarrel led to the two of them splitting as well. Rousseau could not make a go of this philosophical relationship either.

Hume is the towering philosophical figure of the Scottish Enlightenment. He was concerned with the limits of human reason and also the scepticism that inspires such critique, arguing that ultimately our judgements are based upon our sentiments not our logic. He expounded upon such thoughts in books including *A Treatise of Human Nature* (1739) – later to become *An Enquiry Concerning Human Understanding* (1748) and *An Enquiry Concerning the Principles of Morals* (1751), as well as *Dialogues Concerning Natural Religion* (1779).

So, what does he add to the question of the nature of human beings? Hume's take on the matter begins with a common assumption of the Enlightenment philosophers that he then pursues to its logical conclusion. The assumption is that in any scientific investigation, priority must be given to the senses – sight, hearing and so on. The name given to this approach is empiricism. Empiricism holds that experience through the five senses is what counts because it is this 'sense-data' that it is necessary to contend with if the world is to be revealed to us without human interpretation, and therefore free from any kind of mistaken distortion. Our minds process and can reshape the sense-data we receive for sure; we can make mistakes about the world around us. But the empiricist believes that through experimentation and testing, our concepts and ideas can be explored to determine what is true about the world as it is in itself. In other words, empiricism is the philosophy that most commonly lies behind science.

However, Hume noticed that relying on the senses is not as straightforward as it may seem. For example, if I look at a tree, I do not experience the tree but experience the sense-data that I receive from the tree. The tree as an object in the world is quite separate from me vis-à-vis the experience. The same is also true when I love someone. It might be thought that this is an alternative, direct way of experiencing the world, and a very intimate one at that. However, again, strictly speaking I only know of my experience of the love. The beloved, as another person, remains quite separate from me since they are mediated to me by my feelings. The implication is that empiricism might be wrong: any experience of the world as it is in itself falls from our grasp.

It is as if scnsc-data docs not conncct us with the world but stands between us and the world, and it might be thought that Hume conceives of the human condition as a kind of prison on an existential island. However, worse was to come. For Hume takes his logic a step further. He says that even our experience of *ourselves* must be an experience of sense-data. We are isolated from ourselves too – or to put it another way we cannot perceive ourselves as we are in ourselves, anymore than I can directly see my eye with my eye or smell my nose with my nose. Hume sums up this state of affairs in a famous passage from his *A Treatise of Human Nature*:

> There are some philosophers who imagine we are every moment intimately conscious of what we call our self ... For my part, when I enter most intimately into what I call *myself*, I always stumble on some particular perception or other, of heat or cold, light or shade, love or hatred, pain or pleasure. I can never catch *myself* at any time without a perception, and never can observe anything but the perception.

He concludes that this sense of 'myself' is, therefore, really just a bundle of different perceptions and ideas. There is, in truth, no self at all.

Scepticism and backgammon

To put it another way, and in contrast with Rousseau, Hume has a radically anti-essentialist idea of human nature. And it might be thought that there is not much point in discussing him any further, given that his philosophy seems so opposed to this key element within humanism. It seems as if Hume has reached a philosophical impasse, a kind of limit of thought. The implication would be that someone who goes along with him is left with one of two options: they either accept his radical scepticism and fall into silence, to say no more about this illusory self, or they effectively ignore him, and simply pick up where they otherwise left off on the humanist themes of human freedom, progress and so on.

The second option is the one Hume took himself. In a comment at the end of his sceptical reflections, he perhaps deliberately recalls, and twists, the image associated with the Enlightenment that we began with – that of the sun of reason dispelling the clouds of ignorance. Hume wrote: 'Most fortunately it happens, that since reason is incapable of dispelling these clouds, Nature herself suffices to that purpose.' In other words, where reason fails – such as in understanding what it is to be human – Nature herself shows us what is the case. This led Hume to a thoroughly humane way out of the corner into which he had apparently argued himself. He wrote that after too much philosophy:

> I dine, I play a game of backgammon, I converse, and am merry with my friends; and when after three or four hours amusement, I wou'd return to these speculations, they appear so cold, and strain'd, and ridiculous, that I cannot find in my heart to enter into them any farther.

In fact, and as an aside, there are rational ways around Hume's impasse – though they diverge from the strict empiricism he was examining. One possibility is to point out that while an individual may only receive perceptions of himself or herself, they are still his or her perceptions, and not anyone else's. This would seem to imply that there is, after all, a perceiving self which knows those perceptions as their own. However, this also suggests that the self is somehow separate from any sense-data, i.e. the self is some disembodied thing. This notion is what would upset the strict empiricist.

Another possibility would be to argue that the sum total of an individual's interactions with the world around them is not, in fact, gained only via sense-data perceived in the mind. Rather, we are embodied creatures, who interact with the world not just via mental impressions but with our physical bodies and, in particular, with ourselves as existing in particular times and places. This is why it makes sense to say that men and women can experience the world differently, though they have the same sorts of eyes, ears and the like.

The ethics of sympathy

So much for the problems with human nature and empiricism. However, Hume examined human nature in another way that is perhaps more straightforwardly illuminating and important for humanism, this time in relation to ethics. Ethics is the study of good and evil, motivations, decisions and moral foundations. It is clearly a crucial issue for humanism, particularly as humanists often want to identify a basis for their actions apart from a belief in God. If religious people can say they act in such and such a way because of their faith, on what basis can the humanist say they act, particularly if they are agnostic or atheistic?

It seems natural to assume that human beings do things – right or wrong, good or bad, benign or malign – for reasons. A typical model of how such ethical decision-making works goes something like this: if someone is a good person, they calculate the virtuousness of any particular action they might take, or make choices between two courses of action that they could take, and opt for the more virtuous and/or less vicious course.

But again, Hume is iconoclastic in this respect. He denies this is how humans operate. He believes that it is not *reason* but *passion* that lies at the heart of ethics. Reason plays a part, but only in channelling the passions that power what we do. His famous summary of why this is the case makes the bold claim that reason is not actually capable of making ethical decisions at all: 'Tis not contrary to reason to prefer the destruction of the whole world to the scratching of my finger.'

In general, Hume argues that moral behaviour is more a question of what *feels* right rather than what is *judged* right. Ethics is a question of pleasure – not the pleasure-seeking of the hedonist, but the pleasure that comes from doing something praiseworthy and without thought of personal gain.

It seems a little shocking – suggesting that mature adults are no more in control of what they do than a baby who cries when hungry and smiles when satisfied. But Hume is not so down on the passions, and explains that some of the 'best' of them are calm, even reason-like. So, there are people who are naturally kind, and others who are in possession of an innate *joie de vivre*. Others again have an appetite to spread goodness throughout the world. These tendencies reveal a very positive side to human nature. Or, to put it another way, an ethics based upon the human capacity to feel goodwill towards the world – an ethics of sympathy – which might be a very good one for the humanist to adopt.

Having said that, it might further be thought that a rather vague trust in benevolence, as this model of ethics seems to suggest, offers a shallow foundation upon which to base a moral system. Particular problems come to mind:

1 **Justice** What about the place and need for justice in the world, lest it be overrun by the many evil individuals who simply do not desire the pleasures of good behaviour? Hume replies that justice is necessary and that it is based upon self-interest. It is a kind of convention that we agree to because it makes for a stable society, something that is ultimately in everyone's interests whether they are good or bad.

2 **Motivation** A second problem that may come to mind is that even for the good, behaving ethically is often personally costly and may well go unrewarded. What is it that motivates people to act well in these cases, as clearly they often do? Hume thinks that there is a fundamental feature of human nature that stands us in good stead when it comes to acting morally, namely that we have a natural sympathy for others. This empathy is what tells us that it is wrong to harm others, since we feel something of that harm in ourselves. Sympathy is what drives people to act benevolently.

3 **The problem of praise** A related issue is whether Hume's ethics might actually be a form of self-love in disguise. This would be because of the link between moral behaviour and the desire for approbation: someone does something not because it is in itself good but because in doing it others will think well of them. Hume refutes this charge by saying that while many people may do good things in the hope of being honoured or respected for doing them, this does not detract from the fact that they want to be remembered for doing good things. 'To love the glory of virtuous deeds is a sure proof of the love of virtue,' he averred. After all, if someone's aim was solely to be remembered, or solely to benefit themselves, then there are many bad things they might do which would bring about these aims more effectively than doing good.

So Hume's foundations for ethics can appeal to contemporary humanists because of the goodness of human nature upon which it is based. However, if that were not enough, there is something else about it that commends it to many and that we should explore a little further. This is that it does away with the role that religion has traditionally played in morality.

Godless morality

Thinking about the links between religion and morality – whether religion is necessary for moral behaviour, as Voltaire thought, or whether people will do good apart from any belief in God – has become a key issue in humanism. Now, it seems obvious that people can behave ethically without religion. Moreover, it might be better that they do, for then they can say that they seek to act well for its own sake, and not because of any fear they have about disobeying some wrathful deity. What Hume provides is a robust ethical system based upon these intuitions.

However, at the time of the Enlightenment, the thought was revolutionary. In Hume's conception of why people act, they do so not because they fear any hellish punishment should they do bad things; they fear becoming loathsome to themselves, not praiseworthy and so on. Similarly, they do not do good things in the hope of some future, heavenly reward; they do good because it feels right to do so now. Their capacity to act well is not taken to be God-given either. Rather, it is innate in human nature and called human care, concern or sympathy. In short, Hume was perhaps the first individual to offer a plausible account of how it is perfectly possible to live an ethical life without subscribing to any form of religious belief.

But does it work in practice? The opportunity came to prove it by the manner in which this 'virtuous infidel' – as Hume was called – died. By the summer of 1776, he had become a very sick man. He knew he was dying and, writing to his friend, the economist Adam Smith, he imagined himself asking the boatman of Greek mythology, Charon, to stay his journey across the Styx:

> Good Charon, I have been endeavouring to open the eyes of people; have a little patience only till I have the pleasure of seeing the churches shut up, and the clergy sent about their business; but Charon would reply, O you loitering rogue; that wont happen these two hundred years; do you fancy I will give you a lease for so long a time? Get into the boat this instant.

A few days later Hume was indeed dead and Smith grasped that this was an important moment in Hume's life if his ethics was to convince others. Ever since Plato, philosophers had said that to philosophize is to learn how to die. Nothing, then, shows the veracity of the philosophy as much as the manner of the philosopher's death. Smith likened Hume's death to that of

Socrates himself. Plato had written that Socrates was 'a man who, we would say, was of all those we have known the best, and also the wisest and most upright'. Smith thought similarly, writing a moving testimony in which he said Hume approached 'as nearly to the idea of a perfectly wise and upright man, as perhaps the nature of human frailty will permit'. Hume was not just a freethinker; he was a pagan saint.

Defending design

In fact, like a saint, Hume spoke from the dead too. For he had another assault on religion up his sleeve, this time not in relation to ethics, but in relation to the central question of the existence of God. During his life, he had written another book, his *Dialogues Concerning Natural Religion*. Though it had circulated in Edinburgh for many years, it had never actually been published. In 1779, three years after his death, Hume's nephew saw that it happened. It actually attracted little attention immediately afterwards, though now the *Dialogues* has become a key text for humanists in the debate about the existence of God. So let us briefly look at it.

The book is a composed exchange between three characters – Demea, Philo and Cleanthes – who debate the arguments and counter-arguments associated with what people have claimed to know about God, not from revelation but reason. Each character represents a different position. Demea, the individual represented least sympathetically, is religiously orthodox. He argues both that God cannot be known through reason and that God's nature is intrinsically unknowable by finite mortals. Philo is a philosophical sceptic and while agreeing with Demea that God is unknown adds that organized religion is morally and psychologically harmful. He ends up adopting a kind of fideism – the belief that since reason cannot tell us anything about God, it forces believers to rely solely on faith in revelation. Cleanthes is a believer and an empiricist. He argues that belief in God is proven by the evidence of design in the world.

Hume gives Cleanthes a subtle version of the argument for the existence of God from design. It proceeds by analogy: if it is the case that all the finely-tuned machines that we know of are the product of human intelligence, then it only makes sense to suppose that the finely-tuned machine that we know the universe to be must be the product of some divine intelligence too. Analogy demands it.

Philo, the sceptic – whom some take to be closest to Hume's own position – presents several counter-arguments:

- He worries that the universe only weakly resembles a machine and so the argument by analogy would fail on that count; as an alternative, he suggests that the universe might be thought of as a body.
- He points out that while a machine is a self-contained entity, the universe is the sum total of everything that is, so the argument seems limited again.
- He continues with the observation that order is not necessarily an indication of intelligent design anyway. Look, say, at plants that are ordered but not intelligent.
- He also throws a couple of logical spanners in the works. First, by showing that the design argument would work better with a repeated series of observations; and since the universe is a one-off, this cannot be provided. Second, by highlighting the fact that even if design were true, it would tell us nothing about God who is unlike the world in every respect, being perfect, infinite and immaterial.
- At another moment in the dialogue Philo raises the problem of evil, asking whether the mess of pain and suffering does not counter the idea that the universe exhibits design anyway.
- Finally, he demonstrates that the design argument doesn't add anything to our understanding of the universe. It is at least as difficult to understand how God's mind is ordered as it is difficult to understand the order found in nature, such as it is. In other words, attributing apparent design to a superhuman intelligence explains nothing.

These arguments still do the rounds when the proof for the existence of God is discussed. But having said all that, Philo for one admits that the reasons for and against hang in the balance. '[I] believe that the arguments on which it is established exceed the objections which lie against it,' he concludes. Philo, probably like Hume, is against organized religion but is an agnostic when it comes to the particular question of God.

Dare to know!

Hume had died. His passing in some ways marks a halfway point in the history of the Enlightenment. D'Alembert, Diderot, Rousseau and Voltaire outlived him for a few more years, but the generation of which they were all a part was giving way to the next. With it, came new ideas about the issues they had explored, another wave of Enlightenment thought.

No figure was more important then, or now, than Immanuel Kant (1724–1804). He is arguably the greatest philosopher of modern times. Echoing Hume – who he said awoke him from his 'dogmatic slumbers' – Kant thought we can only know of the world as it appears to us, not as it is in itself, since our cognition of objects forms what we experience. This led to his doctrine of transcendental idealism, namely that human knowledge is limited to the things we can detect, or phenomena. Behind that lay a noumenal world that we can think about but not know by acquaintance. He wrote about these matters in several books of great importance, *Critique of Pure Reason* (1781), *Critique of Practical Reason* (1788), *Critique of Judgement* (1790), *Religion with the Boundaries of Mere Reason* (1793), and *Metaphysic of Morals* (1797). For a man whose thought spans centuries, it is somewhat surprising to learn that he spent his entire life without leaving his hometown, Königsberg, in East Prussia.

Kant's *Critiques* rank among the greatest philosophy books ever written. However, it is a more modest piece of work that can provide us with a way into his philosophy. It is also one that often draws the attention of the contemporary humanist.

In 1784, Kant responded to a competition run by a German newspaper. It had asked for answers to the question, 'What is Enlightenment?' Various members of the great and the good had replied. Kant's essay has become a classic statement of Enlightenment and, therefore, humanist values. However, it is a subtle piece. While eminently quotable, it also buries some of its richer insights in the difficult phraseology that Kant could never quite shake off even when writing for a wider audience. His answer bears a closer look.

He begins boldly: 'Enlightenment is man's emergence from his self-imposed immaturity.' Immaturity is depending on others for your own understanding. Such dependence may manifest itself as parroting from learned books, following a pastor instead of your own conscience, or submitting to the latest fads of diet prescribed by a doctor. (This last example really is one of Kant's: some things never change!) The resulting immaturity is self-imposed because such behaviour involves a lack of resolve and courage to think for yourself. Hence, Kant declares, the motto of the Enlightenment is: 'Have courage to use your own understanding!' – or more succinctly, '*Sapere Aude!*', Dare to

Know!

Kant continued by pointing out that people are afraid to be enlightened, to walk unaided for themselves, because at first it is difficult and even dangerous. Immaturity has become part and parcel of many people's nature, and they rather like it that way. Rules are easier, more comforting, than the freedom of a cultivated mind.

Nevertheless, Kant believes that Enlightenment will come, if slowly, because it looks irresistibly attractive once individuals have had a taste of freedom. It entails nothing short of new habits of thinking. In fact, there is no revolution when it comes to Enlightenment since violent change does not provide the necessary space for freeing the mind; revolutions require the imposition of exactly the opposite of Enlightenment, namely new prejudices and submission to new authorities.

Freedom's allure

Kant believes that the taste of freedom that draws us along this tricky path is of two types. One is the free use of reason in public debate; the other is the free use of reason in private deliberation. It is public debate that counts for Enlightenment – the processes of scholarship and scrutiny that take place in the open. When done there, for all to see, the body politic can move forward together as a whole. Should individuals move as they will, willy-nilly – as the turbulent currents of their free thought would carry them – then a kind of anarchy would ensue. Like revolutions, this would not instill freedom but chaos.

Kant underlines the point with more examples. He argues that citizens should pay taxes, though they may question the government. Soldiers should obey orders, though they may wonder why. Pastors should teach what their church requires, though they themselves may doubt it. In order that Enlightenment may nonetheless occur, it is the duty of the guardians of a society to exercise their freedom in public debate. Progress will thereby be made – as indeed is 'man's divine right', 'essential destiny' and 'dignity' – but progress by consensus, after the difficult work of new thinking, and thinking through its ramifications, has been done. So human beings can be rallied with the call to dare to know. But they should never think that this is easy. After all, self-knowledge is arguably the most difficult kind of knowledge there is.

Reason and responsibility

By the end of the essay the careful reader is left with an overriding impression – Enlightenment is good, very good; but it is nothing if not difficult. Moreover, the late eighteenth century itself, for all its questioning and free-thought, was not enlightened, at least by Kant's reckoning. The best Kant could say was that it was in the process of Enlightenment. The reason he thought this is because it had yet to resolve what he believed to be the toughest test of true Enlightenment, namely the matter of religion. This is the one area of immaturity that Kant highlights as being particularly crucial, if also vexed.

In other words, although the early Enlightenment atheists had disparaged religion, Voltaire had marginalized it, and Hume had provided cogent arguments as to why we could do without it, Kant thought the argument was far from over. What was it that bothered him? Why is religion a touchstone for Enlightenment?

That is not entirely clear from his newspaper piece alone. Simplistically, it might be thought that religion is key because it entails submitting to an authority other than yourself – that is, it is a quintessential case of the immaturity that Enlightenment urges us to discard. However, Kant was not against religion per se. In fact, it turns out that religion was essential to his understanding of morality. Rather, it is the relationship between the two that lies at the heart of his concerns. For what Enlightenment requires – at least according to Kant – is a more sophisticated attitude towards religion, not an automatic and therefore adolescent-like rejection.

Religion was essential to Kant's understanding of morality because he believed it underpinned the maxims that he thought the moral person should live by – maxims such as, do not treat other human beings as means but only as ends in themselves. In other words, Kant has a completely different understanding of morality from Hume: he does nothing short of reversing it. It is not feeling that takes priority but reason. Hume's appeal to sympathy was one of the things that disturbed Kant; that awoke him out of slumber. He felt it needed to be replaced by something more robust, a rational system to which all could assent. That can be summed up in one word, duty.

Duty not sympathy

Consider another of the best-known of Kant's maxims: to do to others as you would have them do to you – or to put it more generally, to act in ways that can be applied to everyone universally. For example, lying is not a moral way of acting because most individuals, most of the time, would not want people to lie to them. Your duty, therefore, is to tell the truth.

Such maxims are all well and good, but why should we obey them? Here's one reason. Take the case of lying again: if I lie to others then I cannot complain when they lie to me, and such a world would be an impossible place in which to live. In other words, obeying the maxim makes sense in practice. Or as Kant put it, the maxim is one of practical reason. Nevertheless, this does not explain why sometimes people feel they can and should lie. Worse for ethics, in reality, there are not infrequent occasions when it seems better to lie than to opt for the brutality of coldly speaking the truth.

This is where the religious foundations of Kant's morality come in. He recognizes that people are flawed and that the pressures of life lead us into compromises. Nonetheless, it remains the case that ideally we should never lie, never deviate from the maxims. What sustains this idealism – what prevents the best (no lies) becoming the enemy of the good (white lies) – is the existence of a place in which the ideal is actually realized. 'Ought implies can', Kant summarized. Since such perfection is clearly not possible in this world, Kant turns to God. It is God who embodies the actual existence of moral perfection, either as part of the divine nature or, for mortals, as a promise that it will be achieved in the next life. To put it more rationally, we cannot actually come up with a completely watertight, strong set of reasons for why we should always and invariably act morally – beyond the thought that on the whole it tends to work in practice. Rather, Kant thought, we should act morally because of what God promises.

God again

Now, it might be thought that to insist on theological foundations for morality is a retrogressive step away from Enlightenment. After all, does that not imply that we should submit to the priests and pastors and not think for ourselves? If you go along with Kant, though, this is not what he is insisting on. Rather, Kant is arguing that individuals should work out for themselves what it means to obey God by working out for themselves what it means to follow the maxims that God has given. In other words, Kant is appealing to another theme within humanism, that is its individualism, and rational, individual responsibility in particular. For, according to Kant, the supreme tool at our disposal in this task is not human sympathy but reason.

So, someone who merely follows what a priest says by, say, attending mass so many times a week, in the hope that his or her behaviour will please God, is deluding themselves. They are unenlightened because it is moral rectitude in which God delights. This may well not involve going to mass at all. Likewise, someone else who feels they are favoured by God because of some inner feeling or sense that they have been blessed, is similarly deluding themselves. According to Kant, it is not what you feel that counts, but being dutiful in what you do.

The bar for what counts as moral is therefore set very high by Kant. He goes so far as to say that any action which benefits the individual in any way at all cannot count as moral behaviour – though that is not to say that they are necessarily immoral either, just morally neutral. For example, the things that friends do for each other can never be moral, only non-moral, in this ethical system, since friends always hope for something in return – for all that they love to give to each other too.

That the demands of Kantian morality are severe, often undermined by our complicated intentions, is another reflection of the difficulty of becoming enlightened. Hence people do prefer to go to mass several times a week or search for some inner sense that they are doing OK. Parroting books, following pastors, adhering to food fads is easy by comparison. Immaturity consoles. But what Kant gives to humanism is an ideal that human beings can do better.

Critical attitude

Having said that, Kant concedes that while the goal of the moral life is to do moral things, being moral is not only about your *actions*. It is also about the *attitude* you have. So rather like the person who is on the way to Enlightenment, but still carries vestiges of immaturity with them, someone can be on the way to becoming moral, though they may still act with mixed motives. It is their orientation that counts. And the key to having the right moral orientation is the sincere effort to act according to reason, according to the right moral maxims. A person who is becoming morally enlightened will not only be struggling with the maxims but will also embody a certain spirit, a *critical* spirit. They will be striving to throw off their old superstitions, or habits of submitting to various authorities, by exercising their own understanding.

To put it another way, Enlightenment does not lie immediately before us. If Kant trusts the sun is behind the clouds, the clouds have not yet pulled back to reveal it. We are not like Moses, on the verge of the Promised Land. We are still in the unenlightened wilderness. The first task, then, is to sharpen our critical faculties and learn to find our balance. We can then take some steps out of immaturity. To imagine, like an adolescent, that we are more mature than we are, is to fool ourselves and look stupid. It is to claim to know more than we do – another definition of being unenlightened.

This might seem depressing, even pessimistic – and not worthy of a humanist who has faith in humankind. In fact, when Kant published an account of why he thought human beings were so frail, immature and flawed, no less a person than Goethe accused him of reinventing the Christian doctrine of Original Sin, with its implication that human beings need 'outside help' to be truly saved. But although Kant thought human beings generally immoral, he also thought them capable of understanding what duty required and of choosing to do it. He is not a pessimist but a realist. He does not underestimate the enormity of the task. We live in an age of Enlightenment not in an enlightened age. There is still a lot of work to be done. And being critical, having courage – particularly in the face of temptations stemming from moral weakness – is key.

This critical attitude is something all humanists would endorse. As we saw, critiquing sources of authority, and even reason itself, is something that was celebrated by many Renaissance humanists, as it is by humanists today. However, Kant's resort to theological foundations upon which to build the edifice of his moral philosophy is something that humanists today would want seriously to question, even in those who are otherwise religious. Hume provides an alternative: replace duty to God with the sympathy of human nature – though as we shall explore in later chapters, this can seem naively optimistic in the century after the Holocaust and the terrors of Stalin and Mao.

For now, let us note that there remains a problem to address: on what does morality rest when the theological foundations are eroded? Or to put it in terms that any parent would recognize: how often can you answer the petulant question, 'Why should I?' with the imperial answer, 'Because you should!'?

Revolution

We have said that Kant represents a second wave of Enlightenment thought. In some ways, he refined what the first generation achieved, particularly in relation to knowledge and science. In other ways, he opposed the directions in which they had gone, particularly in relation to ethics and religion. However, there was something else that marked a turning-point in the Enlightenment, and this time it wasn't a person but an event.

That event was the French Revolution. At first, many who held what would now be considered humanist values welcomed the storming of the Bastille in 1789. The *philosophes*, like Rousseau, who called for social and political reform undoubtedly influenced events. And the French 'Declaration of the Rights of Man and of the Citizen' that followed the uprising embodied the same Enlightenment values as the earlier American 'Declaration of Independence'. The first article read: 'Men are born and remain free and equal in rights.' Freedom of religion and freedom of speech were guaranteed in subsequent clauses. The humanist theme of the separation of political powers, and Rousseau's concept of the state's role in representing the general will of the people, were woven into the document.

However, within a couple of years, a newly reborn France was at war with her neighbours. And then a year later, she was at war with herself, and her leaders launched their Reign of Terror. Tens of thousands were executed, and ten times that number arrested. Is this what it was to be enlightened? It seemed that Kant had been right. Revolution does not free minds, it imprisons them again.

Rights of man

Thomas Paine (1737–1809) was a key figure in these tempestuous years, and is another champion that humanists remember today. He was born in Norfolk to a Quaker father and an Anglican mother, a religiously-mixed household that no doubt contributed to him feeling at home amongst the colonists when he arrived in America aged 37. He had been persuaded to cross the Atlantic by Benjamin Franklin who told him that his anti-authoritarianism would find an eager audience there. Franklin was right, at least initially. Within a year Paine had become a founding member of the first anti-slavery society in America. Within two years he was up to his eyeballs in the American Revolution, having penned the propagandist pamphlet, *Common Sense*.

However, Paine's popularity rose and fell with events on the other side of the Atlantic, where he returned in 1787. In 1791, the first part of *The Rights of Man* was published in London, a defence of the French Revolution against the attack made by the conservative Edmund Burke in his *Reflections on the Revolution in France*. It sold 50,000 copies in just a few weeks. However, Paine's timing was unfortunate for it was in the same year that the high hopes of those who had stormed the Bastille began to trouble people in England and America as political turmoil ensued. He fled to France, while in London he was tried for sedition, convicted, and had his books and effigy burned. Part two of *The Rights of Man* appeared in 1792 in France and America only. Ironically and horridly, Paine was himself imprisoned for nine months under the Terror because he had declared his opposition to the beheading of the king, Louis XVI.

The Rights of Man articulates many themes that were to become characteristic of liberal democracies. He argued that welfare services such as universal education, redistribution of wealth, maternity benefits and pensions for the elderly should be part of a very practical solution to the evils that had precipitated the French Revolution. The mark of civilization was the poor being happy.

Paine's next book *The Age of Reason* was another populist call, this time against organized religion and for deism. He described how every religion and national church pretended to have 'some special mission from God, communicated to certain individuals' – Moses for the Jews, Jesus for Christians, Mohammed for Muslims. Though he believed in God, he disbelieved all God's self-proclaimed, ecclesiastical servants. 'My own mind is my own church,' he wrote and called Christianity 'a fable'.

This too got a mixed reception and when Paine later died a famous obituary opined: 'He had lived long, did some good and much harm.' However, since then his reputation has revived. In America, he now stands squarely in the humanist tradition of freethinkers. In Britain, he has been called 'the English Voltaire', and is closely associated with human rights.

A note on human rights

Human rights are a crucial tool in the protection of individuals against immoral acts of organizations and governments. They grew out of the notion of Natural Law found in Ancient Greco-Roman and Christian philosophy. The key thought is that human beings have absolute rights that they possess simply by virtue of being human. These rights can be thought of in terms of the right to not be *interfered* with, as say in the right to freedom of speech or freedom to worship. Or they can be thought of in terms of the right to *possess* certain things, such as education and employment.

Alongside Thomas Paine's *The Rights of Man* (1791–2), other key texts include John Locke's *Second Treatise of Government* (1690), the American Declaration of Independence (1776), and the Universal Declaration of Human Rights (1948).

Today, there is a substantial critique of human rights on the grounds that they emphasize differences between human beings and major on often-conflicting entitlements, leading to social fragmentation. What may be proposed alongside rights is the need for an ethos based upon common responsibilities and shared principles.

Religion of humanity

Paine was not the only one to hold onto humanist values across the tempestuous years of revolution. After them, another figure led a campaign to reinvigorate the spirit of Enlightenment, championing the empirical pursuit of human knowledge, the development of social institutions based on science, and the progress of humankind in history in strikingly practical ways. He made a lasting impression on the history of humanism as a result. This individual was Auguste Comte (1789–1857).

Comte began life as a secretary to someone with whom he shared his name, Comte Saint-Simon. Saint-Simon articulated an early form of socialism. It included the management of capital and labour for the good of society as a whole, a society in which he envisaged equality between men and women.

Positive philosophy

If that seemed radical enough, Comte's own contribution to humanism was even more startling. He called it 'positive philosophy' and it is remembered today for its powerful doctrine of human progress. In essence, Comte believed that human history passed through three stages of existence – theological, metaphysical and positive. Not all the changes in human society and knowledge that cluster together to form each stage are necessarily advances in themselves. But overall, the effect is progressive.

1 **Theological** The theological stage is one in which human beings do not understand the world around them in anything like a scientific way. So, the explanations offered for events and phenomena are supernatural and the means of interacting with this strange world are magical. There is nothing wrong with this stage in its proper place and time, namely before the Reformation. It is merely a period marked by human immaturity, and a reliance on spirits and gods.

2 **Metaphysical** The theological stage gives way to the metaphysical. This is a transitional phase, according to Comte lasting up to the French Revolution. It describes the world in terms of abstractions like essences and final causes, though they turn out to be as dark and mysterious as the theological concepts that preceded them.

3 **Positive** Finally comes the positive phase, the early years of which Comte believed his time enjoyed. It is marked by a philosophy that abandons the transcendent pseudo-explanations for things which characterized the previous stages, and adopts instead the scientific study of phenomena and the establishment of rational laws.

Apart from this general schema, Comte's other great contribution was to articulate how science might be applied at the socio-political level. He gave the new discipline a name, sociology. It would study the forces that hold society together and those that provoke it to change. It would be the science of social enlightenment.

Interestingly, Comte was a great admirer of Roman Catholicism, not for its theology but in its capacity to shape and sustain a global organization through the imposition of a hierarchy to which people were obedient. In his account of the positive society, *System of Positive Polity*, he borrowed from the Church to describe a 'religion of humanity'. It included doctrines and liturgies in a system of structures and symbols stripped of superstition, substituted for by science. Sociologists would replace bishops, businessmen government, and women would become the custodians of morality. Indeed, individuals were encouraged to meditate upon an idealized image of a mother.

Limits of liberty

Comtean humanists followed the injunction to 'live for others'. And humanity itself was venerated in the threefold guise of *Grand Etre* (Great Being), *Grand Fétich* (Earth) and *Grand Milieu* (Destiny). This was another kind of humanist essentialism, though unlike Rousseau whose figure of Man was located at the beginning of time, Comte's Man was the goal of humanity and lay in the indefinite future.

If such innovations appear faintly ridiculous now, many were actually put into practice during the Revolution. And for a while Comte was as influential in Europe as Marx and Darwin. His ethical religion appealed to novelists such as George Eliot, Emile Zola and Thomas Hardy – not in all its systematic finery, but as a powerful articulation of the belief that humanity should become the focus for life and thought. Writers such as Oscar Wilde commended his vision of a socialism that might liberate the individual's soul. His exemplary, domesticated woman resonated with Victorian essayists such as Ruskin and finds echoes in figures such as the submissive heroine of *Middlemarch,* Dorothea.

John Stuart Mill (1806–73), the greatest English philosopher of the nineteenth century, took his idea of progress from Comte and linked it to his hope for a better future. Mill also recognized that limits had to be set on an individual's liberty if society as a whole were to be free, though unlike Comte, Mill also saw that limits had to be set on society's ability to interfere with the lives of individuals too.

Finally, we can note that Comte's hostility towards superstition and traditional religion began to fix the association between humanism and atheistic secularism in the popular imagination. His positivism was described by the Victorian fathers of modern atheistic humanism as their 'scientific Bible'. Though by the time the National Secular Society, and subsequently the Rationalist Press Association, was founded in the mid- to late-nineteenth century, ecclesiastical pretensions – the excesses of his 'religion of humanity' – had wisely been ditched.

Summary

We are at the end of the Enlightenment centuries and it is possible to view them as launching a burst of optimism in the transformative power of the new human learning. This spirit of hope and enquiry drew its energy from the tremendous success of the sciences, particularly Newton's advances in physics and mathematics. The fundamental nature of the material world seemed to be within the grasp of human beings, and what counted as knowledge was shaped to fit this possibility as a result. Hence the distance that is still felt between what we now call modernity and the Middle Ages.

The dream that was never far from the surface during the period was one in which the science that had worked in relation to understanding the natural world could be applied to understand human affairs, social, moral and – if it survived the onslaught – religious. To put it another way, a revolution was underway that would achieve nothing less than reshaping what it was to be human. But then Enlightenment figures like Hume and Kant appeared, suggesting that this dream was further off than people thought. It might even be a delusion. So though the optimism persisted, it became more and more qualified as the decades proceeded. This shift of mood was played out in double-quick time during the last decade of the eighteenth century in response to the French Revolution.

Much of this remains in the humanism of our day: the debates about religion, about ethics, about progress, about human nature all draw on what was explored so richly during the Enlightenment. We are now in a position to move towards the present. However, in order to continue the story, our exploration will change in style now. So far the book has adopted a more or less continuously narrative approach, weaving in the key figures and how their philosophy relates to humanist concerns. Once we get into the mid-nineteenth and twentieth century, however, I think a different approach is better. This is the period during which thinkers actually start to call themselves humanists, as opposed to being philosophers pursuing what we retrospectively think of as humanist concerns. However, with that development also comes strikingly different ways of articulating what counts as humanism. So it is more helpful to know them, and describe them, by their different names. In the next three chapters we will explore these new 'humanisms', and the reaction to them, in turn.

04

contemporary humanisms 1: Marxism, utilitarianism and pragmatism

In this chapter you will learn:

- what Karl Marx contributed in the disaster of communism and the humane politics of socialism
- how utilitarianism, a new theory of ethics, evolved and why it is important to humanists
- about the American pragmatist philosophers and their contribution to humanism.

From the mid-nineteenth century onwards, various post-Enlightenment thinkers started to refer to their philosophy as humanist and, soon after, others started to refer to themselves as humanist or humanistic. In other words, various systems of thought emerged that were self-identified as humanism. In this chapter, we will look at what were historically the first three of these developments, Marxism, utilitarianism and pragmatism.

1 **Marxism** The first is, of course, associated with the philosophy of Karl Marx. As far back as 1844, before even Burkhardt had identified the Renaissance as humanistic, Marx had written of an explicitly modern idea of humanism in his *Economic and Philosophical Manuscripts*.

2 **Utilitarianism** The second development is associated with the philosophy of utilitarianism, the idea that an action is right if it tends to produce happiness and wrong if it does the reverse. This approach actually reaches back into the eighteenth century, but here we will pick it up in the work of John Stuart Mill, who published his seminal text called *Utilitarianism* in 1861.

3 **Pragmatism** The third is a tradition of humanism that developed first in the US, in the shape of the pragmatism of William James. He argued that usefulness and practicability are the criteria by which to judge the merit of ideas. Pragmatism was dominant during the first quarter of the twentieth century, and it still has its champions today.

In each case we will consider the origins of the philosophy concerned and then how it manifests itself in humanism now.

Marxism

In some ways Marxism can be seen as originating in a criticism of one tendency within the Enlightenment and humanism alike, namely the valuing of the individual. The worry is that a society which gives itself over to such individualism rapidly turns into one where it is only the powerful and wealthy who can exercise their free choice. The Marxist critique therefore suggests that what is required is not a theory of ethics and the individual, but ethics and society. In other words, what is sought is a socialist theory of the human condition – socialist in the broadest sense.

In fact, before Marx appeared and made this approach his own, socialist theories of various sorts had been associated with the humanist tradition. It could be said to reach back to Plato who was fond of the Ancient Greek aphorism: 'Friends hold all things in common.' His exploration of the ideal society, *The Republic*, revolves around the belief that nothing is more damaging to human beings than social division.

Thomas More's *Utopia*, one of the great products of Renaissance humanism, reflects on socialist ideals too. On his eponymous island, there is no such thing as private property or even privacy; doors are kept unlocked. Everyone shares in the work that must be done – except scholars, lawyers and priests, that is – and this makes light of it; citizens only have to labour for six hours a day.

Of course, both Plato's *The Republic* and More's *Utopia* are also implicit critiques of such socialist ideals. Plato paints a picture of common life that is at least as disturbing as it might be appealing. More's neologism – utopia – literally means 'no place'. And it was not until the nineteenth century that Marx picked up the baton and tried to iron out the difficulties to arrive at a socialist theory that could be put into practice on a large scale. In his early work at least, he explicitly associated the word humanism with his version of socialism, namely communism. (I say 'at least' because some scholars have argued that in his later work, Marx denies that there is any such thing as a human essence and so drops the reference to humanism.)

Alienation

In the *Economic and Philosophical Manuscripts*, Marx identifies the damage that is done to human beings who live under individualistic capitalism and explores the human potential that he imagines would be liberated under a socially-based, communist regime. He sees the issue as coalescing around a tension that human beings have always struggled to resolve, namely the tension between the fact that they are 'of nature', though live in often very unnatural societies.

In some ways this is the issue with which Rousseau battled when he developed his notions of the state of nature and the social contract. However, Marx took it in a very different direction. He believed that human beings find their self-realization in nature: through labouring on the land they change the world and change themselves in the process. However, he also saw that the needs of human beings can only be met when they cooperate. A tension arises because this social side of human life is opposed to the former naturalism. In other words, we must learn to labour *together* if we are to thrive.

But this is a struggle, and it gives rise to ever-more complex modes of production and patterns of interaction, such as those we call capitalism. However, they are also a source of problems. For under capitalism, human beings are alienated from themselves because the satisfaction that might be gained from being productive is lost. Why? Because capitalism distances people from the fruits of their labour. They work for a capitalist boss who creams off the profits. This exploits the worker and leaves them not only without much to live on but possibly in outright poverty. The result is a sense of alienation. It is experienced not just materially but existentially as well. Our social essence has become separated from our natural existence. We are alienated from ourselves.

Religion as opiate

Incidentally, this explains the origins of religion according to Marx. Religion arises as the 'opiate of the people', in the famous phrase, a palliative against the horrors of alienation. It is the 'sigh of the oppressed creature, the heart in a heartless world, the soul of soulless conditions,' as Marx also said of theistic belief. However, although Marx was avowedly atheistic, he did not believe that simply identifying the causes of religion, or exposing its fantasies, would be enough to throw it off. Only when the realities of humankind's alienation had been practically addressed would religion disappear, for it would then be no longer necessary. Conversely, it would be ridiculous to believe that religion could simply be 'thought away' if people's material conditions were left unchanged.

Marx believed that the time when this would happen was coming. The form of that coming was communism. He thought that the pressures of living under capitalism were becoming unbearable. The moment was arriving when human beings would rise up and communism would be born, the period of history in which people's material natures would be reconciled with their social natures. It is this reconciliation that he calls a form of humanism in this passage from the *Economic and Philosophical Manuscripts*.

> Communism as completed naturalism is humanism, and as completed humanism is naturalism. It is the genuine solution of the antagonism between man and nature and between man and man.

Totalitarianism

Of course, we now know that communism did arise, but not with the happy results for which Marx longed. Far from reuniting the essence of human beings with the lives they could lead, it propagated atrocious violence. The combined activities of Stalinism, Maoism and other totalitarian communist regimes amounted to the slaughter of tens of millions of human beings during the course of the twentieth century.

For humanists, it is important, therefore, to ask where Marx went wrong. Philosophers have pointed to the way Marx underestimated the capacity of capitalism to reinvent itself, and so keep human beings' revolutionary tendencies at bay. Others have pointed to economic flaws in his system.

However, another area that might be of particular interest to humanists concerns his misunderstanding of human nature. We have outlined his belief in its productive, labouring essence. What is striking about his insistence on the centrality of labour in human nature is that it appears to ignore the many other characteristics that philosophers have thought equally important, such as, say, personhood, language or indeed religion.

Marx's argument is that these are important too, but labour always takes priority: personhood, language and religion depend upon labour as their source. In other words, they all depend upon our productive capacity. So, inasmuch as Marx was wrong, it seems that labour as the key feature of human nature is perhaps not as fundamental as he thought: personhood, language and/or religion might be as basic too.

Universality

Marx also argued that human beings share a universal nature. By this universality he meant that all things being equal – notably under a communist regime – people would experience a powerful sense of solidarity with one another. His hope was that this fellow-feeling would eventually transcend all the barriers between peoples that exist under capitalism; barriers such as nationality and religion – a hope that is captured in the famous slogan that concludes the tract which Marx penned with his friend and collaborator Frederick Engels, *The Communist Manifesto*: 'Workers of the world, Unite!'

Again, though, it seems that this force of sympathy is just not substantial enough to power the emergence of global communism. Or since that would now seem to be an undesirable outcome anyway, one might wonder whether human fellow-feeling even has enough potency to overcome the excesses of capitalism that continue to flourish in the modern world. Which takes us back to the original question: is there a socialist ethic that could appeal to contemporary humanists and that can be made to work?

Socialist humanism

Modern socialism can be thought of as the political philosophy that draws on Marx's analysis of capitalism – which is powerful and lasting for all the failures of communism – whilst rejecting the specifics of his communist solution. In fact, what was called 'socialist humanism' was a self-conscious reaction to the horrors of communism as they became obvious midway through the twentieth century. Instead of developing a full-blown existential critique of capitalism, as Marx did, it points to capitalism's moral flaws. Instead of championing wholesale political revolution, as Marx did, modern socialism therefore advocates piecemeal socio-economic reforms.

Bertrand Russell was one humanist who professed such a socialism. He drew a distinction between himself and communists by arguing that following Marx needn't be a 'gospel of proletarian revenge'; it needn't be violent. In his essay, *The Case for Socialism*, he continued:

> I regard it primarily as an adjustment to machine production demanded by considerations of common sense, and calculated to increase the happiness, not only of proletarians, but of all except a tiny minority of the human race.

Russell highlights several flaws in capitalism with which others agreed. They are moral failures in the sense that they are detrimental to human flourishing, at least in a majority of cases. They include:

- Substantial disparities in wealth, opportunities and power between the rich and the poor that creates a permanent underclass, and keeps women and children in subjection.

- Rampant individualism that has no thought for vulnerable members of society, particularly the unemployed or unemployable.
- Leaving the production of all goods and services to market mechanisms in the belief that this turns the market from being a means to deliver these goods and services to being an end in itself; choice and competition come to be seen as virtues in their own right.
- Discrimination against minority groups in society since all people have a right to be part of the society to which they belong.

To these Russell added some other critiques of capitalism that also seem to hold:

- Inequalities in leisure time, since instead of mechanized means of production freeing up time for all to enjoy, it is the capitalist owners who take it at the expense of the workers. He shared this sentiment with Oscar Wilde, who in his essay *The Soul of Man under Socialism*, opined: 'Cultivated leisure is the aim of man.'
- Poor quality art, since commercial pressures are at odds with artistic expression. Not only does the market more often than not reward poor quality art but it prefers variations on profitable themes not untested departures. Socialism, though, liberates people from these compromises, according to Russell. Again, Wilde concurs when he avers: 'The true artist is a man who believes absolutely in himself, because he is absolutely himself.'
- Russell also believed that the 'unemployed rich' of capitalism were a curse – people with much wealth but little real value to society. The problem is that by virtue of their wealth, they can worm their way into positions of influence though without the moral, intellectual or artistic abilities to exercise that influence well.

As an economic system aimed at achieving better ends, socialists believe in the state ownership of production (to avoid the excesses of the market); the redistribution of wealth (to avoid the creation of an under class); a major role for governments in economic decision-making (to ensure that the market works for people and not people for the market). Economic central planning has also been suggested, though it is arguably more characteristic of communism than socialism.

So where has socialism got to now? Is it a viable option for the contemporary humanist? In the West at least, socialism is nearly as redundant a philosophy as communism. It lost much credibility after the collapse of communism. Critics have also argued that to function properly, socialist policy-makers need to have access to more information about a market than can possibly be provided in any real situation. The resulting lack of information upon which to make decisions only increases amidst the dynamism of global markets – militating against the possibility of a successful international socialism, a dream that socialists like Russell shared with Marx. (Russell thought it was the key to ending war.) According to this critique, socialists are, therefore, always condemned to make mistakes, for which the people they would otherwise champion pay the price.

Having said that, social market economics – a sort of compromise between socialism and capitalism – is widespread. It is a set of policies ranging from government funding of a welfare state through to protectionist tax regimes in support of national industries. They are aimed at mitigating the inhumane effects of market forces and providing safety nets for those who would otherwise fall through them. In other words, socialist ideas can be said to still play an important part in the world for some humanists. It is one strand in contemporary humanism.

The origins of utilitarianism

If Marxism is dead, and socialism a shadow of its former self, then the second of the humanisms for this chapter – utilitarianism – is still in rude health. Jeremy Bentham (1748–1832) is the father of utilitarianism. Bentham was an eighteenth-century English philosopher, very much part of the Enlightenment, who argued that government should aim at the greatest happiness for the greatest number of people. Incidentally, although a contemporary of Thomas Paine, he also thought that the concept of natural rights was a contradiction in terms, calling it 'nonsense on stilts'. However, it was his godson, John Stuart Mill who, a few years after Marx's early work, put together a robust form of utilitarianism that is still highly influential today.

Mill was an extraordinary figure – though he never thought of himself as in any way remarkable. He was learning Greek and maths at the age of three, philosophy and ancient history at six, literature at ten, and economics and logic at 14. Perhaps unsurprisingly, given such a head start, his writings had an enormous impact upon nineteenth-century Britain.

- He was an early advocate of women's rights, writing 'The principle which regulates the existing social relations between the two sexes – the legal subordination of one sex to the other – is wrong in itself, and now one of the chief hindrances to human improvement.'
- Mill also championed liberalism. His formula for what it means to live in a liberal society is still recited. If liberty consists of doing what you desire then it also follows that: 'The liberty of the individual must thus far be limited; he must not make himself a nuisance to other people.' As we saw, he provided a vital rider to Comte's more authoritarian humanism.

His key work on utilitarianism as a theory of ethics came in 1861, with his seminal work on the subject called *Utilitarianism*.

Utility as well-being

Bentham had written that, 'The greatest happiness of the greatest number is the foundation of morals and legislation.' In other words, the word utilitarian refers to those 'utilities' that make life worth living, and utilitarianism is a theory about what people do, how they decide, and how they should act – that is, so as to produce as much well-being as possible.

Bentham interpreted utility to mean happiness, and then took the further step of equating happiness with pleasure. Conversely, unhappiness meant pain. So in his version of the theory, the question of how to live is answered by increasing the amount of happiness in the world.

He then took this logic to its natural conclusion. If the question of life is how to increase the amount of happiness, then this implies a need for a way of measuring the amount of pleasure associated with different kinds of activity. He called this 'felicific calculus'. His aim was to measure the amounts of pleasure for different activities and attach numbers to them. Then people would have a scientific basis upon which to conduct their ethics, simply by choosing the activities that had the highest numbers.

Problems with happiness

At one level, felicific calculus appeals to a natural intuition that
we can choose between options on the basis of the pleasure and
pain they may cause us. We tend to go for those things that are
more pleasurable, and avoid those things that are painful. But
when taken as a scientific principle, this hedonism soon runs
into absurdities. For example, pleasures come in very different
forms. So to compare different pleasures is like comparing the
taste of an apple with that of a pear and deciding which is better
by asking about the 'appleness' of both. The apple would fair
well; the pear not at all. On this scale the pear would not be
regarded pleasurable at all. Basically, you cannot compare
apples and pears.

Also there is the complicating factor that sometimes pleasures are
closely associated with pain. Consider learning to play the piano.
The effort it takes a child to bash a melody out on the keys may
result in much pain, not only for them but also for their parents.
However, the pleasure the child may eventually gain from being
able to play later in life could be substantial – though unless they
go on to become a concert pianist, the difference between the
pleasure and the pain may in retrospect always hang in the
balance. But parents, of course, do not decide along these lines at
all. Rather they force their children to have lessons because they
believe music to be valuable and good.

Happiness and humanism

Mill noticed the problems with utilitarianism as Bentham had
formulated it. To those we have just discussed, he added
another: 'Ask yourself whether you are happy, and you cease to
be so.' In other words, there seemed to be something self-
defeating in the very calculated nature of utilitarianism.

But Mill saw something worth rescuing in utilitarianism which
led him to write his book. He argued that the problems existed
because Bentham had only properly considered one part of life,
the empirical, practical part. What had been missed was that
human beings also have an emotional life, the side of life that is
satisfied by the arts, literature and music. Both aspects are
necessary for a humanly rich existence. What he sought to do
was integrate both sides of life into a revised account of
utilitarianism.

The key change was the ability to distinguish between higher and lower pleasures. Higher pleasures are things like the arts or friendship. Lower pleasures are things like being fed or keeping warm. This led to another famous observation. In *Utilitarianism*, Mill wrote: 'It is better to be a human being dissatisfied than a pig satisfied; better to be Socrates dissatisfied than a fool satisfied.' What he meant was that a dissatisfied Socrates is a better state to be in than that of a satisfied pig because even with its frustrations, Socrates's life allows him to access higher pleasures. Moreover, even a small taste of the pleasures of such a philosophical life are worth more than being sated on the pleasures of mere consumption.

Contemporary utilitarianism

Mill's reform was the first important one in the history of the idea and, in the intervening years, philosophers have added a number of further refinements. Peter Singer (b.1946) is one contemporary philosopher closely associated with utilitarianism, being well known for his writing at both a popular and academic level. He has responded to a number of critiques of the theory and is well known for his campaigning work on the welfare of animals. In fact, one of his modifications arises directly from this work. Strictly speaking, utilitarians do not believe in rights since rights imply that there are universal values to which human beings and others should have access. This undermines the notion that it is utility that counts. Singer, though, believes that whilst establishing the foundations upon which rights might rest is a futile task, the language of human and animal rights is a useful shorthand behind which many of his utilitarian concerns can be addressed and progressed.

He also updates the notion of pleasure and pain with the idea of satisfying preferences. People and animals have preferences that may be natural or, in the case of human beings, rational. And it is the ways in which those preferences can be thwarted that Singer's version of utilitarianism seeks to challenge. For example, an animal has a preference to avoid pain, so that should be the guiding principle in animal husbandry. Alternatively, while a human being might seek to avoid pain, their rational self might calculate that some pains are worth suffering for a greater good. For example, if you go to the dentist you know you might suffer, but you also know that the benefit of having healthy teeth outweighs that temporary setback.

Critics of utilitarianism

So utilitarianism is an active ethical theory today, not least among humanists. However, that is not to say it is without its critics, too. For example, if maximizing happiness is the key imperative then consider the following scenario. Surely, it is better to kill one healthy person, remove their organs, and give them to five or six unhealthy people who would be restored to full, happy lives after the transplants? To put it in utilitarian terms, one person's pain and loss would lead to half a dozen's pleasure and gain. We intuitively react against this thought, but within the parameters of its own theory, utilitarianism appears to find it difficult to say why we should not act in this way.

Similarly, consider the issue of torture. Surely, utilitarianism would suggest that it is better to torture one individual who might have information about some pending atrocity, than risk hundreds of people's lives who might be saved? Again, there is something about torture that seems fundamentally wrong. It is just that utilitarianism doesn't help us identify what it is.

Life in the round

The utilitarians have responded to these problems by saying both scenarios represent immoral acts because of the effect they have on others. In the case of the transplants, the practice of killing healthy people would cause very many people to worry that they might be next, so it would actually increase unhappiness in the general population. Similarly, the practice of torture should cause widespread discontent because it is such a hideous thing to do.

There is a further point that follows from these ripostes. When thinking about what makes life worthwhile, we do not actually consider what makes us happy by examining our various activities in isolation and then only doing those that carry some pleasure. Life is more connected than that. For example, going to work is an activity that includes both happy-making things, like being paid or finding friends, and unhappy-making things, like having to sit in an office or stand in a factory for hours on end. The two aspects, though, are two sides of the same coin. What we need to do is consider life in the round, in its whole context.

This thought has led some utilitarians to the paradoxical conclusion that the best way to live as a utilitarian – that is to maximize well-being in the world – is actually not to make the calculations that would otherwise seem to be characteristic of utilitarianism. Rather, it is better to follow your common sense for most of the time, and only resort to utilitarian decision-making in extreme situations. This has been called rule utilitarianism – the conviction that for most of the time it is better to follow moral rules, only breaking them when the consequences would clearly be bad.

On why bad things lead to worse

However, another philosopher, Bernard Williams (1929–2003), has pursued this paradox further and identified a more profound problem with utilitarianism.

Williams argued that the problem with utilitarianism is that it treats people instrumentally. They become objects of the theory's calculations, and so serve those calculations, rather than being treated as human individuals in their own right. This is why utilitarianism finds it hard to answer why a healthy person should not donate their organs and, similarly, why one person should not be tortured. If it had a conception of each and every human being as an end in themselves, and not as a means to other ends, even other human ends, then it could reject these cases with force.

To put it another way, the problem is that utilitarianism justifies doing one bad thing in the name of achieving a greater good. However, in the real world, one bad thing often leads to another bad thing. In response, the utilitarian then argues for doing a further bad thing to rescue the good thing they were aiming at originally. But that next bad thing causes further bad things to happen, and so on.

If you want an example of this tragic outcome then you need look no further than the Iraq war of 2003. Proponents of the war made a utilitarian case for it. They argued that while war itself is a bad thing, it would lead to the greater good of freeing the people of Iraq to live democratically. However, war itself unleashes resentment, revenge and rage, so the successive bad things that must be done to combat the realities of the war came to swamp any good that the initial aggression might have provided.

Having noted the critiques, there are a number of features of utilitarianism that its proponents continue to find compelling. Humanists in particular are drawn by a number of core elements:

- The clarity of the theory.
- It is down to earth and very practical.
- It is not reliant on religious traditions or belief in an absolute good or evil.
- It does not depend on obeying the rules of any received authority.
- It strives to reduce the amount of pain in the world, as much as increase the pleasures of life.
- By focussing on reducing suffering as the central moral task, it is able to embrace concerns about the well-being of animals as well as humans.
- It incorporates a sense that progress can be made in ethics and in terms of improving people's lives.
- It is amenable to scientific interpretation.

Since these elements are key starting points in moral philosophy for many humanists, utilitarianism is always likely to be held in high regard.

Pragmatism

It has often been noticed that there is something quite European, even English, about utilitarianism. It advocates moderation in thought and a focus on the happy, contented life. It is as if it suits many of the intellectual tastes and national characteristics found on the eastern coast of the Atlantic.

The third of our humanistic philosophies in this chapter, pragmatism, has been called the American philosophy. There is something in its focus on what works, in its synthesis of the practical and philosophical, that chimes with the 'just do it' element in the American character. It is even quite accommodating of religion, the revivalist feature of life on the other side of the Atlantic that is often so incomprehensible to European humanists. It has had a distinguished history throughout the twentieth century, and into the twenty-first, particularly in America. It is still a lively strand within humanism today.

The person who first popularized it, and thereby provides a way into it for us, was William James (1842–1910). James was a likeable man; his success as a philosopher in his own lifetime was as much due to his character as his thought. In his *History of Western Philosophy*, Bertrand Russell notes that James was almost universally loved:

> On the scientific side, the study of medicine had given his thoughts a tendency towards materialism, which, however, was held in check by his religious emotions. His religious feelings were very Protestant, very democratic, and very full of the warmth of human kindness. He refused altogether to follow his brother Henry into fastidious snobbishness.

Philosophically, James's thought can be broken down into three tenets. First, his beliefs about subjectivity and objectivity; second, his thoughts about what it is to take a decision when it comes to believing in something; and third, his adherence to the so-called principle of pragmatism.

1 **Any radical distinction between subject and object is false.** This first tenet is perhaps the most difficult to understand. For example, it seems natural to assume that someone knows something – the 'someone' being the subject, the 'something' being the object that they know. James argued this is illusion. The reason is that there can be no radical difference between mind (subject) and matter (object); rather, all the world is made up of the same stuff which James called 'pure experience'. Those who say that mind is different from matter 'are clinging to a mere echo, the faint rumour left behind by the disappearing "soul" upon the air of philosophy.'

This disappearance of the soul might appeal to humanist sensibilities. But the necessity of denying any radical distinction between subject and object brings problems with it. For example, what might 'pure experience' itself be? It is an idea that many philosophers since James have found unsatisfactory.

2 **We often have to make decisions about beliefs for which there are inadequate rational grounds.** If the first tenet is difficult, the second is more straightforward. For it is surely the case that in practice, we often have to make decisions about beliefs for which there are inadequate rational grounds. James called it the 'Will to Believe', in an essay of the same title. He thought that religious belief was the quintessential example. For example, a sceptic may decide that they cannot believe in God, not because the evidence is against deities, but because having concluded that the evidence alone is not enough to

decide one way or another, they would rather avoid the error of believing in God when it might well not be true. According to James, though, the religious believer may also conclude that though the evidence is inadequate, there is a duty to believe in truth as much as there is to shun error. This first imperative is what the sceptic ignores at the risk of not believing something that is in fact true. Of course, both the believer and the sceptic may be duped. But James suggests that being duped 'through hope' is better than being duped 'through fear'.

The weakness of this tenet is that it doesn't take much account of the *probability* of whether things may or may not exist. So, someone may think that it is overwhelmingly unlikely that God exists and so call themselves an atheist. It is not so much that they fear committing what they regard as the error of theism as simply that they regard theism itself as enormously improbable. (Whether or not God can be judged to exist as a question of probability is another question entirely.)

3 **Something can be said to be true if it works – that is, if it has the virtue of making people happy.** This is called the principle of pragmatism. It can be summarized by saying that the value of a theory is not primarily whether or not it is true, but whether it works. James wrote: 'We cannot reject any hypothesis if consequences useful to life flow from it.' And even more strongly: 'The true is the name of whatever proves itself to be good in the way of belief.'

This relationship between truth and utility needs clarification. For example, it might be thought to imply that truth simply does not matter; even that it doesn't exist. James denied such nihilism. Instead, he argued that if something worked for him then it was not just true but was truth. Conversely, he sought to draw a different kind of distinction, namely that truth is not the same as reality. 'Realities are not *true*, they *are*; and beliefs are true *of* them.' So it is not so much that truth corresponds to reality, as if facts were always the same as truths. Rather, our ideas about what is true can point us to reality. There is always a need to cross the bridge between ideas about reality and reality itself.

Problems with 'what works'

A number of difficulties are raised by James's pragmatism. Bertrand Russell rejected it on several grounds:

1 **The difficulty of saying what is good.** Russell argued that to apply the principle of pragmatism you must first arrive at a true idea of what is good, which is notoriously hard to do. (The situation for pragmatists seems even more complicated, Russell continued, if for them the truth of something is already intimately related to its goodness – which is tantamount to tautology, arguing that what is good is good because it is good.) James, though, could reply that much of the difficulty of deciding what is good stems from the presumed need to have an *objective* account of it. *Subjectively* speaking, this is not necessarily hard at all. And he has already denied the difference between the two.

2 **The fact that some truths do not depend upon their efficacy.** Russell argued that some things simply are true, notably historical facts such as that Columbus sailed across the Atlantic in 1492. The idea that the truth of this dating depends upon whether or not it is good for humanity is clearly ridiculous. However, I think that James escapes this ridicule since his pragmatism is directed at truths for which there isn't enough evidence *in principle* to decide. This is not the case for historical facts where there is evidence.

3 **The accusation that it avoids certain fundamental questions.** Russell argued that when applied to religion, pragmatism avoids fundamental theological questions, such as whether God is, or is not, actually in heaven. For James, though, this thought would be a prime case in which there is not enough evidence upon which to make an objective decision.

4 **It tries to circumvent fundamental scepticism.** Finally, Russell argues that, 'James's doctrine is an attempt to build a superstructure of belief upon a foundation of scepticism, and like all such attempts it is dependent on fallacies.' In relation to religion, Russell's accusation is that for most believers, who are by definition not sceptics, the correct thing to say about their convictions is, 'I believe in God and therefore I am happy.' James, though, reinterprets the believer's faith, converting it into the statement, 'If I believed in God I would be happy; therefore, I believe in God.' Little wonder, Russell notes, that the Pope condemned pragmatism. In short, you cannot have your sceptical cake and eat it.

The priority of experience in religion

As an aside, I am not sure this is what James is saying of belief at all. Rather, in his most important book, *The Varieties of Religious Experience*, is he asking what it *feels* like to have a religious experience? Or why such experiences should be called religious and not, say, existential or artistic? In other words, James realizes that what primarily counts in religion is not the *belief* but the *experience* – the difference it makes. So people's descriptions of their religious experiences form the primary material for the study of religion, even when explanations of these experiences are subsequently offered. Religious feelings and impulses are nothing if not subjective.

Therefore Russell's accusation – that James advocates the justification of religious belief because of its utility – makes the mistake of giving priority to the religious *belief*. Rather, belief comes after; it tries to make sense of the *experience*. Incidentally, this is something that all religious institutions, such as churches, understand if only by their failure to keep a cap on what people make of their experiences: it is for this reason that heterodoxy and heresy are at least as resilient as orthodoxy.

Incidentally, a related and important fact that James draws attention to, even in the title of his book, is that religious experience is nothing if not various. It cannot simply be equated with a peak experience, or a sense of connectedness, or a creative urge, or a loss of self, or a feeling of bliss. At different times, religious people have said it is all these things and none of them.

Ignoring or forgetting this is the mistake that James's successors, present-day neuropsychologists of religion, often appear to make. They seek physiological explanations for religion, typically by monitoring activity in the brain, and thereby assume it is one thing or the other, normally some kind of peak or exceptional experience. James, though, would say that religious experience always exceeds any one of its manifestations. It can be studied by science but is ultimately entirely beyond science's ability to grasp.

Pragmatism as a humanism

Explicit links between pragmatism and humanism were not championed until a generation after James, notably by the philosopher F. C. S. Schiller (1864–1937). Schiller made the connections explicit in his book *Humanism: Philosophical Essays*, published in 1903. His version of humanism is based upon pragmatism and, in particular, the notion that for something to be true it must at least have some practical application in life. In fact, positive practicality is key to something being thought of as humanistic. Schiller is also at pains to show what a waste of valuable philosophical time, as it were, it has been to speculate on intellectual matters that can have no possible bearing upon what works. He wants to show that wordy metaphysics is pointless unless its meaning has some application and its thought some purpose.

Other pragmatists

Dewey

Another pragmatist and contemporary of Schiller – and someone who, philosophically speaking, is more important – was the American John Dewey (1859–1952). Bertrand Russell thought Dewey the most distinguished living philosopher at the time. Dewey sought to turn pragmatism into a systematic theory. He did so by rejecting all dualisms – mind/body, fact/value, means/ends – and by developing his pragmatism on evolutionary principles: he envisaged philosophy as a continually self-correcting process, not unlike evolutionary change. He also thought that philosophy makes progress like science, though is limited in the sense that this progress is only ever in relation to current experience. In fact, he was an advocate of what is called 'fallibilism', the view that no fact, rule or idea is ever certain. This means that philosophy differs from science on two counts:

1 **Experience** It embraces a wider range of experiences than science can, including moral and aesthetic dimensions of existence in particular.
2 **Truth** It is also different in terms of its understanding of truth. Dewey wrote: 'Truth is the opinion which is fated to be ultimately agreed to by all who investigate' – showing his indebtedness to the pragmatic principle. In other words, truth is judged by its effects.

It should also be added that Dewey has been an inspiration to some humanists for his contribution to society at large, particularly for his tireless work in the sphere of education.

Rorty

To bring our account of pragmatism up to date, we should mention a philosopher who died during the writing of this book, namely Richard Rorty (1931–2007). He was another pragmatist advocate of deflationary accounts of truth – offending many when he argued that most of philosophy since Plato has been interesting but useless. He preferred philosophy that contributed to a wider conversation between human beings on justice and truth without worrying about the grounds for justice and truth: it would aim at accounts that work in terms of delivering practical goods. 'Time will tell, but epistemology won't,' he wrote in one book. To put it another way, he saw philosophy as an essentially creative and imaginative exercise.

It is also a collective one, since the greatest utility philosophy might have – its aim therefore – is solidarity. He wrote:

> If we could be moved solely by the desire for solidarity, setting aside the desire for objectivity altogether, then we should think of human progress as making it possible for human beings to do more interesting things and be more interesting people, not as heading towards a place which has somehow been prepared for us in advance.

This vision is clearly humanistic, being focused on the betterment of human beings. However, Rorty found himself at odds with other humanists, even those who could be called pragmatic. For example, he might be thought naïve in thinking that human beings can simply give up their longing to find things that are true with a capital 'T'. Critics of Rorty might reply that Plato has lasted for a very good reason: he is not just creative and imaginative but aims to be right. Also, there are many humanists who could not or would not give up on all objective criteria for truth, no matter how hard they might be to ascertain.

Summary

In this chapter, we have moved into the post-Enlightenment history of humanism, the period in which thinkers actually called themselves humanists. However, we have also seen that what humanism might be can vary radically. We have considered three versions here.

- The first was an approach to humanism inspired by Marx which majors on the belief that philosophy must not focus on the individual, or only on the individual, but on the social. It is arguably the least important kind of humanism in operation today, though still carries some weight in social economics.

- The second was utilitarianism, an ethical approach to humanism which seeks to maximize the greatest happiness for the greatest number. It gained great weight in the form developed by Mill and, in the philosophies of utilitarians like Peter Singer, is a major force amongst humanist thinkers today.
- The third humanism was pragmatism. Summed up as 'what works', it too has developed into a major strand within humanism, appealing particularly to those who believe that the old aims of philosophy, to ascertain what is true, are less important than developing ways of thinking that better allow humans to live together.

Before leaving this chapter, it is worth just referring to two other kinds of humanism that relate to those we have encountered.

Literary humanism

Literary humanism, also call the New Humanism, was a literary movement that emerged in the early decades of the twentieth century, soon after pragmatism. It argued that human beings are unique in the natural world, that experience is fundamentally moral not natural, and that human beings are free, though subject to natural laws. An important advocate was Matthew Arnold, who wrote books including *Culture and Anarchy* (1869) and *Essays in Criticism* (1888). He looked back to writers like Chaucer who he believed had gained 'the power to survey the world from a central, a truly human point of view'. For Arnold, Chaucer was the first to explore everyday experience, as opposed to that of the clergy or aristocracy. Added to this, Chaucer, though a great poet, had the virtue of being an ordinary human being too – an observation that celebrates the uniqueness *and* universality of the human condition.

Feminism

A second kind of humanism can be linked to Marxism, and is based upon feminist philosophy. It can be linked to Marxism inasmuch as if Marx had critiqued the individualistic line of thought from the Enlightenment, then feminists critiqued the fact that it was not just individualistic but decidedly male too.

Feminism has developed into a broad philosophical movement that it is not possible to do justice to here. However, broadly speaking, it seeks both to establish equality for women and to understand the patriarchal roots of culture and thought.

For humanists, a key feminist issue is that of the traditional association between women and irrationality, which if humanism stresses the rational nature of Man [sic], can perpetuate patriarchal patterns of thought. Similarly, a humanism that stresses the 'human animal's' place in nature can also import a social determinism which ascribes particular roles to women, curtailing their freedom. Much has been written on feminism and some seminal texts include Mary Wollstonecraft's *A Vindication of the Rights of Women* (1792), John Stuart Mill *The Subjection of Women* (1869) and Carol Gilligan's *In a Different Voice* (1982).

In relation to feminism, an interesting conundrum for humanists today is the wearing of the veil by Muslim women. These women claim it as their right, arguing that it is a sign of respect and honour. They sound almost like feminists in so doing. Humanists, though, will see the veil as symbolic of a repressive religious social order and want to reject it.

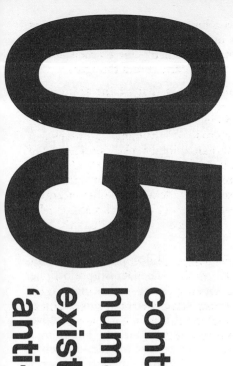

05

contemporary humanisms 2: existentialists and 'anti-humanists'

In this chapter you will learn:

- how another new kind of humanism emerged in the twentieth century based upon the thoughts of the existentialists
- about figures including Sartre, Nietzsche and Foucault
- why various critics of humanism, the so-called anti-humanists, are arguably an important part of the humanist tradition.

In the twentieth century the humanist philosophies of the nineteenth century, notably utilitarianism and Marxism, were sustained, developed and often enriched. There was also the American invention of pragmatism. However, that was not the only humanist innovation of the twentieth century. In continental Europe two more important developments emerged. The first is existentialism, the philosophy that acclaims the absolute freedom of the human individual. The second is sometimes called anti-humanism, though I shall argue it has a proper place within the history of humanism because it offers criticisms of humanism that are important to engage with. It is to these strands that we now turn.

Radical freedom

Strictly speaking, existentialism is a philosophy whose roots reach back into the nineteenth century. The Danish philosopher Søren Kierkegaard (1813–1855) is usually identified as its founder. He argued that the subjective, personal dimension of life is what matters. 'What use would it be if I were to discover so-called objective truth?' he asked in his journal. 'The thing is to find a truth which is truth for me, to find the idea for which I am willing to live and die.' It is this subjectivity that became central to existentialism.

With this human centeredness, one can see the immediate appeal of existentialism as a form of humanism. However, it was not until the twentieth century and the existentialism of Jean-Paul Sartre (1905–80), that it became explicitly identified with humanism. Sartre was famous in France and the world over as a novelist, playwright and philosopher. He was also awarded the Nobel Prize for Literature in 1964, though he declined it. However, his importance to humanism can be focused on a lecture he gave in 1946. It was entitled *Existentialism is a Humanism* and has become another seminal text in the history of humanism.

Sartre begins by identifying various charges that, at the time, had been laid against existentialism:

- It had been accused of being quietist; encouraging people to contemplate their existence, not act to improve it.
- It was accused of being ignominious and individualistic – the first because it dwells on the darker side of life, the second because it begins with Descartes' famous 'I think therefore I am,' a solitary account of humankind.

- It was accused of being anarchic, propagating a moral code of 'each to their own'.

It is to combat these charges of pathetic inaction, dismal pessimism and dangerous solipsism that he appeals to the word humanism. No small part of the problem, Sartre continued, is that existentialism as a philosophy has come to mean everything and nothing; it has become a victim of its own success, used almost synonymously with words like 'expressive' or alternatively in wholly alien contexts such as 'existential crisis'.

So what does Sartre think humanism can deliver, and what does existentialism mean to him? In a word, freedom. And this is what people find so alarming about existentialism: 'It confronts man with a possibility of choice.' To put it in a more technical way, what lies at the heart of existentialism is the belief that '*existence* comes before *essence*' – that is, when thinking about what it is to be human, existentialists begin with the subjective experience of being human, not some kind of objective understanding of human nature. 'We mean that man first of all exists, encounters himself, surges up in the world – and defines himself afterwards … and then he will be what he makes of himself.'

Dignity as self-determination

Sartre calls this capacity for self-realization the first principle of existentialism. Therein lies the dignity of humankind – that long-standing theme within humanism – for it distinguishes people from mere things. 'Man is, before all else, something which propels itself towards a future and is aware that it is doing so.' Various things follow from this dignity:

- With it comes a tremendous personal responsibility. If every person is capable of self-realization then the onus for doing so rests squarely upon each person's shoulders.
- With it also comes a tremendous collective responsibility. For when one person defines themselves, they also define what it is to be human and this has some kind of impact upon all other humans' sense of themselves. Thus, the image that we fashion for ourselves 'is valid for all and for the entire epoch in which we find ourselves'.

It is because of this collective responsibility that many of the supposedly pessimistic characteristics of existentialism follow. Take anguish: this is the burden of asking what might happen if everyone did as you yourself are now doing. It is the concern that every leader understands. For what that means is this:

If I regard a certain course of action as good, it is only I who can choose to say that it is good and not bad ... Everything happens to every man as though the whole human race had its eyes fixed upon what he is doing and regulated its conduct according.

Abandonment

Another key word for Sartre is abandonment. This refers to his atheism and the desire to understand the consequences of the non-existence of God 'right to the end'. He thinks this is important since if the ramifications of a Godless universe are avoided or finessed in some way then this denial threatens the very foundations of morality. In other words, the existentialist understands very well that with the disappearance of God also disappears the possibility of locating human values in some transcendent realm. 'It is nowhere written that "the good" exists, that one must be honest or must not lie, since we are now upon the plane where there are only men.'

One thing to note about Sartre's atheism is that it is not obsessed with showing that God does not exist. Towards the end of *Existentialism is a Humanism*, Sartre says:

> Existentialism is not atheist in the sense that it would exhaust itself in demonstrations of the non-existence of God. It declares, rather, that even if God existed that would make no difference from its point of view. Not that we believe God does exist, but we think that the real problem is not that of His existence; what man needs is to find himself again and to understand that nothing can save him from himself, not even a valid proof of the existence of God.

To put it the other way around, as Dostoevsky wrote: 'If God did not exist, everything would be permitted' – and that is precisely the position that the existentialist understands human beings to be in. It means both that we cannot find anything to depend on apart from ourselves, and that we have no excuses: we cannot explain our actions with reference to human nature for there is no such thing as human nature. 'There is no determinism – man is free, man *is* freedom.'

This, Sartre explains, is what he means when he says that people are *condemned* to be free. We did not create ourselves but upon finding ourselves thrown into the world, we are at liberty. And this liberty is frightening because there are no rules as to how we should live; no commandments that can tell us what to do.

Worse still, we cannot turn in on ourselves to find our 'true' selves and then try to realize that. People are not born heroes, they make themselves heroes. People are not born cowards, their cowardice is their responsibility. Sartre states: 'I can neither seek within myself for an authentic impulse to action, nor can I expect, from some ethic, formulae that will enable me to act.' So we are abandoned to decide what to do for ourselves, to work out how to be. It is another source of liberative anguish. Sartre continues:

> This is humanism, because we remind man that there is no legislator but himself; that he himself, thus abandoned, must decide for himself; also because we show that it is not by turning back upon himself, but always by seeking, beyond himself, an aim which is one of liberation or of some particular realization, that man can realize himself as truly human.

Action

Such thoughts might lead to despair, to the pessimism that his accusers level against him. However, Sartre argues the opposite. It means, for example, that if someone has been cowardly, then they are also always free to be heroic now. If someone has been a liar, they can start to speak truthfully. Conversely, someone else who refuses to be free, say, by arguing that they are following an authority like the Church or that their actions are determined by some imagined inner nature, are susceptible to the existentialist's judgement: they are cowards.

Sartre cannot have hope for the future of humankind because he does not believe there is any natural goodness within human beings that will automatically win out. However, because he as one person can choose to do good, at least as he sees it, he can work fiercely for a better tomorrow. This is why existentialism is not quietist. Quite the opposite: properly understood it leads to action. In fact, without action, human beings are nothing. Sartre states: 'Man is nothing else but what he purposes, he exists only in so far as he realizes himself, he is therefore nothing else but the sum of his actions, nothing else but what his life is.'

Moreover, because every other individual is in the same boat as I am, they become invaluable sources for understanding my own predicament, and I theirs. 'The other is indispensable to my existence, and equally so too any knowledge I can have of myself.' The truth of this is reinforced because although there is no essential human nature, there are very widespread conditions of human existence in which people live. For example, the time in which someone is born will decide whether they are a slave, a baron or a proletarian. And that will be the same for everyone else born in that time. This again is a source of solidarity.

Existentialism rebuts the charge of relativism with a similar line of thought. Sartre admits that it is the case that existentialists do not have any universal maxims or conception of morality like, say, Kant did. However, he also thinks that such universals are more or less useless in practice, since in practice, ethics is always particular, always specific. So, a maxim like 'love others' has to be *applied*, and it can mean such different things in different circumstances that the universal maxim ceases to have any meaningful content. It becomes a platitude.

Problems with existential humanism

Sartre's account of existentialism as a humanism therefore has many qualities that other humanists would admire: the dignity of humanity; the freedom to choose; the sense of connection with others; the seriousness of its moral purpose and so on. However, there are some facets that are more problematic:

1 Anti-essentialism

Perhaps the most fundamental issue concerns Sartre's anti-essentialism. He explicitly denies that human beings should be regarded as of supreme value. There is no essence of humanity to which human beings must return or be resolved towards – like Rousseau's state-of-nature, or Comte's religion of humanity. Humanity, as opposed to individual human beings, cannot be an end in itself, for human beings must define themselves.

Elsewhere, Sartre had ridiculed even the possibility. He says it is absurd to declare 'Man is magnificent!' simply because, say, we can build aeroplanes that fly higher than mountains. It would make equal sense to conclude that the mountains are magnificent and human beings are poor flying creatures like gnats.

Sartre also points out that there is a grave danger in essentialist conceptions of humanism. They result in all sorts of crimes being committed against actual groups or individuals in the name of an oppressive ideal of humanity that finds certain groups or individuals marred or polluting. Nazism obviously comes to mind, though in *Existentialism as a Humanism*, Sartre continues:

> And we have no right to believe that humanity is something to which we could set up a cult, after the manner of Auguste Comte. The cult of humanity ends in Comtian humanism, shut-in upon itself, and – this must be said – in Fascism. We do not want humanism like that.

2 Atheism

Sartre's humanism is fundamentally atheistic. In fact, he believes it is theism that has encouraged people to make the mistake of putting essence before existence. This is based upon the myth that God designed human beings before creating them. 'The conception of man in the mind of God is comparable to that of the paper-knife in the mind of the artisan: God makes man according to a procedure and a conception, exactly as the artisan manufactures a paper-knife, following a definition and formula.'

A similar notion is found buried in the humanistic essentialism of the eighteenth century. There, the belief in God may be wholly or partially suppressed. And yet the concept of Man persists. Sartre believes this needs to be expunged – for fear of the fascistic consequences – and the acceptance of atheism is a crucial part of that corrective.

However, not all existentialists followed Sartre in thinking that theism was the fundamental problem. In particular, the Christian existentialists argued that those who believe in human essentialism do so on the basis of a mistaken conception of Christianity. The key doctrine should be the one which states that God created human beings *ex nihilo* – out of nothing. So, rather than myths of divine creativity being the enemy of existentialism, the doctrine of creation is in fact the guarantor of existentialism's central doctrine: that human beings are created free.

This theism allows these existentialists to be even more radical than that. For the '*ex nihilo*' itself becomes the fundamental feature of human existence, that is, in short, nothing. This contrasts with the atheistic existentialist who, like Sartre, declares that freedom is the fundamental feature of human existence, which leaves him open to the accusation of reintroducing an essentialism through the back door.

Another point that Christian existentialists have made is that religion provides many resources for pursuing an existentialist way of life, not least because many of the greatest figures in religion have been so remarkably self-determined. For Karl Jaspers, a leading Christian existentialist, the Buddha and Jesus, along with Socrates and Confucius, are paradigms of human beings who have discovered the human task as the existentialist sees it:

> In them human experiences and aspirations are manifested in the extreme ... They became sources of philosophical thought and a stimulus to resistance, through whom the resisters first gained self-awareness.

3 Progress

Finally, Sartre denies human progress – something that is a touchstone for many humanists. He denies it because in order for progress to occur some of the predicaments that human beings face would have to improve. According to the existential worldview, this does not happen, particularly in relation to all important moral issues. It is implicit in radical freedom that human beings have an on-going, continuous choice between good and evil. The specifics of those goods and evils change, of course: slavery is banned or health improves. But then slavery reinvents itself and, of course, people always ultimately face the frailty of their bodies and death.

However, for all that humanists might reject some of Sartre's conclusions, they can learn much from existentialism without necessarily embracing it in its entirety. There is the stress on the value of human subjectivity and the supreme value of freedom. And alongside these obviously humanistic themes, Sartre might also be remembered for arguing that humanism is not a static project. It is more like a way of life, an attitude towards the human condition that is based upon subjectivity and freedom. This makes it an open-ended pursuit, and one that will never come to an end.

'Anti-humanist' philosophy

Utilitarianism, pragmatism and existentialism have all tended to embrace the notion of humanism positively, if very differently. However, running alongside the twentieth-century explorations of humanism is another strand to explore. This one has not had such a good press, at least amongst humanists. Indeed, it is usually referred to as 'anti-humanist'.

The expression anti-humanism arose when thinkers appeared to attack one or more of the elements that could be taken as key to any humanist philosophy. In fact, my feeling is that the so-called anti-humanists were often engaged in a committed critique of the humanist tradition. There aim was not to overthrow it but deepen it, in one way or another. After all, most were atheists, or at least atheistically inclined. Given that they were not harbingers of any alternative ideology, like religion, it is not as if they had much of an alternative but to stick with humanism in some shape or form.

Here, we will discuss in detail just two figures, Friedrich Nietzsche (1844–1900) and Michel Foucault (1926–84). Their aim was radical: to reinvigorate humanist ideas and rid them of faults or weaknesses. In other words, they are the inheritors of the sceptical tradition that reaches back through the eighteenth century in the work of Kant and Hume, and to the Renaissance in the writing of Montaigne and Machiavelli. Indeed, both Foucault and Nietzsche have been called 'Masters of Suspicion'.

Friedrich Nietzsche

Nietzsche provides a good place to start, not least because it was he who proclaimed what many people at the time were thinking: God is dead. However, before coming to that let us first consider some of the other elements that he denounced at the same time. It is these that give rise to the anti-humanist accusation.

First, Nietzsche loathed Christianity. This might be thought the mark of a good humanist by some, not an anti-humanist, but it was the way in which Nietzsche denounced Christianity that can disturb even an atheistic humanist. He argued that Christianity encourages a slave mentality. This is partly because of the necessity of submitting to a deity, but also because of Christianity's ethical requirement to serve others. Nietzsche thought this dehumanizing. For example, to have pity on others is patronizing to them and self-indulgent of you. He wrote in *The Gay Science*:

> When we see somebody suffer, we like to exploit this opportunity to take possession of him; those who become his benefactors and pity him, for example, do this and call the lust for a new possession that he awakens in them 'love'; and the pleasure they feel is comparable to that aroused by the prospect of a new conquest.

Instead, Nietzsche encouraged people to rejoice together even in the midst of suffering. This, though, runs the risk of appearing inhumane. It might challenge the humanist virtues of solidarity and fellow-feeling.

Questioning progress

Second, Nietzsche attacked scientific progressivism, the notion that through science, human knowledge advances and progresses. This seems like a more direct attack on humanism. Nietzsche identified three phases through which this positivist doctrine has passed since the advent of modern science.

- The first was that of Newton, who believed that science would reveal the goodness and wisdom of God. As an atheist, Nietzsche thought this self-evidently untrue.
- The second was that of Voltaire, who believed that science would elicit knowledge that would improve human morality and happiness. This might have been possible to believe in the eighteenth century, but no more.
- The third is perhaps typical of many scientists now who see their discipline as the pursuit of objective, disinterested knowledge, and not tainted with the flaws of most other disciplines. This, though, becomes unsustainable, according to Nietzsche, as soon as you observe the processes of science, which are driven by competition and power. Further, a little philosophy of science, drawing on the work of someone like Hume, shows that science rapidly loses any easy claim to objectivity.

So, Nietzsche thought that all three positivist attitudes to science were based on fundamental errors.

Historical perspectivism

The examples above point to more profound critiques that Nietzsche had of humanism. For example, he thought it lacked a proper historical sense, which might manifest itself in a number of ways. The doctrine of progress is one, in that it fails to see both that it has been undermined before and that its origins are possibly quite unpalatable to its contemporary adherents. Philosophically speaking, a related but more substantial complaint is that the moral virtues held by humanism are themselves historically conditioned.

Consider the dignity of humankind. Pico, the author of the phrase, appears to have located man's dignity in occult knowledge that would enable him to become divine. The eighteenth-century humanists saw man's dignity in a kind of post-Christian understanding of humankind as the pinnacle of creation. This was dashed with the discovery of evolution, but was reinvented again in the twentieth century by conceptions of dignity as freedom or spirit. Nietzsche's point is that a value like dignity depends on your historic time and place. This doctrine is sometimes called 'perspectivism'. Without this sense of time and place, Nietzsche would say that championing man's dignity becomes as much empty rhetoric.

Character and dignity

This, in turn, matters because empty rhetoric is corrosive. It lacks honesty. It corrals human beings as herd-like animals rather than cultivating their individual dignity. In *The Gay Science*, one of the books of Nietzsche's so-called middle period, when these themes are articulated very accessibly, he writes of one thing that is needful for the modern individual, that is, 'To "give style" to one's character – a great and rare art!' What Nietzsche argues is that the dignified individual is one who can turn an eye on themselves and survey their weaknesses and strengths. Both facets, once admitted and understood, can be knitted together to form one's character, to lend it style. It takes a long time and much practice, but these are admirable people. They find satisfaction in life. They are able to throw off the resentment of those who do not have the courage to examine themselves. For such resentment, with its desire for revenge, makes for the most undignified of human creatures.

In many other examples that could be taken from Nietzsche's books, similar imperatives are extolled. Tenets of humanist faith are scrutinized for sure, often with a knife-like wit. But the overall aim is to make more of what it is to be human. This is humanism as a brave work on yourself, not an abstract philosophy.

The death of God

Nowhere is this courageousness more needed than in Nietzsche's exploration of what it means to live in an age without God. Nietzsche makes his announcement of the death of God in a rather unexpected way. He tells the story of a madman who one day went to the marketplace. His fellow human beings were about their everyday, secular activities – living already in an age that had left God behind. And the madman cried out: 'I seek God! I seek God!' They laughed and mocked, asking whether God had got lost, or whether God is hiding, or if God is afraid of us? But then the madman turns on his tormenters. 'I will tell you,' he cries. 'We have killed him – you and I.'

Nietzsche's point is not to plead God's cause; rather it is to indicate the ramifications of God's departure from the modern world. They are not unlike the way the world shatters when someone is murdered. The madman continues his articulation of this horrifying state of affairs in cosmological terms:

> How could we drink up the sea? Who gave us the sponge to wipe away the entire horizon? What were we doing when we unchained this earth from its sun? Whither is it moving now? Whither are we moving? Away from all suns? Are we not plunging continually? Backward, sideward, forward, in all directions? Is there still any up or down? Are we not straying as through an infinite nothing? Do we not feel the breath of empty space? Has it not become colder? Is not night continually closing in on us?

And so the 'madman' continues, for he is not really mad but a prophet. He understands the atheistic human condition more clearly than those around him. It may have been inevitable that God died. It may have been desirable. Presumably Nietzsche thought so, as an atheist. However, this did not blind him to the great problems it would throw up for humankind, and humanism – problems of how to ground morality, how to locate a sense of meaning, how to orientate ourselves through life.

The disillusionment of Enlightenment

This, then, is another of Nietzsche's criticisms of humanism. Its atheism – or at least its sense of having moved beyond the superstitions of our medieval forbears – can be so glib; as if all that is required is to breathe deeply of Enlightenment air and watch as the sun dispels the clouds! The humanist call, as Nietzsche sees it, is actually far more tremendous than that. Nietzsche is rehearsing the warning of Kant, that Enlightenment is tough, that in political revolutions and personal delusions it can go wrong. It would be better to say this was an age of Enlightenment rather than an enlightened age.

Later in *The Gay Science*, Nietzsche offers his own estimation of how long Enlightenment might take. Centuries, he muses. And in the meantime, human beings will be constantly tempted to fall back on old superstitions and old faiths, often without even realizing it. Chief among these will be the conviction that they are enlightened already.

Michel Foucault

Michel Foucault is another philosopher frequently tarred with the anti-humanist brush, because he takes issue with rigid conceptions of 'man'. Foucault objects to this essentialism because he believes it is actually constructed – constructed through various discourses, of ambiguous benefit to actual human beings, which developed in the modern period. For example, psychiatric discourses constructed increasingly complex ideas of what it is to be mad and what it is to be sane. Legal discourses did the same in terms of what it is to be criminal and law-abiding. Moral discourses constructed ideas of what it is to be deviant and normal.

The reason these discourses are of ambiguous benefit is that real people fall across the categories they create – perhaps being somewhat mad and somewhat sane, somewhat deviant and somewhat normal. The robust idea of 'man' disciplines us into normative behaviour, so that we might think of ourselves as sane, law-abiding, normal individuals. And for many, much of the time, that is fine. However, those who fall outside of the boundaries – the mad, criminal deviants – are more fiercely disciplined, propelled to the margins of society by modern institutions like the penal system, and held in other modern institutions like the psychiatric hospital.

A recent invention

It is this legacy of eighteenth- and nineteenth-century humanism to which Foucault objects. In a famous passage at the conclusion of his book, *The Order of Things*, he writes:

> One thing in any case is certain: man is neither the oldest nor the most constant problem that has been posed for human knowledge. Taking a relatively short chronological sample within a restricted geographical area – European culture since the sixteenth century – one can be certain that man is a recent invention within it ... As the archaeology of our thought easily shows, man is an invention of recent date. And one perhaps nearing its end.

It is this talk of man being a 'recent invention' that annoys some humanists. It questions essentialist understandings of human nature, like those of Rousseau that argue for an innocent 'state-of-nature' lying underneath the corruptions brought about by living in society. Alternatively, it seems to suggest that some of the advances made by science, such as modern psychiatry, or developments in what would usually be thought of as social progress, like the modern penal system, are actually more suspect than they might first appear.

Power-knowledge

Foucault's phrase for this was 'power-knowledge'. It aims to capture the sense in which any claim to have knowledge about people, such as that they are mad or deviant, also entails an exercise of power over them. So someone whose is declared mad can be locked up in the madhouse. Someone who is found guilty can be incarcerated in a prison. Obviously, there is some reason to do this, some good that might result. But it is deluded of the champions of progress to presume that the good of humanity is the only result.

The insane become institutionalized and may never be capable of living in the wider world again. Are they better or worse off for that? It is a question that must be asked, in the name of humanity. Similarly, the imprisoned may be led into a life of crime by being locked up. Indeed the chances are that they will be, if the evidence of organizations like the Howard League for Penal Reform is anything to go by. In a typically strident phrase Foucault concludes that: 'Humanity installs each of its violences in a system of rules and thus proceeds from domination to domination.'

So is there any chance of a philosophy of humanism with a hope that things can get better? Foucault asked this question by asking one that had been asked by Kant: what is Enlightenment? His essay of that title was published in the year Foucault died, suddenly and as a relatively young man. It is perhaps for this reason that it is often overlooked, but to my mind humanists would find much in it to inspire them.

Questioning yourself

Foucault turns back to Kant's answer and assesses it. He writes: 'Kant, in fact, describes Enlightenment as the moment when humanity is going to put its own reason to use, without subjecting itself to any authority.' From this follows Kant's project of critique which Foucault thinks is interesting because it is a self-critique: Kant tries to reflect upon 'the contemporary status of his own enterprise'. He questions himself. He tries to understand what is different about his own philosophy and where it might fall short.

This, then, Foucault continues, should be the task of the enlightened humanist today. It is not simply to accept the eighteenth-century construction of man; rather it is to forge an understanding of what it is to be human that fits our times. This becomes a 'practice of liberty' because it also seeks to transcend the limitations of what our generation has received, notably the neat divisions between the normal and deviant. And this can be thought of as a creative task, one even of invention.

Coming out

A useful case in point is one that was close to Foucault himself, namely that of sexuality. Foucault was homosexual – a category of human sexuality that has only existed since the nineteenth century. This is not, of course, to suggest that there were no men who loved men, and no men who had sex with other men, before then. Rather it is to point out that understanding oneself as *a* homosexual is a recent conception. The Ancient Greek man who had a relationship with another man did not think of himself as different from other men, as the contemporary gay person does, at least to some degree.

Now, this modern turn has brought about many benefits for gay people, from gay bars to civil partnerships. However, Foucault also believed they come at a price, namely the risk of categorizing yourself as a gay man or woman, as if that were somehow a defining feature of yourself. This is to enjoy a freedom – the freedom to be gay – by imposing a kind of limit upon yourself. So, Foucault argued, the real goal of gay liberation should not be just to 'come out' but ultimately to find a 'way out' of the business of calling people gay or straight altogether – that would be truly liberated. He hoped that was happening, and it was part of what he meant when he wrote that man was a recent invention and perhaps nearing its end.

Summary

There are other figures we could point to that have been thought anti-humanist. Sigmund Freud (1856–1939) would be one, the inventor of psychoanalysis, as well as interpreter of dreams, 'discoverer' of the unconscious and brilliant essayist. The paradox is that although Freud can be a figure of hate and ridicule among humanists, and his work branded a pseudo-science, he saw himself as an 'Enlightener', a rationalist who sought to throw light into the darkest corners of the human mind.

The same would be true of the other 'anti-humanists'. They were masters of suspicion because they sought to leave their fellows less deluded. For Nietzsche, this meant trying to see things in an historical perspective and realizing that the death of God did not imply any automatic liberation, anymore than simply heralding an age as one of enlightenment meant that the people in it were enlightened. For Foucault, a crucial issue is to understand that progress is not always what it seems to be. Moreover, while humanists quite rightly seek knowledge, they might also be aware that what they believe to be true has ramifications for others that can actually be oppressive.

These are all useful critiques of humanism. To my mind, they have as much of a place in the recent history of humanism as the more straightforwardly positive doctrines of utilitarianism, pragmatism and the other humanisms we have introduced in this chapter, namely existentialism – the humanism that advocates freedom.

06

contemporary humanisms 3: Darwin, organized humanism and Christians

In this chapter you will learn:
- how the theory of evolution caused everyone to think again
- about the story of modern atheistic and organized humanism that began in the nineteenth century
- why religious humanism lives on in spite of it all.

Our examination of post-Enlightenment humanism, or rather humanisms, has now revealed not only advocates of the themes that reach back through the Enlightenment and to the Renaissance, but also critics of them, too. What is humanism? It is a human-centred concern with science, reason, personhood, happiness and freedom – and it is nothing if not richly diverse.

But there is perhaps one figure that the astute reader will have noticed has been missing until now. Moreover, he is particularly important since he plays a key role in debates about humanism that not only took place during the twentieth century but are alive and kicking in the twenty-first, right up to the present day. That figure is Charles Darwin (1809–1882).

The Darwinian revolution

In the history of humanism, there are few commemorative dates. The year Pico published *On the Dignity of Man*, 1486, might be one; the day David Hume died, Sunday, 25 August 1776, might be another. But there is one more to add: 24 November 1859. On this day Darwin's *On the Origin of Species by Means of Natural Selection, or the Preservation of Favoured Races in the Struggle for Life* – the *Origin of Species* for short – was published.

His book is the foundational text for the scientific theory of evolution. Its key idea is that in nature, advantageous physiological variations are preserved according to whether an organism survives and whether it mates. This is called natural selection and sexual selection respectively. In fact, Darwin was not the first to propose a theory of evolution; that accolade goes to the pre-Socratic philosopher Empedocles of the fifth century BCE. However, the book is a landmark in modern humanism on a number of counts:

1 **Science** Darwin's big idea, evolution, is one of the most important theories in modern science. Its essence is that natural processes can account for the extraordinary diversity of living creatures on earth through adaptive selection. Darwin had amassed very substantial evidence in support of his theory, evidence that has only increased as evolution has developed since.

2 **Religion** If evolution provides an explanation for the complexity of the living world, it also provides a rebuttal to proofs of God's existence by design. Although many

philosophers, including individuals like David Hume, had suggested reasons as to why design might be doubted, the lack of an alternative explanation for the intricacy of the living world was a weakness in their critique. After all, the variety and mutual dependency of living organisms is extraordinary. Darwin allows atheists to propose why without resorting to God.

3 **Controversy** The book has been followed by wave after wave of controversy from the moment it was published. The arguments it sparks fall into two categories. First, the theory is probed on scientific grounds. For example, many scientists wondered what the mechanism for passing on changes across the generations might be. Darwin called his own theory of inheritance 'pangenesis' and it was roundly criticized by his contemporaries. The real answer emerged in two stages. First, genes were discovered in 1865, by Gregor Mendel and, second, the role played by DNA in genetic inheritance was revealed in 1943. That was an important gap in the theory filled – though other details of evolution continue to generate substantial and often fierce debate amongst biologists. Having said that, it should also be noted that none of them doubts the basic insights of evolution.

That no mainstream biologist doubts the fundamentals of evolution is important to underline because the second category of controversy – on religious and moral grounds – can involve the denial of evolution. Darwin's theory is quite as earth-shattering as the Copernican revolution of the sixteenth century and the revolutions in relativity and quantum physics of the twentieth. It took centuries for some to accept that the earth was not the centre of the universe. Arguably the philosophical implications of the work of Albert Einstein and quantum physicists like Niels Bohr and Werner Heisenberg are still hardly understood. So perhaps it is enough that the work of today is to come to terms with what Darwinism means for human beings.

The religious and moral controversies about evolution took shape very quickly and have remained pretty constant over the years. The questions that the debates revolve around include:

- What does evolution mean for the status of human beings alongside other animals?
- If it undermines any designing role for God in the universe, does it also undermine any human sense of meaning in the world?

- Since natural selection is purposeless, does that mean that all human life is purposeless too?
- If the dominant law among natural organisms is 'survival of the fittest' then does that release human beings from all moral constraints?
- If nature selects those creatures that are best adapted to their environment, then maybe human beings should follow suit and select people that they regard as superior too – the science of eugenics?

The Scopes trial

These controversies came to a head in the first decades of the twentieth century when they clashed, sometimes violently, with a new phenomenon: Christian fundamentalism. The word fundamentalism comes from a series of pamphlets called *The Fundamentals* that were published by American evangelicals during the 1910s and insisted on Christians believing certain things like the inerrancy of the Bible. Evolution came to be pitted against one of the tenets of such fundamentalist belief, namely creationism. Ironically, few people in Darwin's day – a generation or two before – believed in biblical literalism and whether or not, say, the Garden of Eden actually existed. It was not until the mid-1920s, most strikingly at the John Scopes 'monkey trial' in Dayton, Tennessee, that lines were drawn between this new strain of Christianity and the new science.

The trial concerned the prosecution of a science teacher for teaching evolution in a state school, which for a short while was illegal. Clarence Darrow, the agnostic defence lawyer, won the day. He humiliated the leading anti-Darwinian, William Jennings Bryan – though some commentators rather lament that Bryan was made to look so foolish. They suggest that thereafter the trial only served to entrench positions. Its memory still fans the flames that burn about the issue a century later.

Having thrown all these questions up in the air, it is no surprise that Darwin supposedly called himself the 'devil's chaplain'. He has certainly become little short of a secular saint for many humanists, celebrated for the painstaking scientific work that blossomed into his theory and for the intellectual courage that could face its profound ramifications. Here, though, let us focus on two questions. First, what is the philosophical status of evolution as a scientific theory? This is important given that evolution is such a prominent bone of contention in the debates

humanists have with their opponents in the modern world.
Second, what exactly is the impact that evolution has on the
philosophy of religion and the question of the existence of God?

Creationism and intelligent design

Understanding evolution's status as a scientific theory has
become so important because of the battle pitched against
evolution by creationists, alongside the proponents of a variant
on creationism, so-called intelligent design. Though both have
changed in the last century or so, the difference between
creationism and intelligent design is roughly as follows:

- Creationists believe that the world was created in six days, as
  a literal reading of the book of Genesis in the Bible appears
  to imply.
- Intelligent design does not hold to that, but rather believes
  that there are gaps in the scientific account of evolution
  which can only be explained by God's agency. For example,
  they argue that science itself has thrown up examples from
  the anatomy of certain creatures that are simply too complex
  to have evolved by natural selection. In this way, intelligent
  design presents itself as scientific.
- Mainstream science responds to these challenges in two ways:

  First, by demonstrating that all the examples the advocates
  of intelligent design provide in support of their theory are
  mistaken. Evolution can in principle explain them all.

  Second, by stating that God is not a scientific explanation
  of the natural world, being scientifically inexplicable
  himself. In short, intelligent design is not science.

  (Incidentally, mainstream biblical scholars provide the best
  response to the creationist's literalism by pointing out that
  there are actually two creation myths in the book of Genesis,
  and so to take either literally is in fact unbiblical).

The politics of evolution

However, if that is how reason can dismiss the challenge of
creationism and intelligent design, rhetoric often steals the show
– and spreads confusion. For example, there is a tendency
among some Darwinists to debate as if evolution was simply
and indisputably true in all its parts. This strategy, I believe,

actually prolongs the controversy. In reality, while there is an overwhelming amount of evidence to support certain aspects of Darwin's theory, there is less to support others. These aspects of the theory remain genuinely scientifically contentious. Not admitting this allows the creationists and their allies to seize upon these more weakly-established aspects and thereby call the whole theory into question.

Hence the need for a proper appreciation of evolution. It is vital to see beyond the crude blacks and whites of this increasingly politicized debate. And in order to do so, I offer just one philosophical consideration of Darwin's theory, that of the philosopher Karl Popper (1902–94).

Evolution as a theory

Popper was a leading philosopher of the twentieth century and is remembered for the way he thought science proceeded, as articulated in his book *The Logic of Scientific Discovery* (1934). According to him, scientists come up with theories based upon their intuition. These are then tested empirically. However, it is never possible to totally verify these theories – any more than it is possible to say for certain that the sun will rise tomorrow solely on the basis of the observation that it has risen for countless, previous yesterdays. Rather, Popper thought, the best scientific theories last because they are not shown to be false. To put it another way, the best scientific theories are those that would be the most easy to falsify. That they stand up makes them all the more likely.

Popper examined the theory of evolution for the parts that are, on his account, scientifically robust and for others that are based more on conjecture and/or are difficult to test. According to him, the indisputable aspects of evolution are those that concern adaptation. After all, it is almost tautologous to say that the offspring of an organism which, through random variations, turn out to be better adapted to their environment are bound to survive better. This is not to belittle evolution but to emphasize its power. What Darwin added – and this is his greatest scientific achievement, according to Popper – was showing that the evolution of a species will take place over very long periods of time.

Just how long, and whether perhaps there are periods in which evolution speeds up, or even appears to make jumps, is one of the contentious areas of modern evolutionary research. However, the basic timeframe is enormous – and note, quite long enough to throw the creationist's beliefs into disarray.

Alongside such strengths, Popper also raised several weaknesses. Take just one, the origins of life. Darwin himself did not discuss this matter in his book. It was as theologically a sensitive issue then as now, but more importantly in terms of science, natural selection presupposes that life exists already for it to work (hence the title *Origin of Species*, not *Origin of Life*). So strictly speaking, evolution can have nothing to say about the origins of life.

Having said that, a working theory that many biologists do try to test is that life arose spontaneously from some kind of primordial soup, perhaps in the forging of complex, organic molecules as a result of electro-magnetic reactions in the ancient terrestrial atmosphere. This notion is supported by Darwin in that he famously used the image of the tree of life to picture how species diversify. It suggests a common ancestry for life, hence the primordial soup theory. Popper thought this image leads to poor science since it is impossible to falsify. Conversely, it could be the case that life spontaneously emerged several times on planet earth. We just don't know and, at the moment, it looks like we probably never will.

Incidentally, there are other moments from within the history of evolution that are not easily accounted for by Darwin's theory. One is the appearance of eukaryotic cells, that is cells with nuclei and other features. These cells are those that make up nearly all multi-cellular organisms like animals and plants, including ourselves. The problem here is that their emergence seems fantastically unlikely, though obviously it has happened.

The emergence of consciousness seems to be another highly improbable event, though clearly it, too, exists. It will not be until science has a far clearer idea of what consciousness is that just what is at stake in this will itself become clearer. Though again, it is possible that science will never understand consciousness at all, as is believed by some philosophers.

Language

Other philosophers as well as Popper have highlighted problems with evolution. A striking one is the origins of language. Language is based upon rules and conventions. It is fundamentally different from the grunts and calls of non-human animals, so it cannot exist apart from the prior existence of a community of people who already share those rules and conventions. In other words, it seems that there can never have been an isolated individual who used language.

Natural selection, though, occurs as a result of variations embodied in isolated individuals. In order to have an evolutionary explanation for the origins of language, you would need to imagine an isolated individual first speaking. Again, this appears to be something of an impossibility.

Incidentally, there is evidence that some animals, like apes, can be taught some rudiments of language. They then communicate by, say, touching pictures. But that makes the same point: language must be taught; it has not arisen spontaneously, at least in these cases. This is to say that it already exists – in the communal capacities of the animals' human keepers.

Darwinism and purpose

So much for the achievements and gaps in evolutionary theory. What of its philosophical implications for religious belief? These can be broken down into two parts. First, on its implications for the purposefulness of life; and second, on its implications for the design argument and the existence of God.

The sense in which Darwinism can be taken to challenge the sense of life having a purpose concerns what is called teleology. Teleology is the idea that organisms and activities have a goal or end. Such final causes would drive an organism or activity forward. The search for them had been a tenet of the explanation of things since the time of Aristotle, who first systematized teleology in his metaphysics. Moreover, Aristotle talked about such goals and ends as good for the organism or activity concerned.

Darwin undermines this purposefulness because evolution by natural selection has no final goal. It happens randomly in the now with no thought for the morrow. Evolution cannot even be said to have the goal of survival: rather it is that those creatures which happen to survive that pass their characteristics on. So, the proto-spider developed the capability of spinning webs not because that would then enable it to catch flies – as if that goal was always pulling the evolution of the spider in that direction.

Rather, the proto-spider gradually developed the capability of spinning silk which as it turned out is good for catching flies. Thus, put crudely, the best spinners of webs survived.

It should be noted that it is easy to forget that evolution is purposeless. The move from saying simply that such and such a feature evolved, to saying it was adaptively advantageous, to saying it evolved because of the advantages it conferred on the organism is a small one, especially when such features seem truly extraordinary viewed with hindsight. And yet that move reintroduces a false sense of teleology into the equation. It seems a hard belief to put down.

Values

There is another factor to remember here. Even if it is acknowledged that Darwinism renders natural life purposeless, there is a long tradition in philosophy of recognizing that values cannot be found in the natural world anyway – the so-called naturalistic fallacy. David Hume summed it up by saying that an 'is' does not imply an 'ought'. In other words, we are our own source of values. It is not that an exquisitely beautiful flower or wonderfully made insect in themselves has meaning, it is that *we* see meaning in the exquisitely beautiful flower and wonderfully made insect. As Bertrand Russell put it, when it comes to values, 'We are kings and we debase ourselves if we bow down to nature.'

Having said that, if meaning and value are not found in the natural world itself, it is hard to know how to explain the emergence of meaning and value in human animals which are, after all, themselves the products of natural evolution.

Evolutionary ethics

This raises another aspect of evolutionary theory – one that aims precisely to answer this question – namely evolutionary ethics, the attempt to understand morality from within an evolutionary frame. The driving idea is that given human beings evolved, then their moral sensibilities must have evolved too – in the Darwinian sense. Thus, it should be possible to understand ethics in evolutionary terms.

In general, this is taken to mean that things are afforded ethical value in accordance with their adaptive advantage. For example, human beings assign friendship a high moral worth because friendly behaviour among evolving human beings was beneficial to their survival. Similarly, altruism is widely regarded as a good trait but only because considering others served the self-interests of individual members of the human species at some time in the past. However, there are substantial scientific and philosophical problems with evolutionary ethics:

1 **History** Explanations of moral behaviour tend to presume specific knowledge of the social life and conditions of human beings in the Pleistocene period in which they are said to have evolved. However, scientific knowledge of this period at this level is very sketchy. So, as a general rule, the conclusions that evolutionary ethics draws when assuming knowledge of this period is highly speculative and almost wholly untestable.

2 **Reductionism** A related criticism is that evolutionary ethics often crassly reduces complex human feelings and decisions to fit it into the Darwinian frame. Considering friendship again, friendship is taken to be defined as something like mutual goodwill resulting from mutual benefits exchanged – that is, as something essentially instrumental. The philosophers of friendship, though, all agree that the best kind of friendship is not instrumental at all. In fact, if it is perceived primarily as such then it is undermined – as in someone feeling that they are 'being used'.

3 **Purpose** Another problem with evolutionary ethics is that evolution itself is neither good nor bad; it is purposeless. So to ascribe ethical feelings to evolutionary processes is mistaken because it introduces meaning into the system. To put it another way, it is an occasion of the naturalist fallacy, the mistake of deriving a value from a fact. For example, the society of humankind is a biological fact, but its moral significance – given that it is taken to have moral significance – has other origins, in sentiment or politics.

4 **Determinism** From these critiques come others that might be even more concerning for humanists. For example, evolutionary ethics is deterministic. It sees human beings as biological animals that are controlled by their genes and the environment. This means that human beings are merely 'survival machines', robots without any real subjectivity. The self is an illusion; autonomy is no more than self-control. We are predestined, as it were, to act in certain ways – an understanding of human nature that bears a striking resemblance to the predestination theologies of the Reformation when human free will was similarly denied.

Paradoxically, then, although evolutionary ethics is pursued in the name of rational humanism, its highly reductive, deterministic account of human morality actually removes any role for reason in ethics. In this sense, evolutionary ethics is actually anti-humanistic.

Complexity as a goal?

A second area in which teleology is vigorously debated concerns a different science, that of cosmology. The question here is whether the universe itself is goal-directed – whether by mechanistic means, it works towards the end of producing living creatures – and living creatures with self-awareness too.

Some biologists believe that there is a tendency in evolution to produce ever-more complex organisms that then find its greatest expression in the evolution of consciousness. Others deny that possibility, arguing instead that consciousness is an evolutionary exception but no more significant than, say, the marsupial's pouch or a giraffe's long neck.

The possibility that the universe itself might have goals is kept alive by the work of cosmologists. For example, they notice the fine tuning of many of the fundamental constants of nature. If these values had differed by even the tiniest fraction – fractions far too small to visualize – then the universe as we know it could not exist. This so-called anthropic principle, the idea that the universe appears tuned to allow humans to appear, can be refuted by pointing out that if the universe were not as it is, then we would not be here to observe it and imagine that an anthropic principle existed. Perhaps there are millions or trillions of universes, the refutation continues, where the constants are not as they are here, and there is no life to notice it. Proponents of the principle reply that speculation about the multiverse may or may not be right but, if it is, then it commits you to believing that there are not just trillions but zillions of universes 'elsewhere' – which seems at least as fantastical as any belief in teleology.

The debate continues.

Darwinism and God

When it comes to the design argument and the existence of God, Darwin's questioning presence is powerfully felt. Again, the controversy goes back to the earliest days. One infamous incident concerns Thomas Henry Huxley (1825–95), the Victorian anatomist and staunch defender of evolution. He approved of his sobriquet, 'Darwin's bulldog'. According to reports, in 1860, the year after publication, Bishop Samuel Wilberforce, son of the anti-slavery campaigner, had enquired of Huxley in a debate whether he was 'related to an ape on his grandfather's or grandmother's side?' Huxley's reply was equally withering. He said he would rather have an ape for a grandfather than a man who substituted ridicule for science. Incidentally, Huxley himself was an agnostic. Indeed, he invented the word to describe his position.

The argument for God's existence by design has been described as the one 'proof' that survived the Enlightenment onslaught against the other ontological and cosmological arguments. For example, even a sceptic like David Hume affords a respectful consideration of it in his *Dialogues Concerning Natural Religion*. However, with Darwin that final prop appears to collapse. The nub of the issue is usually taken to be that evolution undermines divine design, in the world of living organisms at least.

And yet, the situation is not quite so simple. For example, theists have argued that Darwin did believers a service in revealing the mechanisms by which God forged the living world. Or, as another contemporary agnostic and philosopher, Anthony Kenny puts it, the belief of Christians and others that they are the children of God has never been seen as incompatible with the belief that they are also the children of their natural parents. So why not of apes too?

Darwinists reply that the most important element against design is the purposeless of evolution. Adaptation positively excludes the possibility of input from any intelligence. But the theist can reply: actually what Darwin's theory shows is that any *particular* adaptation is devoid of intelligence. The *ultimate* reason that adaptation occurs at all, though, can – if someone so wills – still be put down to a divine intelligence.

Again, the philosophical argument is far from resolved.

Organized humanism

Let us take a step back now and pick up the story of humanism more directly and, in particular, of humanism in its organized forms. Societies and organizations with explicitly humanist aims and goals began to take shape in the nineteenth century. An important date, and a good starting point for us, is 1851. For in this year, George Jacob Holyoake declared a 'secularist doctrine' from what he called the Central Secularist Society in London.

A note on secularism

The word 'secular' alone simply relates to worldly things. It marks the contrast with sacred things. It comes from the Latin for temporal. In politics, it identifies the separation of the state from the control of the Church – as in a 'secular state'. Secularization is the process by which this comes about. It is a settlement that the vast majority of people in the West – religious or otherwise – would subscribe to.

'Secularism' takes the meaning of the word a step further. It implies a rejection of religion, particularly in ethics. Having said that, a rational foundation for moral philosophy is something that many religious people would subscribe to as well – though they might add that religion provides a powerful motivation for behaving morally.

Hence while sometimes 'secular humanism' is taken to mean a humanism that rejects religion and is atheistic, Christian humanists would call themselves secular too – believing in the secular state and rational ethics. Here, then, I will use the phrase 'atheistic humanism', a phrase once used by the philosopher Antony Flew, to refer to those who explicitly reject any kind of religious worldview.

Holyoake's secularist doctrine featured elements such as that science and reason are the only authorities for empirical and moral knowledge; that morality should be guided by utilitarianism; and that the positive philosophy of Comte should be 'the scientific Bible of secularism'. Throughout the 1850s, Holyoake organized conferences and published newspapers and books promoting these causes. He garnered support from individuals and other societies with related aims, and campaigned on various issues from allowing park bands to play on Sundays to the repeal of the blasphemy laws.

Another key person emerged at the end of the decade, Charles Bradlaugh (1833–91). In his *Autobiography*, John Stuart Mill described Bradlaugh as 'a man of ability', who shared 'the democratic feelings of the working classes, judged political questions for [himself] and had courage to assert [his] individual convictions against popular opposition'.

Bradlaugh was instrumental in founding the National Secular Society in 1866 – a society that still thrives. As its first president, Bradlaugh championed the principles of promoting human happiness, and removing religious and legal barriers to free thought and life. And its establishment was hard fought. The humanists were involved in public events, some controversial and stormy, and campaigned on various social issues including birth control, poverty, religious education and religious broadcasting. Being involved could be dangerous. On occasion humanists were imprisoned. One individual, Annie Besant, had custody of her child removed on account of her views.

Perhaps unsurprisingly, given what was at stake, individual humanists often disagreed on questions of strategy and ideology. Should they campaign directly against religious beliefs or just the hold that religious policies have on society? Should they adopt Comte's positivism as Holyoake believed, or some other version of humanism? Bradlaugh argued for attacks on theology and was against Comte's positivism (which was labelled 'Roman Catholicism minus the Christianity'). He won the day.

Publications

By 1885, Charles Watts had begun publishing Watts' Literary Guide, a publication that was revised, and lives on now as the magazine, *New Humanist*. Watts also organized the Propagandist Press Committee that is now part of the Rationalist Press Association. The *Thinkers' Library* was another landmark in the history of modern humanism. It published 140 volumes over 22 years, including works by Mark Twain and H. G. Wells.

Across the first years of the twentieth century, the National Secular Society reached new peaks in terms of membership and attendance at the public events it sponsored. It had entered the mainstream. And then, a particularly notable event occurred. In 1927 the celebrity British philosopher Bertrand Russell lectured the society on the theme of 'Why I am not a Christian'. The lecture was subsequently published and ever since Russell has been held in high regard by humanists, atheist and otherwise.

Russell the man

Russell liked to keep people guessing about his personal convictions. While he popularized many arguments against organized religion and theistic belief, he described himself not as an atheist but as an 'atheistically-inclined agnostic': there is always room to doubt the non-existence of God, he teased. Similarly, whilst he became closely linked to the secularist movements, he once told a journalist that he felt uncomfortable with humanism since 'I think, on the whole, that the non-human part of the cosmos is much more interesting and satisfactory than the human part.'

This wit is exhibited throughout Russell's essays on religion, too. In one he notes how bizarre it is that although the biblical injunction about keeping the Sabbath is to do no *work* on a Saturday, certain Protestants reinterpret this to mean do not *play* on a Sunday.

Russell's objection to Christianity is robust and rests on two pillars of scepticism. First, he argues that to be a Christian requires belief in God and immortality. Second, he argues that it necessitates holding, 'that Christ was the best and wisest of men'.

1 Proofs fail

Russell does not believe in God for the reason that the traditional proofs of God do not persuade him. He is not alone in this: they have not persuaded many others, before and since. Nevertheless, as it happens, some of Russell's reasons for not believing the proofs have fallen out of date. Consider the 'first cause argument' – that God was needed to kick the world off. Russell followed the astronomers of his day who suggested that 'there is no reason to suppose that the world had a beginning at all'. However, astronomers do now say that the universe had a beginning – though whether or not it needs a 'first cause' to prompt it into existence is currently a moot point.

When it comes to immortality, Russell had addressed the issue in an earlier essay, *What I Believe*. He found against it on the grounds that human life seems so intimately tied up with material existence that it is just inconceivable that life could continue after the body dies. He also felt the belief that humans have immaterial souls made little sense since if they are immaterial then they would not be limited to one place but would presumably extend throughout the whole of space. That human beings always experience themselves as being only in one location would appear to be evidence against the existence of souls.

Russell went on to consider various moral reasons for belief in
God – from the need to have God in order to determine what is
right and wrong, to God's role in establishing justice. He finds
them all at fault, and explains his deeper concerns too.
For example:

> What really moves people to believe in God is not any
> intellectual argument at all. Most people believe in God
> because they have been taught from early infancy to do it,
> and that is the main reason.

This objection to the teaching of religion to children, widely
observed to be the most usual cause of religious belief, is one
that reaches across twentieth-century atheistic humanism. As
the Jesuit motto has it: 'Give me a child until he is seven and I
will give you the man.'

2 Jesus the man
When it comes to whether Jesus is the best and wisest of men,
Russell actually finds much to commend Jesus as a moral
teacher. For example, he thinks 'Judge not lest ye be judged,' is
excellent advice, and he opines that a very good principle is:
'Give to him that asketh of thee and of him that would borrow
of thee turn though him not away.'

However, for all that some of Jesus' ethical maxims are good, he
finds his moral character abhorrent. For example, the idea that
some people will be cast into outer darkness for all eternity goes
against every humanist principle, even when thinking about the
most evil of people. All in all, Russell thinks that Jesus' tone can
be strikingly intolerant – and not becoming of a sage.

Fear – the root of all religion

In fact, if there is one thing that Russell objects to in religion
more than any other it is the way it rests on fear – fear of being
cursed, of death, or eternal damnation. Fear is objectionable not
only because it makes people fearful but because it is the father
of cruelty. Thus, for Russell, religion is behind all inhibitions on
moral progress, if moral progress is defined as promoting
human happiness.

It is something to do with this violent tone that Russell connects
to another objection, namely that faith in Christ has made
people in history distinctly wicked. He writes:

The more intense has been the religion of any period, and the more profound their dogmatic belief, the greater has been the cruelty and the worse has been the state of affairs.

Russell can be forgiven for not knowing about the excesses of the atheistic regimes of communism in Russia and China; he was writing in 1927. So, the philosophical refinement of Russell's point is that it is not the object of someone's faith that deepens their capacity for evil, but the irrevocable nature of their commitment to that faith which counts. Someone who utterly believes in the supreme truth of science can be as heartless as any believer – as history subsequently showed.

Similarly, when Russell rages against, say, the Church's objection to birth control – which contributed to the spread of deadly diseases – he is right to blame that evil on blind faith, but wrong to present it as if ignorant ethical dogmas are a peculiarly religious vice. Russell himself held what he regarded as an 'enlightened' educational philosophy, based upon allowing children to be free. However, going to the school where he started to propagate this philosophy all but destroyed his son John.

Of his time, and timeless

However, for all his flaws, there is no doubting the thrust of Russell's argument and the appeal that it has had to the humanists of his audience then and since. Russell ends with a typically purple passage that explains why he still inspires a following:

> We ought to stand up and look the world frankly in the face. We ought to make the best we can of the world, and if it is not so good as we wish, after all it will still be better than what these others have made of it in all these ages. A good world needs knowledge, kindliness, and courage; it does not need a regretful hankering after the past or a fettering of the free intelligence by the words uttered long ago by ignorant men. It needs a fearless outlook and a free intelligence. It needs hope for the future, not looking back all the time toward a past that is dead, which we trust will be far surpassed by the future that our intelligence can create.

Scientific humanism

We have had a short interlude to consider the contribution of Bertrand Russell. Returning again to the story of organized humanism from where we left off: after Russell, another crucial figure in its development was the British biologist Julian Huxley (1887–1975), grandson of 'Darwin's Bulldog', T. H. Huxley.

A biologist, philosopher, author and educator, Huxley was the first director of UNESCO and the first President of the International Humanist and Ethical Union. These two sides of his work he saw as intimately connected, hoping that UNESCO would develop a 'scientific world humanism' that could underpin a 'single world culture'.

He picked upon the phase 'scientific humanism' as it had previously been favoured by many socialists. They argued that the broader 'free thought' movement needed to coalesce around left-wing aspirations that they felt were captured in the term. Huxley liked to think of scientific humanism as a new 'religion of life'. He argued that if the scientific element was that which attended to matters of reason and fact, the humanistic would inject a necessary concern with values, spirit and fellowship. Or, to put it another way, science needs to be made humane to counter the default mode of its cold, objectivistic gaze. In a book illuminatingly entitled *Religion without Revelation* he wrote:

> Man can and should begin constructing a new common outlook, a new habitation for his spirit, new from the foundations up, on the basis of a scientific humanism.

Then in 1940 he published another book entitled *The Uniqueness of Man*. Here he explained what he meant further:

> Scientific humanism is a protest against supernaturalism: the human spirit, now in its individual, now in its corporate aspects, is the source of all values and the highest reality we know. It is a protest against one-sidedness and fixity: the human spirit has many sides and cannot be ruled by any single rule.

This position, nonetheless, kept Huxley open to religious influences. In the 1960s he showed his debt to the mystical thinker Teilhard de Chardin, writing an introduction to de Chardin's seminal work *The Phenomenon of Man*. And when *Religion Without Revelation* appeared in its final 1967 edition, he called for a 'new and permanent natural religion', that incorporated evolutionary and 'transhumanistic' elements.

Incidentally, Julian's arguably more famous brother, Aldous Huxley, the author and literary critic, coined his own brand of humanism. In 1932, his distrust of politics and technology led to his iconic novel, *Brave New World*. He became increasingly interested in Hindu philosophy and mysticism, wrote about it in another book, *The Perennial Philosophy*, and described his outlook as 'pessimistic humanism'.

Religious humanism

Meanwhile, in 1933, things were happening on the other side of the Atlantic. The American Humanist Association published the first humanist manifesto, which talked of 'religious humanism'. It noted widespread changes in religious beliefs and called for a revision of traditional attitudes: 'the vital movement now is the direction of a candid and explicit humanism'.

By using the word religion it did not want to associate itself with theological doctrines but to adopt a word that had always been associated with 'the highest values of life'. A new religion would form its hopes and plans 'in the light of the scientific spirit and method'. The affirmation of life was its goal.

Forty years later – and after another brutal world war – the second humanist manifesto adopted a different tone. It noted that science can bring evil as well as good. It no longer saw itself as a religious humanism, but while denying supernaturalism and theism, it did not reject religion outright. Signed by hundreds of intellectuals, and including 17 longer points, it embraced several varieties of humanism – scientific, ethical, religious and Marxist – and other positions including atheism, agnosticism, rationalism and liberalism.

Movement, manifesto or creed?

To put it another way, at this stage, organized humanism was struggling to embrace a dizzying array of positions. This is perhaps why, after the war, in England there were moves to adopt a less inclusive stance. Events helped to catalyze a new focus. For example, a report from the Church of England blamed what it called 'humanism' for a decline in belief and morality. One humanist, Archibald Robertson, replied with a mini-creed that still sounds contemporary: 'Whatever in the modern world is good, whatever is creative, whatever is hopeful, has its roots in humanism ... The humanist position is alone rational and right.' Then, in 1955, the radio broadcasts of Margaret Knight, later published as *Morals Without Religion*, explicitly defined humanism as against religion.

For all that, though, ambivalence about the word persisted. The British novelist and essayist, E. M. Forster (1879–1970), for one, intervened by asking himself how he defined himself. Not atheist he said: too crude. Not agnostic: too feeble. Not liberal: 'impossible'. The word humanist encourages 'bored withdrawal', though he thought it the best option. 'It expresses more nearly what I feel about myself ... Humanism covers my main belief and my main disbelief.' To put it another way, Forster did not want to campaign for humanism, but rather celebrate it. He continued:

> Humanism could better be honoured by reciting a list of the things one has enjoyed or found interesting, of the people who have helped one, and of the people whom one has loved and tried to help.

There were other humanists who did not agree with Forster – and they would not withdraw either. Harold Blackham (b.1903) was one of them, and another key player in this story. He had been working on what he regarded as the principles of humanism that were necessary if it were to be a serious movement. His 1954 *Essentials of Humanism* concluded:

> Humanism, then, is not a set of opinions, still less a rejection of any set of opinions. It is a body of central convictions about reason and science, freedom and morality, ideas and values, which requires commitment, choice, and action, for it requires the creation of a personal life of one's own and of a world, a human civilization. Therefore humanism is a call to all men, a vision of what is to be achieved.

For Blackham, humanism was not a religion, a philosophy or a political party but an alternative to religion – a vision, a broad reform movement.

Deists allowed

We are now edging towards the present day. The anti-religious version of organized humanism seemed to gain the upper hand again, at least in Britain, when Barbara Smoker became President of the National Secular Society in 1971, a post she held until 1996. She had once called humanism a 'natural religion' based upon 'spiritual communion', but in her 1973 booklet *Humanism* she came out against any association with religion whatsoever.

Another prominent individual who seemed to be lending his weight in the same direction was the philosopher Antony Flew. For him, it was the phrase 'scientific humanism' that appealed again. It implied putting the welfare of human beings first: 'scientific primarily as regards matters of fact; humanist concerning questions of value'. Flew argued that from this a commitment to atheism followed, since religious ethics must put God's will first, whereas humanist ethics prioritize the needs of human beings. Then in 1993, Flew published a book entitled *Atheistic Humanism* based upon his Prometheus Lectures at the State University of New York given in 1991. In it he defended more atheist presuppositions, not least that as atheists human beings gain an 'inalienable prerogative of responsibility'.

But as if to show that the word could never quite be pinned down, in 2004 Flew declared himself no longer an atheist but a deist. Some confusion followed as to just what caused Flew to change his mind, although he has affirmed his new commitment on a number of subsequent occasions. It seems he has been impressed by new arguments from philosophers of religion on the existence of God, troubled by the problems that naturalism has in showing how non-living matter can turn into living organisms, and intrigued by questions about the big bang and fine tuning raised by cosmology.

Nicolas Walter, in his detailed history of the term, *Humanism: What's in the Word* (1997), concludes that whilst there is still debate in humanist circles as to the stance it should adopt, humanism is 'generally seen as definitely separate from and indeed hostile to religion.'.

Since then, with the increased prominence of apparently religiously inspired terrorism, and also because creationism seems to be taught more and more in schools, particularly in America, atheistic humanism has redoubled its energies. The high watermark to date came with the publication of *The God Delusion* by evolutionary biologist Richard Dawkins (b.1941) in 2006. Though ferociously critiqued by believers and atheists alike, it was a runaway bestseller and sold millions of copies worldwide.

A new humanism?

Now that we are up to the present day, I must switch into a more personal mode of reflection. On the one hand, it seems to me that some of the charges being hurled at religion are right on target. For example, it is troubling that in some parts of the world, notably America, creationism is taught alongside modern science as if there were a choice between the two. Also, religions often continue to sanction prejudice against women and homosexuals, which results in untold human unhappiness, to say nothing of violence and deaths.

On the other hand, some of what is written and said by atheistic humanists against religion is either ignorantly simplistic or wilfully prejudiced. It is the tone that the new atheists have adopted – the strategy of vilifying those they see as opponents – that is so telling. Here are some of the things that they say:

- Religious people, without distinction, are against freedom, learning and culture.
- Their faith in God is said by definition to be no more subtle than believing in fairies or pixies.
- They are indirectly blamed for the violence of the terrorists: it is argued that moderate beliefs provide a cover for extremists by placing matters held on faith above contradiction.

The sociologist of religion, Gordon Lynch, has written: 'The sheer ferocity of many of the atheist critiques of religion also suggests that we are not in the territory of reasoned debate, but witnessing the birth pangs of a new, anti-religious cultural identity.' Lynch adds that whether this comes about remains to be seen. Or, as E. M. Forster intimated, it is an open question as to whether humanism can ever be that kind of thing anyway.

There are also atheists who believe that the present wave of religious lampooning is unhelpful, even opposed to the spirit that led them to atheism. Julian Baggini, author of *Atheism: A Very Short Introduction*, writes:

> I think that my opposition to militant atheism is based on a commitment to the very values that I think inspire atheism: an open-minded commitment to the truth and rational enquiry … Hostile opposition to the beliefs of others combined with a dogged conviction of the certainty of one's own beliefs is, I think, antithetical to such values.

The point is not just an important personal reflection but carries political weight: in an era of religious fundamentalism and violent extremism, Christian and atheistic humanists should surely be working towards a common cause to combat growing intolerance. If hardening positions are antithetical to the values that might inspire atheism, they are also antithetical to those that lead many to call themselves humanist at all, atheistic or not.

Christian humanism

In fact, humanism inspired by Christianity – and humanists who are Christians – have been integral to the humanist tradition ever since the Renaissance. Moreover, in recent years Christian humanists have been putting every bit as much work into redefining themselves as their atheistic peers. They argue that many of the elements within religious belief that non-believers find so objectionable are ones that repel them too. So who are the key figures in Christian humanism and how do contemporary Christian humanists define themselves?

The problem of sin

There is a sense in which Christianity might be thought to be an almost naturally humanistic religion. Its central figure is a man, Jesus. Moreover, this human being is said to be divine. On the face of it this incarnation would seem to provide an excellent framework within which to place many of humanism's great themes – its celebration of the dignity of humankind, human solidarity, freedom and knowledge. These elements do capture the essence of the beliefs of Christian humanists.

However, not all traditions within Christianity have interpreted their faith in the God who became man as so effusive of humanity. For example, Calvinist theology does not recognize the innate dignity of human beings. It surveys all the evil that exists in the world and concludes that human nature is depraved by sin. Martin Luther similarly thought that free will is delusional since human beings are corrupted. That God had become man was to rescue humanity from this fatal predicament, not to endorse it. For these Protestant theologians, Jesus saves human beings, not sanctifies their humanity.

It is a question of degree. There is one tradition in Christianity, reaching back to the great theologian of the fourth century, Augustine, which views humanity as 'a mass of sin, waited upon by death,' as Augustine uncompromisingly put it. Humankind's present state is a product of the Fall, the mythical original sin of Adam and Eve. It was catastrophic. However, there is another tradition in Christianity that is inspired by the words of God in Genesis. After having created the world and all that lives in it, the story goes that God looked and declared it was good.

Creation is good

The great theologian of the medieval period, Thomas Aquinas, was more inclined in this direction. For him, the great capacities of human beings – to love, to reason, to create – reflect the nature of God. Moreover, God sustains life every moment of the day. It is hard to have a completely negative view of something with which the all-good God is so actively involved, though Aquinas undoubtedly thought that God's needful grace was part of that activity if human beings are to be perfected again.

Christian humanists today might also believe that God's intervention, in some shape or form, is necessary for human beings to live fulfilled lives. Far from seeing this as a weakness, though, they argue that it is a serious response to a serious problem within humanism – the fact that humanity has such a tremendous capacity for evil. If the atheistic humanist objects to the Christian humanist that this need for salvation from 'outside' compromises humanity's autonomy, the Christian humanist's response is that this necessity is only a reflection of the apparent inability of humanity to redeem itself.

Theological humanism

To flesh this out a little further, consider now some of the key figures in Christian humanism, starting first with Dietrich Bonhoeffer. Bonhoeffer (1906–45) was a German Lutheran theologian. During the rise of Nazism, he was a member of the Confessing Church that tried to oppose fascism. In 1943, Bonhoeffer was arrested for his involvement in a plot to overthrow Hitler. This led to his imprisonment and execution in 1945, aged 39.

Bonhoeffer is distinctive because of his radical interpretation of the incarnation of God in the person of Jesus Christ. He eschewed speculative theology about God's otherworldliness, as well as highly spiritualized religious ideas of God within us. For him, God *was* the human being Jesus Christ. This person vicariously suffered for others and thereby showed humanity at its best to be 'being for others'. After Christ's death, Bonhoeffer believed Christ was resurrected in the Church. So, therefore, all Christians are called to live for their fellow humans.

This humanistic theology led to a polemic against religion. In fact, Bonhoeffer thought that organized religion was the product of sin. It inevitably makes God out to be either wholly transcendent or individualistically present in the believer. Both are misconstrued since they result from the selfish desires of men and women. In other words, his Christianity is explicitly non-religious and this-worldly; it is a secular Christianity – to the extent that some of his followers have interpreted him as meaning that Christians should live as if there is no God. Bonhoeffer also declared that the modern world has 'come of age', by which he meant that it could be accountable to itself. In this way we can be mature.

Bonhoeffer is an important figure for Christian humanists because of the example of his life. Other theologians are invoked because they are some of Christianity's biggest hitters. For example, in the early nineteenth century, Friedrich Schleiermacher (1768–1834) wrote explicitly against Christianity's opponents, or its 'cultured despisers' as he called them. He argued that every human being can have what he called 'God-consciousness'. The significance of the person of Jesus is that he perfected his God-consciousness naturally in his own life. This is what makes him so central for Christians. He is the example that all human beings may follow.

Schleiermacher was also against supernatural understandings of faith, writing: 'The idea that the divine revelation in Christ must be something in this respect supernatural will simply not stand the test.' For him, to be religious, is to have a 'sense and taste for the infinite'. Monotheism was simply the purest form of this feeling for the absolute.

Alternatively, the Catholic theologian Karl Rahner, a leading twentieth-century figure associated with the Second Vatican Council, echoes other humanist sentiments on the dignity of humankind:

> Only someone who forgets that the essence of man is to be unbounded ... can suppose that it is impossible for there to be a man, who, precisely by being man in the fullest sense ... is God's existence in the world.

Sea of Faith

Christian humanism took a distinctive turn in 1980 when a Cambridge academic and priest, Don Cupitt, published a book, *Taking Leave of God*. In it, Cupitt presented a history of Christianity that exemplified the so-called 'death of God' theologies. Taking Nietzsche's exploration of the emergence of the modern world seriously, he reinterpreted the incarnation again – this time to mean that the centre of religious concern has moved from God to humanity, from heaven to earth. This changes what Christians might think about God. Instead of being a supernatural entity, Cupitt wrote that God becomes 'a unifying symbol that eloquently personifies and represents to us everything that spirituality requires of us'. As a result, Christianity comes to celebrate selflessness in life and not belief in the objective reality of God or life after death.

Cupitt develops his form of Christian humanism in other ways. For example, he acknowledges that the veracity of Christian dogma rests on its moral authority as opposed to its objective truth. The objective truth of God – theological 'realism' – simply cannot be ascertained. Christianity matters only in its championing of humanist values. He writes:

> We cannot in fact be realists, for we all of us treat a serious moral objection to a dogma as a weighty reason for doubting its truth. This in turn implies that our real view of religious truth must be ethical.

This non-realism or atheistic attitude towards any objective belief in God is the cornerstone of a network Cupitt has inspired called the 'Sea of Faith' (after Matthew Arnold's famous line and an eponymous television series Cupitt presented). It is important to note that not all Christians who regard themselves as humanists are atheistic. However, Cupitt represents a point at which atheistic and Christian humanism come remarkably close.

Summary

In this chapter we have reached the present day in the history of humanism, and have also come up squarely against the most vigorous current debate within humanism, namely whether or not humanism can in some sense be religious. By way of a conclusion to this chapter, here are some questions that strike me as important to ponder as you consider what you think about this issue:

Three questions for atheistic humanists

1 In your arguments against religion do you examine the best in religion? After all, you look to the best in humanity in your humanism and engage the most sophisticated sources when asking scientific and philosophical questions.

2 Is it really true, considering the whole humanist tradition, that humanism can be straightforwardly defined by its opposition to belief in a supernatural God?

3 Is atheistic humanism not just optimistic but utopian, dangerously deluded about the depths of human depravity that undeniably exists in the world?

Three questions for Christian humanists

1 Is it really plausible to follow so closely – let alone worship – one particular man, Jesus, a Jewish eschatological prophet who lived 2000 years ago?

2 Can you really claim to be humanist when Christian churches, even liberal ones, still fall foul of central humanist causes such as rights for homosexuals and women?

3 Let us say that, at best, the question of God's existence remains an open one. Is that adequate grounds on which to build the great edifice of a faith?

07 ten pressing issues

In this chapter you will learn about humanism and:

- humanism after Auschwitz
- faith schools and religious education
- climate change
- good without God
- gay rights and identity politics
- blasphemy
- progress
- mind-body problem
- namings, weddings and funerals
- mystery and wonderment.

We have seen that contemporary humanism is shaped by a number of philosophical traditions. We have also seen that it is not just represented in various schools of philosophy but has become an organized force in the world in its own right. This has led to much debate about just what humanism is, a reflection of the diversity that has always been part of its tradition. In particular, the most obvious point of contention today is whether humanism is explicitly anti-religious, the issue with which we ended the last chapter.

However, contemporary humanism faces other issues particular to our times. So now that we have completed our history of humanism, and surveyed the content of its philosophies at some length, let us now turn to ten matters that are particularly pressing.

1 Humanism after Auschwitz

The twentieth century witnessed many horrors meted out by human beings, great and small, on their fellows. Three individuals were particularly successful at filling the world with their monstrous terrors – Mao, Stalin and Hitler.

The biography of Mao by Jung Chang and Jon Halliday reveals that the Chinese leader was responsible for 70 million deaths, and all in so-called peacetime, too.

Alongside the trials and purges that killed tens of millions of his political opponents, Stalin's industrial policies led to famines in which 10 million peasants also perished. The American scholar George F. Kennan has called Stalin great in his 'criminality effectively without limits'.

And there is something uniquely disturbing in the genocidal policies of Hitler. They reached their ghastly climax in the 'Final Solution' of Reinhard Heydrich to 'cleanse' Europe, from West to East, of its Jews. This is how Heydrich chillingly described it:

> In the course of the final solution of the Jewish question, 11 million Jews are involved. Under appropriate control these are to be brought to the East for employment. In large labour gangs, with the sexes strictly segregated, they are to be employed in these areas for road construction, in which task undoubtedly a majority will disappear from natural diminution. The evacuated Jews will at first be conveyed in trainloads to transit ghettos from where they

will be further transported to the East. The remnant that is able to survive all this must be regarded as the germ cell of a new Jewish development and therefore destroyed. In the course of the final solution, Europe is to be combed for Jews from West to East.

The extermination of the Jews, alongside gays and gypsies, poses such a problem for humanism for the simple reason that after such an event it seems difficult to imagine how any kind of confidence in human goodness can ever be regained again. Auschwitz and the other death camps represent the secular equivalent of an issue with which religious believers have long struggled: the problem of evil.

Worse still, the political philosophies that lay behind Nazism, Stalinism and Maoism can be called atheistic and humanistic. They were fundamentally inspired by the adulation of an essentialist humanity, science and the freedom gained from throwing off the shackles of primitive superstition and belief.

A note on the atheism of Hitler and Stalin

So difficult are the implications of twentieth-century crimes against humanity, that some contemporary atheists have argued that atheism itself is irrelevant when trying to grapple with the evils perpetrated. As Richard Dawkins puts it in his book *The God Delusion*, 'Even if we accept that Hitler and Stalin shared atheism in common, they both also had moustaches, as does Saddam Hussein. So what?'

Of course, a scientific and atheistic ideology does not *necessarily* lead to pogroms, any more than religious belief *automatically* produces suicide bombers. However, it surely will not do to treat the atheism of these individuals so lightly – anymore than the Christianity of the medieval crusaders can be regarded as a trivial detail in relation to their atrocities.

There is plenty of evidence that both Stalin and Hitler were inspired by atheistic humanism, albeit grossly distorted. Given the extent of the crimes, it seems far better to recognize this than to dismiss it as someone else's problem. As the commentator John Cornwell has written:

> Marxist-Leninism, it is well known, provided a powerful impetus for murderous purges of political dissidents and religious believers alike. Under Stalin, Russia saw the devastating implementation of sociobiological principles

based on Lamarck – the inheritance of acquired characteristics – legitimizing strategies of enforced collectivization and ruinous systems of agricultural production.

Or, in relation to Hitler, while the relationship between his regime and religion was more ambiguous, there can be little doubt that he aimed to purge religion from his Third Reich. In *Hitler's Table Talk*, author Norman Cameron records Hitler's words, including:

> The dogma of Christianity gets worn away before the advances of science. Religion will have to make more and more concessions. Gradually the myths crumble. When understanding of the universe has become widespread ... then the Christian doctrine will be convicted of absurdity.

The end of the human?

Tony Davies captures the depth of the crisis in his book *Humanism*. He writes:

> In the face of this, it seemed, not only humanism – the rational self-assertive, world-changing humanism of the Greeks, the Renaissance and the Enlightenment – but the very notion of the *human* was called to account. Confronted with the death camps, George Steiner has argued, language itself falls silent. Theodor Adorno, for whom they only made explicit the ruthless will to power that had always been implicit in the project of rational 'enlightenment', believed that they had cancelled the possibility of poetry, the unconstrained voice of humanist individuality. For the camp commanders, like their masters in Berlin, were lovers of poetry, not brutes; and language itself, Hamlet's 'discourse of reason', could not be acquitted of complicity in their monstrous undertakings. For the post-war generations, what has come to be known as the *Shoah* or Holocaust represents the vanishing point, the absolute zero of what is thinkable.

The crisis of Nazism for humanism is that it appears to represent an impasse – a nightmare featuring the violent figure of man from which there is no redemption, no end.

If this is humanity

Surely, there is no easy answer to the presence of Auschwitz in history. However, one way forward might be gleaned from the writings of Primo Levi, the Jewish writer, chemist and survivor of the concentration camps. In his autobiographical account of life in Auschwitz, *If This Is a Man or Survival in Auschwitz*, he exemplifies to an extraordinary degree at least three invaluable qualities that in the face of great evil add up to a remarkable humanism:

1 **Detachment** He is able to analyze the atrocities he witnessed and keep at least part of himself detached from it in order to understand it. A case in point is when, in his book, Levi realizes that the whole purpose of the camp is to dehumanize people. 'A man deprived of everything he loves ... will be a hollow man, reduced to suffering and needs, forgetful of dignity and restraint, for he who loses all often easily loses himself.' Elsewhere he calls it the 'demolition of a man'.

2 **The human face** Second, for all that he knows the camp guards would take away even his name if they could, Levi persists in seeing that they are human beings too, brutalized by the brutality in which they are engaged. He keeps a human face on this evil and thereby maintains the possibility of redemption, as opposed to falling into defeat or seeking out vengeance. Levi writes: 'Their humanity is buried, or they themselves have buried it, under an offence received or inflicted on someone else.'

3 **Belief** Levi sustains a conviction of who he is as a human being, and who those around him are as men, which transcends the horrors of even the worst nights. 'I was also helped by the determination, which I stubbornly preserved, to recognize always, even in the darkest days, in my companions and myself, men, not things, and thus to avoid that total humiliation and demoralization which led so many to spiritual shipwreck.'

Having said all that, it is also important to remember how Levi's life ended. It seems that he committed suicide. That his death occurred over 40 years after his liberation makes his end all the more poignant. There are no easy answers, and perhaps ultimately no answers, to the terrible things that human beings have done to their fellows.

Speaking personally

It is particularly important to remember and face the implications of these events since today extremism is arguably again on the increase. This is clear in the case of religious fundamentalism and is to be rejected and abhorred. But verbal militancy – if not physical – is disturbingly easy to find among atheist humanists too.

For example, religious belief is compared to a mental illness demanding treatment. Alternatively, it is referred to as a cultural virus, conjuring up images of eradication. Or again, Sam Harris, in his best-selling book *The End of Faith*, contemplates a future in which an Islamist regime has nuclear weapons. He argues that it may be necessary to launch a pre-emptive strike 'to ensure our survival' with a nuclear weapon of our own. He continues: 'Needless to say, this would be an unthinkable crime – as it would kill tens of millions of innocent civilians in a single day – but it may be the only course of action available to us, given what Islamists believe.'

This is dangerous, gung-ho talk dressed up as rational. It envisages whole populations of human beings as driven by uncontainable, violent religious beliefs – sidelining the political and economic factors at play in the process. It turns a perceived enemy into a faceless 'other' that can be killed with impunity. It serves to escalate a sense of crisis. To my mind, it is the antithesis of a humanist approach that – learning from history – should strive to de-escalate tension, comprehend the subtleties of religious belief, and put a human face on ideological conflict.

2 Faith schools and religious education

The continuance of so-called faith-based educational institutions at the start of the twenty-first century has become a subject of increasing scandal for many humanists. Before exploring why, a little historical context may be helpful.

The British settlement

The links between Christianity and education reach back at least to the eighth century when cathedrals established institutions to teach Latin and Christian doctrine to clergy.

During the medieval period, these schools taught wider and wider sections of the population, ordained and laypersons, an expansionist trend that continued through the Renaissance and the Reformation. It was only in the eighteenth century that the school system began to separate itself from religious authorities and became attached to the state.

In some countries, the state took over the school system in its entirety. In others, a compromise was reached, whereby the state developed new schools, and the churches maintained their own – though what was taught in both was controlled by the state.

This mix of church and state is the settlement that was reached in the UK: that many schools in modern Britain are faith schools is a product of history. About a quarter of all primary schools in the UK are Church of England. Somewhere around half that figure are Roman Catholic or other denominations. Less than ten per cent of all secondary schools are faith-based.

An old argument

Some humanists have always held controversial views on the perceived evils of faith schools. Bertrand Russell, a great campaigner on education, believed that the Church was a master at, 'giving instruction without stimulating mental activity – a technique in which, long ago, the Jesuits led the way'. He believed that an education influenced by clergymen was bound to be one in which the freedom to learn was limited, and possibly absented, since the Church inevitably wishes to impress its authority upon its pupils, not the joy of pure discovery. Thus, religiously educated pupils will not learn of the diversity of opinions that can be found on all matters. Further, Russell thought, they will be inculcated with an ethos of intolerance and the habits of the herd.

Having said that, Russell believed more or less the same could be said about state schools; the only thing that changed in the secular case was the nature of the authority: government replaced God. Instead, he advocated a radical freedom in education, including the freedom *not* to learn, the freedom *what* to learn, and the less contentious freedom to hold opinions.

The debate today

In more recent times, new and more persuasive arguments have been developed against faith schools:

- Humanists have argued that faith schools are unfair, since by only admitting pupils of particular religions, they discriminate against others whose parents have no faith or a different faith.
- If faith schools receive state subsidies, this implies that the state is effectively condoning and sponsoring a system of unjust selection. Many humanists argue that faiths should be entitled to run their own schools, but without financial support from the state.
- There is a requirement in Britain for schools to hold regular acts of worship. Although the vast majority of schools do not, either on principle or more commonly through lack of resources, the law is said to be anachronistic.
- There is also a concern that because religion is often aligned to ethnicity, faith schools effectively encourage sectarianism and undermine pluralism. This, it is argued, is particularly problematic in places like Northern Ireland.

Many humanists, including those who are religious, agree with or at least acknowledge the concerns behind these complaints. In fact, in recent years, the churches have been taking steps to address some of them. However, a second set of arguments against faith schools takes the debate into more contested territory.

A more radical agenda

Some atheistically inspired humanists are now arguing some or all of the following:

- Children in the UK and other parts of Europe increasingly show no interest in having a personal faith, and so to assume they do, by sending them to faith schools, is, at best, to ignore the trend; at worst, to tyrannize them.
- Many who support faith schools argue that they are necessary for the preservation of values in schools. Humanists strongly contest this assumption, not least because the education system itself should be underpinned by liberal values.
- Moreover, if morality is closely tied to religion, and children reject religion – as well they might – then there is a concern that they will reject morality too.

- The United Nation's Convention on the Rights of Children states that children should receive an education that allows them 'to seek, receive and impart information and ideas of all kinds ... in the spirit of understanding, peace, tolerance, equality of sexes, and friendship among all peoples'. Religious schools compromise this right by educating children in a particular worldview.
- There has also been a concern that creationism is being taught in some faith schools as an alternative scientific theory. This is evident in the USA, although is hard to substantiate in the UK where the national curriculum should prohibit it, at least in science lessons.
- Religious education (RE) is taught as part of the national curriculum. However, faith schools are able to structure RE as they wish, leading to the fear that it might not be objective, fair and balanced – perhaps again fostering sectarian feeling. Humanists have also argued that humanism should be taught alongside different religions.
- Most controversially of all, it is claimed by some atheistic humanists that to raise children as religious is tantamount to child abuse. They say that it forces a set of beliefs on young people that might be damaging to them on a number fronts:
  - Their own sense of themselves might conflict with the beliefs of the religion, as in the case of the homosexual child, leading to a loss of self-esteem.
  - Alternatively, it is said that religious belief is superstitious and/or ridiculous and should no more be taught than that the world is flat or that a monster will eat a child who steps on the cracks in the pavement.
  - Further, it denies the child's right to make up his or her own mind.

The case for faith schools

Apologists for faith schools have rebutted these latter claims in a number of ways. They have said that:

- The argument about faith schools and the preservation of values in education is not about whether people of no faith do or do not have values, since clearly they do. Rather, it is pragmatic, in that it just seems to be the case that a religious ethos in a school helps to counter an otherwise homogenous, dominant secular ethos. This, in turn, tends to see education only as a matter of gaining qualifications for work rather than gaining an education for life.

- For people of faith, there are many advantages to receiving a religious education, not least of which is that religion seems to be a source of value and meaning for many, if not most, human beings. Why, the believer replies, would you want to deny a child an understanding of that enriching possibility?
- Religion may also be part of a child's ethnic and national inheritance. It is therefore important to teach them something of it, not only for their sense of self, but also so that they are equipped to reject any intolerant manifestations of such traditions.

The most contentious claim, that a religious education is tantamount to child abuse, is equally strongly contested on a number of fronts:

- For one thing, it is asked, who is to decide whether religion is an abusive idea or not? Presumably, only one person can supply a satisfactory answer for the atheistic humanist, namely another atheistic humanist, which makes the charge something of a circular argument.
- Further, for most religious people, religion is not primarily a matter of believing certain things but being in a relationship with their fellows and God. So to deny children an opportunity to learn about this relationship, which includes being open to experiencing it, is as undesirable as excluding them from any other loving relationship.
- The implication that raising children within a faith denies them choice is disproved by the evidence. Children plainly *are* able to reject the beliefs of their parents, as any parent will know. If parents do genuinely abusively force their religion upon their children, say, by insisting on an arranged marriage, then the law is in place to protect the rights of the child.
- Having said that, it is surely right to keep the interference of the law in the relationship between parents and children to a minimum. Acting on the belief that raising children in a religious setting is abusive would demand police intervention in vast numbers of families across the country.
- It is not possible to raise children without some sense of conveying what the parent or teacher believes is right. Religion is just one of many examples of this. Others include the value (or not) of sports, music, books, scouts or ballet. If the same principle that the atheist wants to apply to religion were applied universally then, in practice, no adult would be able to teach a child anything.

- Similarly, children cannot be taught *how* to think without being taught something of *what* to think. That is in the nature of being a child as opposed to an adult.

Speaking personally

I think that there is a case for continued reform of the relationship between the state and faith schools, particularly when they are shown to be discriminatory or to foster sectarianism. However, I think that the charge that a religious upbringing is tantamount to child abuse is not only wrong but is unhelpful to wider humanist goals. The analogy is so inflammatory as to detract from the justifiable complaints about religious education.

3 Climate change

Science tells us that climate change is already upon us. Temperatures are rising in various parts of the world and the number of extreme weather events is set to increase. The human cost will be terrible and, if nothing is done, catastrophic.

Climate change can be a challenging ethical issue for humanism when there is a basic assumption that ethics should be human-centred. For example, in many versions of utilitarian ethics, the fundamental premise is that ethics should be directed at delivering the greatest happiness to human beings. Within this framework, environmental issues are, therefore, secondary: they matter only inasmuch as they affect the quality of life of human beings. Concerns about animals and nature as a whole are subservient to this central goal. It is, of course, possible, even essential, to argue that the human species, being animal, depends upon the natural environment as well, and so should use it sustainably. This might be presented as the obvious humanist position to adopt because of its anthropocentrism. However, other philosophical approaches challenge this assumption and raise a series of questions to an exclusively human-centric humanism.

Deep ecology

One key alternative approach is sometimes referred to as deep ecology. Essentially, the argument is that environmental ethics is inadequate to the challenge it faces if the human-centred point of view is not relinquished. Minimally, the welfare of other higher sentient, 'human-like', animals must be embraced, too, such as the apes. Alternatively, as an even 'deeper' approach requires, the whole of nature must be held in view, with the needs of humankind being just one concern to factor in amongst many.

This switch from anthropocentrism to biocentrism radically confronts many basic propositions common to humanism:

- For example, humankind's dignity – whether based upon an individual's capacity to choose a life for themselves or their 'special relationship' to God – is sidelined in favour of the dignity of all life. It is not just that human beings need a flourishing eco-system for they themselves to flourish; it is that the eco-system itself should be allowed to flourish. If required, limits should be imposed on human flourishing, say, in terms of energy consumption.

- Alternatively, whereas humanism has a tendency to place supreme value upon the autonomy of the human individual, and his or her capacity to exercise reason, the deep ecological perspective instead emphasizes the interconnectedness of all creatures. To put it another way, moral value does not just rest with human beings, by virtue of their reason, but is extended to all living things.

- Reason itself is called into question with this shift too. It becomes suspect as a tool by which human beings gain objective knowledge, instead being considered a tool by which they justify and extend their exploitation of the world. Francis Bacon's comments about science having to torture Nature to force her to reveal her secrets and thereby turn them to human use in technology, as discussed above, also comes to mind.

- Finally, there are what might be called the spiritual implications of this, as say captured in the so-called Gaia hypothesis. James Lovelock, the most well-known advocate of this position, describes Gaia like this:

  [There is] a new insight into the interactions between the living and the inorganic parts of the planet. From this has arisen the hypothesis, the model, in which the Earth's living matter, air, oceans, and land surface form a complex system which can be seen as a single organism and which has the capacity to keep our planet a fit place for life.

When Lovelock and others first wrote about Gaia it was widely ridiculed in the scientific community. However, it has gained greater credibility since scientists started to recognize the threat posed by climate change, because climate change science also underlines the interconnectedness of the earth's organic and physical systems.

A spiritual element emerges when a necessity for empathizing with non-human nature is emphasized as a result of the Gaia view. This spirituality manifests itself in 'ecological consciousness' or in expressions of 'ecological solidarity'. The implication might even be that some organisms should sacrifice themselves for the greater Gaia whole.

Humanists have replied to these charges in a number of ways:

- The most common response to the specific matter of climate change would argue that for all that technology has been part of the problem, it is a vital part of the solution too. Without the rapid development and deployment of technologies that offer alternative energy sources, reduce carbon emissions, and allow or encourage human beings to consume less energy, climate change itself cannot be mitigated.

- Utilitarian philosophers have responded to the particular charge against their ethical system by pointing out that a powerful environmental consciousness is actually implied by their way of thinking. For example, it is not just that a damaged environment compromises human happiness; the damage human beings do to their environment is also to their shame, since it undermines the happiness of other, typically poorer, human beings, even compromising their ability to live. Moreover, it is shaming for human beings to behave irresponsibly and purely instrumentally towards other sentient creatures.

- It is also common to criticize the ecology movement for becoming apocalyptic and quasi-religious. The humanist would agree that something needs to be done. However, the best way to proceed is not to promote feelings of guilt and helplessness among people, as if the earth were headed towards some kind of environmental judgement day. Rather, energies should be directed towards gathering more evidence to understand the situation as fully as possible, in order to develop the most effective remedies.

- It is also pointed out that some forms of deep ecology are seen not just to be biocentric but positively anti-human. For example, the more extreme cases can appear to entail an opposition to various forms of humanitarian action, such as sending aid to relieve famine and disease. Deep ecology here would interpret such natural disasters as the ecological organism readjusting the balance, with the loss of human life perhaps being an inevitable part of that readjustment.

Personally speaking

Such humanist responses seem right to me. The only thing I would add is that if climate change is as pressing as science increasingly seems to suggest, then stemming the disaster will require massive changes in human aspirations and consumption. Similar shifts, say, from a feudal, subsistent way of life to the one now found throughout the affluent West, have taken centuries to occur. It is hard to envisage how it can happen in a few years, or decades at most, without some kind of 'deep' sense of the imperative. In other words, I am sceptical as to whether technological and political initiatives are enough, for all that they are necessary. For with climate change, it is as if nothing less than a change in human nature is required.

4 Good without God?

'Without God, everything is permitted.'

This is the fear expressed by Ivan Karamazov in Dostoevsky's famous novel about the Russian brothers, *The Brothers Karamazov* (1880). It suggests that after the death of God, the world is condemned to slide into a moral vacuum in which evil, formerly known as sin, becomes as acceptable as goodness, formerly known as holiness.

Any humanism that claims morality is independent of divinity – perhaps because God does not exist or because of the belief that human beings should take responsibility for themselves – is apparently open to this charge of moral nihilism. Let's consider why people have thought this.

- One argument is that morality is like the law. The law needs a law-giver and a system of punishment to uphold it. If this is right then, in morality, God is the law-giver and his condemnation or blessing expresses the role of the judge.

Moreover, in the same way that people fear punishment and so do not commit crimes, so people will only act morally because they fear the eternal effects of judgement.

- Another more subtle argument was the one offered by Kant. He thought that moral philosophy needed a divine underpinning not because of fear, or because of the analogy with the law, but rather, because the existence of God was required to make following ethical maxims – such as doing to others as you would have them do to you – reasonable. What Kant meant was that it would only be rationally compelling to follow a maxim if there were also the possibility of the good world which that maxim was aimed at actually existing. 'Ought implies can', was his formula. The good world that moral behaviour aims at isn't likely or even possible in the world that we know. So his belief in God served to guarantee it in the next, or at least as existing somehow 'in God'.

- Another reason people suggest that there is no such thing as a godless morality is because of what they take to be the evidence. For example, they might note that it was in the century of the death of God – the twentieth – that human beings inflicted more death and destruction on each other than at any other time in history. Alternatively, they might suggest that the climate change threat of the twenty-first century is a direct product of the loss of piety that people feel towards the environment. Today, people believe that the world exists for humans to do with as they please rather than to be treasured as a gift from God. Or again, they may look at the charitable organizations in the world and observe that the majority of those that seek to alleviate the suffering of others are religious in origin or inspiration.

Humanists have rebutted these charges with a variety of ripostes:

- To the argument that morality is like the law, and impotent without a judge, is the counter-argument that the analogy is wrong. Morality is not like the law; in fact, the law *presupposes* that there is such a thing as morality. Without morality it would not be possible to determine what the law should reward or punish. So morality must rest on standards that can be determined independently of any system of law.

- This leads to a second riposte, summed up in Euthyphro's dilemma. Euthyphro is a character in a dialogue of Plato. In it, he is forced by Socrates to consider whether something is good because God says it is good, or whether God says it is good because it is good already. The difference matters since if something is good solely because God says so, then in theory God might say that, perhaps, torture is good. This would suggest that morality is arbitrary. The conclusion seems to be that what is good is good because it can be shown to be good apart from God. This poses a dilemma to Euthyphro who is a pious young man, because that in turn seems to imply that God has nothing to do with morality – which is precisely what the humanist wants to show when arguing for a godless morality. Euthyphro's dilemma seems to clinch it.

- Kant's charge – that a perfectly realized good world must exist in order to make it rational for us to follow the maxims of morality – has been rebutted in a number of ways. One is simply to reject Kant's way of doing ethics. This is, in effect, what the other great philosopher of the Enlightenment, David Hume, proposed. For him, morality is primarily to do with fellow-feeling and not rational argument. Others have argued that the existence of a perfectly realized good world is not necessary. Rather, all that is required is the *hope* that such a place might be possible, or the hope that the world made by human beings can edge towards it.
- More aggressively, some atheists say that, in fact, their godless morality has greater merit than the theological versions. This is because the religious system of divine retribution rests on non-moral factors – namely punishment – to enforce it. In godless morality, the individual does what is right because it is right.
- Similarly, Sartre argued that the fact that morality is up to us is key to the freedom of being human. It is that which turns people into either moral heroes or cowards.

These last arguments commend themselves as highlighting the value of moral conviction. However, at the same time, they are weak when taken as a refutation of religion because they rest on a caricature of religious morality. It may be the case that some religious people fear punishment for the bad things that they do – though the Bible is full of complaints that bad people do terrible things all the time and God appears to sit idly by. But many non-believers avoid bad things for fear of the implications which are themselves non-moral too. For example, a man may not sleep with a woman who is not his wife, not because of loyalty to his wife, but because he fears the loss of half his capital if he were to get divorced. Also, the obsession with punishment as the locus of religious morality ignores what is at least as equally important to religious people – namely, that doing good is desirable because it brings them closer to the God with which they believe they have a relationship.

Religion as moral inspiration

There is another reason for humanists to be wary of a radical separation of religion from morality – even if they believe that when it comes to moral philosophy that is necessary or desirable – and that is that religious belief forms people's characters. In particular, it can form people into good characters, willing to make very great sacrifices for the sake of others. This has nothing to do with punishment.

There is, of course, plenty of evidence that religion can form people into very bad characters, too. However, it is the formative power of religion that matters. For if behaving morally is not primarily a rational activity but one that stems from the kind of person you are, as Hume thought, then it is necessary to devise a means for cultivating people's characters in this way. Education and politics can undoubtedly be part of that. But religion does seem to be particularly efficacious.

The character of compassion

The central virtue in this transformation is that of compassion. Again, it is perfectly possible to express why it is good to be concerned for others rationally and without reference to God. For example, it might be said that compassion is a good characteristic to have because then people will show compassion to you. Less self-interestedly, it could be argued that a compassionate world is far more likely to function well, because other virtues like trust and kindness will flourish within it.

However, the religious person has another arguably more powerful reason to be compassionate. They believe that to be compassionate is to imitate God. They might say that life itself is a gift from God and that the best use of this gift is to pass it on, as a gift, to others. This is desirable not only because God is good, but because it takes the individual on a path to the greatest fulfilment of their humanity.

A note on enlightened self-interest

It is perhaps worth adding at this point that evolutionary psychologists claim to have found a scientific basis for compassion. This is in so-called enlightened self-interest. Roughly speaking, it turns out that if a member of a group acts in the interests of someone else in the group then that turns out to be the best strategy to win their own interests too. This may be the case, but it misses the central point of the religious understanding of compassion. Here the goal is not to realize your own interests but is precisely to leave them behind – to become genuinely selfless rather than 'altruistically selfish'. This is not just a semantic difference since the religious traditions teach that transcending the self – not just cultivating its happy existence alongside some do-gooding – is the key to human fulfilment.

It is perhaps the powerful witness of religious people who are willing to sacrifice everything for others that makes people worry that a godless world might become less good, less moral. Of course, there are atheists who make sacrifices, even sacrificing all, and they deserve anyone's admiration. But without reference to God, it just seems less easy to explain why they might do that, and why we should follow suit.

Personally speaking

I find the argument about compassion compelling. The evidence that a non-religious world would be one in which people are, on the whole, less willing to sacrifice themselves for others seems more probable.

However, I believe that the argument for compassion can inspire individuals who do not seek to imitate God. The compassionate person is someone who steps out of themselves to sympathize with others. This can be tremendously liberating since it simultaneously takes you away from a solipsistic, self-centred existence to one orientated around love – the love of others.

I suspect that religious people have every right to claim as religious the principle that it is in love that human beings find their fulfilment. However, compassion does not require you to be religious to pursue it.

5 Gay rights and identity politics

Championing the rights of gay men and lesbians – along with those of women and people from ethnic minorities – is a tenet of contemporary humanism. It was not always so. It took John Stuart Mill and Harriet Taylor's book, *The Subjection of Women*, and the activism of the suffragettes, to persuade even humanists that women should be treated as equals. It took the campaigning of the Christian humanist William Wilberforce alongside others like Thomas Paine to abolish slavery, the foul outcome of pernicious racism.

Similarly, before the 1980s it was not uncommon for humanists of various sorts, notably Marxists, to argue that homosexuality was wrong – in the Marxists' case because it was deemed degenerate; the seedy outcome of a bourgeois culture. The evidence of history is that circumstances can turn against homosexual people quickly, too. Weimar Germany offered a relatively tolerant environment for gay men and women, as immortalized in the musical *Cabaret*. Nevertheless, within a few short years of the republic's collapse, Hitler was carting homosexuals off to the gas chambers.

So a crucial part of any humanist politics is the recognition of the rights of minorities such as gays – the point about rights being, that once written into the law, they are more resistant to the changing attitudes of people and populations.

Multiculturalism and diversity

But there is a tension implicit in identity politics. Identity is typically taken to be a matter of fate, not choice. It expresses a demand to be recognized as fundamentally different. The basis for the rights requested are often biological, ethnic or religious – in the case of homosexuals, the scientific evidence is that people's orientation is fixed, even made that way.

The eighteenth-century humanists, though, saw things rather differently. For them, it was the unity of humankind, the singularity of civilization that mattered. They thought that people were not fundamentally different, but fundamentally the same. It was on this basis that all human beings should be included and protected.

The differences of approach are keenly felt in current debates about the value of multiculturalism. In short, should society be plural and afford different people protected places within which to express their different identities? Or should it be plural but with an underlying set of unifying institutions that everyone is subject to regardless of biological, ethnic or religious differences?

Gay marriage

In recent European gay politics, the same tension has been manifest in the introduction of gay marriage. In fact, the phrase 'gay marriage' itself embodies the tension. For some champions of gay rights, perhaps most, it is important that the rights afforded to gay couples should be identical to those of traditional marriage and that the resulting institution be known as marriage, too. Any departure from this demand is perceived as an erosion of equality.

For others though – no less believers in gay rights – homosexual relationships are different in certain respects from those of heterosexuals. For example, they do not inherit the history of gender inequality that has coloured the institution of marriage itself. For them, then, gay unions as civil partnerships seems more appropriate, the phrase suggesting something new and equal but different.

Identity as a trap

There is a deeper problem with identity politics in the case of gay people, too, as identified by Michel Foucault. For him, too close an identification with the labels 'gay', 'homosexual', 'queer', 'lesbian' was a diminishment of a person's humanity. With the label there tends to be an adoption of ways of life, even character traits that are deemed appropriate for gays, homosexuals, queers and lesbians. Gayness, this criticism fears, has more to do with a code of behaviour than with individual expression.

In other words, being known for having a particular sexuality – or any other kind of identity – or claiming it for yourself, can become a trap. One can become incorporated, not liberated. A better strategy is to work for these labels themselves to be overcome, particularly once they have served their purpose of winning rights. With that comes a conception of humanity that is inherently diverse and celebratory of originality.

Rights for all?

This multicultural approach itself throws up problems in turn. For example, should humanists support the 'rights' of creationists to teach their beliefs in schools, if such Christians claim it is a fundamental component of their identity? This is not just a theoretical case. Alternatively, if minorities throw off the labels of identity, in favour of individual freedom, then they risk undermining the basis for the rights they have won as members of particular groups. Should the tide turn against them again, then they may find themselves struggling to protect their rights.

Social transformation

What is often missing from this debate about rights and identities is the call for society, as a whole, to transform itself as it embraces those within it. As the writer and broadcaster Kenan Malik has put it:

> Diversity is important because it allows us to expand our horizons, to compare and contrast different values, beliefs and lifestyles, and make judgements upon them. It is important, in other words, because it allows us to engage in political dialogue and debate that can help create more universal values and beliefs, and a collective language of citizenship.

So, identity politics also requires the maturity of discernment and engagement: if different people should be supported in their efforts to understand themselves – by nurturing their sexuality, gender or ethnicity – that must be regarded as only one side of the coin that also values an outward-looking, changing cosmopolitanism.

Personally speaking

I myself have seen how identity politics can become moribund when it denies what people actually think or feel in the name of tolerance and inclusiveness. It is commonly called 'political correctness'.

On the other hand, political correctness is a powerful cultural force against prejudice; and there can be no doubt that prejudice can return as speedily as it can go.

Malik's call for dialogue and debate among diverse peoples seems to me to be an excellent one. It also chimes with the best in the humanist tradition, seeking to understand before making judgements, to tolerate others because it is expansive of one's own humanity as well as right for them.

6 Blasphemy

Blasphemy has become a totemic issue in contemporary British humanism for a number of reasons:

- It seems ridiculously anachronistic for a modern secular state to threaten its citizens with punishment for profaning the name of God.
- In the UK, it is not blasphemy in general that is forbidden but only blasphemy against Christianity. In a pluralist state, this is discriminatory.
- The last successful blasphemy prosecution was against the publication *Gay News,* in 1977. The magazine printed a poem that offended the so-called family values campaigner, Mary Whitehouse, who brought the prosecution. It was the first case in 50 years, suggesting that the blasphemy laws had not simply fallen dormant but positively needed removing from the statute books. The prosecution was doubly offensive for being homophobic too.
- Blasphemy as an issue has come to the fore again in recent years as a result of various religious groups protesting against satirical and fictional treatments of their beliefs or spiritual leaders. Religious leaders have condemned the accused blasphemers, in the famous case of the writer Salman Rushdie, seriously threatening his life. Whilst no cases in Western law have been successful, the protests have resulted in material not being published and in events being cancelled. In other words, the question of blasphemy has come to be linked with freedom of speech.

Historical context

It is perhaps helpful to put blasphemy into historical context. In Christianity, blasphemy is differentiated from heresy. The latter is holding unorthodox beliefs; the former is expressing mockery or contemptuousness of orthodoxy. In Islam it is blasphemous to speak derisively of God or Mohammad.

Blasphemy has been punishable in secular as well as religious law. The reason why it can be a secular offence stems from periods when blasphemy was deemed to be an offence against the state as well as against God. In Scotland, blasphemy was punishable by death until the eighteenth century – which explains some of the historic concern about blasphemy expressed by humanists. In England, the depiction of Biblical characters on the theatrical stage was effectively banned until 1968 when the Lord Chamberlain's powers of censorship were revoked. At the time of writing, blasphemy laws on both sides of the Atlantic remain, if not always in force.

For all these reasons, humanists have consistently argued for a repeal of the blasphemy laws.

Freedom of speech

The tension between showing respect for religion and the matter of freedom of speech is also a critical factor. On the whole, this issue becomes particularly pressing when the believers, feeling themselves to be the victim of blasphemous attacks, also feel themselves to be subject to other forms of persecution.

Humanists would not want to compromise the right to freedom of speech. Having said that, freedom of speech is itself subject to conventions and restrictions. Inciting violence or racial hatred are two obvious cases. In the present climate, it perhaps seems wise to take care when exercising the right in relation to criticizing religion. A good principle is to ask whether speaking freely increases the knowledge of others or actually perpetuates prejudice and ignorance. Conversely, some humanists have argued that in tandem with calls for the repeal of blasphemy laws there should also be renewed assertions of religious freedom and antidiscrimination laws.

Speaking personally

I should perhaps confess, here, that I myself was once investigated by the police for aiding and abetting the distribution of a blasphemous libel. I ran the website of the Lesbian and Gay Christian Movement. From it there was a link to the poem that so offended Mary Whitehouse. After about a year, the investigation ran into the ground.

As a rule I would advocate profound respect for religious beliefs. However, it seems implicit in the notion of God that God cannot be offended by anything human beings might say or do. So blasphemy itself is something of a theological contradiction.

This suggests that blasphemy as a crime is actually a political tool for bolstering the power of a state or clan that is identified with the beliefs concerned. This is why blasphemy appears on secular statute books. And it is for this reason, not out of any disrespect for religion, that to my mind blasphemy laws should be repealed.

7 Progress

The notion of improvement over time, particularly in relation to human society, well-being and knowledge, has always been closely associated with humanism. Inherent in Pico's 'dignity of man' is the idea of human perfectibility. Various strands of Enlightenment in the eighteenth century advocated progress, too, not least in those associated with utilitarianism. 'In civilized nations, and therefore in the whole of mankind, the sum of well-being is perpetually on the increase,' wrote Jeremy Bentham.

Alternatively, the French philosopher Condorcet declared his view of the human race as:

> Emancipated from its shackles, released from the empire of fate and from that of the enemies of its progress, advancing with a firm and sure step along the path of truth, virtue and happiness.

This hope has continued to the present day, bolstered by the attainment of rights for individuals, continuous improvements in healthcare and dramatic technological advances. Ask yourself as a woman, a homosexual, an old person, a poor person, a sickly infant or someone with a disability whether you would prefer to be alive today or even just a hundred years ago and the answer is obvious: today. As they say in business, it is a 'no-brainer'.

Pillars of progress

The twin pillars upon which the belief in progress rests are science and reason.

- Science brings the development of new technologies that improve the lot of humankind, from reduced mortality rates to increased opportunities for pleasure.
- Reason increases human knowledge, thereby dispelling ignorance, a key hindrance to progress.

However, it is the examination of what underpins the ideological belief in progress that also leads to it being questioned. For example, though it is undoubtedly true that science progresses – in the sense that knowledge of the world accumulates – it is far from clear that the same can be said of morality and politics.

- In morality, every person must learn what it is to be ethical in their own generation. This is partly because moral issues change and partly because morality is ultimately an individual matter of desire, behaviour and character.
- In politics, the main motivation is not the application of knowledge or reason but the pursuit of power. Thus, politicians have a tendency to ignore the so-called lessons of history when it suits them. Also, politics takes place in the ever-changing context of events which means that any individual's exercise of power is limited.

Jean-Jacques Rousseau took the argument a stage further during the Enlightenment itself by arguing that implicit in the idea of progress is a force that works to increase human misery and unhappiness. This pessimism stems from recognizing that progress rests on the cultivation of competitive aspirations, and these must, as a rule, be frustrated to keep the engine of social, economic and rational progress moving forwards.

At worst, this logic can lead to a certain fatalism. At best, it seems that belief in progress is the mark of 'a shallow mind', as the philosopher Friedrich von Hayek put it.

Facts and statistics

Often debates about progress come down to arguments about whether people are happier today, or better educated, or healthier. Again, at least in the West, it seems that the answers are either clearly positive, say in relation to education, or are at least debatable, as perhaps is the case for happiness.

When the question of progress is asked in a global context it becomes more complicated again. Here are a number of statistics that challenge the notion of progress, as quoted by the philosopher Alain Badiou in his book *The Century*, which asks how the twentieth century will speak of itself.

- At the start of the twenty-first century, the richest three people in the world possess a combined fortune greater than the total GDP of the 48 poorest countries in the world put together.
- In 70 countries – that is 40 per cent of the countries in the world – the per capita income is inferior in real currency to what it was 20 years ago.
- Alternatively Badiou states that if you see the twentieth century through the lens of totalitarianism then it is one marked by camps, massacres, tortures and state crime. It is populated by political leaders including Stalin, Hitler and Mao.
- Even when looking at the history of liberalism in the twentieth century, and the spread of democracy, the case starts to look weak. The real growth period only began in the seventies, i.e. relatively recently. And it is in this period that inequalities of wealth became vastly larger.

Personally speaking

I am inclined to believe that the model of progress which applies to the accumulation of scientific knowledge does not apply to other areas of human activity. The evidence weighs too heavily against it. Moreover, denying this evidence, in the laudable hope of sustaining future progress, would seem to risk unwittingly cultivating hubris. This in itself is one of the key forces that acts against progress since it leads to sometimes calamitous mistakes. A better call is for the humanist virtue of humility.

The ideology of progress is flawed for other reasons. It implicitly assumes that human nature itself improves, when the history of ethics and politics shows that its capacity for good and evil remains fairly constant. Alternatively, it remembers the obvious fact that human beings can influence their future, and forgets the equally obvious one that they often do not know in what ways they are doing so – the law of unintended consequences. This calls for the humanist virtue of realism.

In other words, an ideology of progress forgets the role of reason, which alongside increasing human knowledge simultaneously shows us the limits of our knowledge. This calls for the humanist virtue of scepticism – which is not, as we have seen, the same as fatalism.

8 Mind-body problem

The mind-body problem is the difficulty of explaining how the mental nature of being human can be made to fit with its physical nature. How, for example, does the immaterial thought that I am going to bend my finger lead to the material consequence that my finger bends? Alternatively, how can the unconscious stuff of organic chemistry, the stuff that fills the human brain, lead to the self-conscious experience of being human?

Clearly, mental states correlate with physical states, as experiments monitoring human activities in brain scanners demonstrate. But is it the case that mental functioning – to say nothing of what people might call the spiritual – is related to but is in some way distinct from the physical too?

This quandary has become an issue in humanism because of what it might imply about being human. For example, in debates about atheism the belief that material stuff is all that there is in the universe has become important since clearly, if that is the case, then there is no place for disembodied souls, spirits or deities.

Then there is the question of life after death. This depends on whether to be human is to be more than just a body, as the mind-body problem might suggest it is.

In fact, this secondary question remains open.

• For example, while there is a deep dependency between brain activity and consciousness activity, this does not mean that brain activity *causes* consciousness, only that it is a *condition* of consciousness. So, it is a condition of, say, emotion that someone has a functioning frontal cortex. But the functioning of the frontal cortex does not cause emotion. That is an infinitely more complex process that, ultimately, involves everything about the individual concerned and the people and world around them.

• Alternatively, imagine the day when neuroscience can map every single neuron that fires when, say, someone experiences fear. That would say very little about the feeling of fear itself, for the very reason that fear is a feeling. It is primarily a *subjective* experience not an *objective* one. We know ourselves from the inside out, not the outside in, as science must do.

- Further, because neuroscience studies consciousness by studying the brain, all the evidence it produces is bound to support the view that the brain is all that consciousness is. Strictly speaking, though, this does not prove that there could not be a consciousness that exists apart from a physical brain – the very thing that people with faith in a personal God do believe. Similarly, just because a corpse emits no brainwaves proves nothing if consciousness is something more than just brain states. Conversely, it also implies that science will never prove that there is life after death or a disembodied consciousness too. Though note: if there is little consolation in this for the conviction atheist, there is little in it for the ardent believer seeking proof either.

- If the science is indeterminate, the philosophy of the mind-body problem is also likely to keep these debates going because it is unresolved as well. Consider, for example, what is implied according to the radical materialist's insistence that mental states are just neural states in the brain. It leads to some extraordinary consequences:

> It has led some to deny that consciousness is real at all. Instead, they call it an epiphenomenon of brain activity. This seems extraordinary for its denial of what most would take to be the defining human experience.

> Others, in order to explain the phenomenon of consciousness, describe a kind of materialism which requires that consciousness is itself a property of matter. This so-called panpsychism argues that consciousness is emergent. It does not find its full form apart from in the complex brains of higher mammals. However, it also implies that all matter possesses quasi-properties of conscious. In short, everything from people, to stones, to individual atoms must have some kind of inner subjectivity.

Personally speaking

It seems to me that trying to solve the mind-body problem through science and science alone is a mistaken project. The experience of mind is nothing if not subjective. The activities of science are nothing if not aimed at objective verifiable knowledge. Thus, science can illuminate what it is to be an individual self, but it will never grasp it in its entirety. Philosophy, literature and art are required for that.

It also seems quite likely that the mind-body problem is a good candidate for one of those metaphysical problems that philosophy will never completely solve. The issue is too caught up in the labyrinthine nature of the self, meaning, consciousness and free will.

This is not to say it should not continue to be studied; quite the opposite. It is an occasion for profound wonder, and anything which deepens that sense of mystery, to my mind, deepens our humanity as well.

9 Namings, weddings and funerals

Rites of passage are those ceremonies that take place at key moments in life. Baptisms, weddings and funerals are the most common three, the 'hatch, match and dispatch' of the clergyman's employment. In Judaism there is also the bar mitzvah, or coming-of-age ceremony. Then there may be other 'occasional offices', as they are also called, such as a ceremony marking a divorce or the scattering of ashes. They have traditionally been the sole preserve of the Church or religious community.

Humanists have protested against the dominance of religious organizations at these moments in life on a number of counts:

- They have made the perfectly reasonable point that for those with no sense of religion or religious belief, the provision of only faith-based rites is inadequate.
- It could be said that non-believers who use the Church for such occasions – believing not a word that is said but merely enjoying the ceremony – are acting somewhat hypocritically.
- For individuals who believe that matters like death are wholly natural events – and it is in understanding them as such that they find comfort – a naturalistic context may be more appropriate than a religious building.
- For many humanists, the whole point of being a humanist is to express the belief that there is no point beyond this life to which it leads, but rather that the here and now is what matters. Ceremonies for humanists should therefore reflect this conviction.

- Similarly, humanists would not look to external authorities, like sacred scriptures, when reflecting on life's turning-points but prefer instead to stress the values of self-determination and personal responsibility.

- Alternatively, while humanists might recognize the value of meditation and silence, they typically would not accept that prayers are made to any supernatural being. Ceremonies should avoid such intercessions too.

- Similarly, humanists will desire to look at many sources of inspiration and comfort, not solely those associated with any particular religious tradition: they may turn to Shakespeare as readily as the saints, to a literary source as much as a spiritual one.

- Humanists may prefer a more stoical mood in their rites of passage, believing that comforts come too easily in a religious setting, and that proffered hopes such as life after death are false. They seek inner strength and human support rather than divine assistance and blessing.

For all these reasons, there is a deliberate movement amongst some humanists to extend the provision of secular rites of passage.

Old versus new

On occasion, humanists and religious leaders clash over who has the right to perform occasional offices, or over the quality of such events offered by each tradition. For the sake of clarity it might be useful to know that:

- If there is ample scope for tailoring services when led by a humanist, there is usually plenty of opportunity to do the same in a church. For example, the use of tributes, music and readings will be encouraged by the clergy as well as the secular officiant. The issue at stake is not that of the personalization of services per se, so much as ensuring they have a good balance. Those who are bereaved or celebrating often appreciate advice on this matter from those with experience.

- In British registry offices no religious content is allowed. At civil marriages and civil partnerships no material may be sung or read out that is explicitly religious. This is the law of the land.

- The Christian churches no longer regard suicide as a sin. People who have committed suicide, and those who grieve their loss, will be treated with all the respect they deserve by religious and secular ministers alike.

- For some rites of passage, such as funerals and naming ceremonies, it is perfectly possible to conduct the service without the presence of any official – religious or humanist. The only occasion on which the proper officiant must be present is when the rite is a legal one, notably in the case of marriage and civil partnerships.
- Humanist weddings can take place in all sorts of places, as desired by the couple. There is also increasing scope for religious services to be conducted outside of consecrated premises.
- Many Christian clergy are actually very sensitive to the needs of non-believers. After all, they are quite used to being in a minority in modern secular countries. Also, they may well believe that the purpose of the Church is not to *convert* others but to *serve* them – particularly in times of need. Added to this, the churches do have access to resources for rites of passage that have not only stood the test of time but are beautiful in their depth and maturity.

Green burials

Some people want to opt for a 'green burial' – a funeral using biodegradable materials for the coffin and without 'extras' like headstones. The main obstacle to overcome when this is desired is the legal one of correctly disposing of dead bodies. An increasing number of geographical sites are being set aside for such so-called natural deaths. They are typically not consecrated, to avoid bureaucratic hurdles apart from anything else, and ministers of all faiths and none are free to conduct ceremonies in them.

Gay ceremonies

The Anglican Church, the Roman Catholic Church and other Protestant Churches, bar the Methodists, are all either clearly against homosexual relationships or torn as to whether or not to celebrate gay love. The situation is one characterized by hypocrisy and homophobia. In short, the Christian churches do not present gay people wanting to affirm their relationships with anything like an unconditional welcome. With exceptions, the same may be said for other religions as well.

However, there are other options for gay people looking for a service to mark a civil partnership. For humanists, humanist organizations offer such resources free of prejudice. And for religious people, there are gay religious organizations that can advise you how to make faith-based arrangements for such celebrations too.

Pastoral care

One of the great strengths of the churches is the network of pastoral care they offer that extends across the country in the shape of parishes. Even today, with parish churches closing, every person in the land has a parish priest. Not that this will be much comfort to many humanists! However, it has prompted the question of whether humanists should attempt to set up a parallel network for those without faith.

In some countries, such as the Netherlands and Belgium, there are humanist counselling services. These are protected by an act of parliament to ensure that those who do not profess a religion can have access to the same support when in need.

Apart from the cost of doing so, the consensus on the whole seems to be that while humanists can always offer pastoral support on a personal or local basis, for many situations of difficulty in life, existing bodies such as the Samaritans, Alcoholics Anonymous and the Citizen's Advice Bureau provide excellent support. They are also well equipped to accommodate humanist beliefs.

Thought for the day

A slightly different dimension to this issue in the UK concerns the BBC's religious broadcasting. By statute, Britain's biggest broadcaster has to provide a certain amount of religious content. This includes various 'God-slots' such as 'Thought for the Day' on Radio 4 and 'Pause for Thought' on Radio 2. To qualify, the authors of these short reflections must express a religious conviction during the broadcast.

In response, there has recently been a campaign by humanist bodies either to abolish this kind of output in the name of removing the religious privilege it represents, or if abolishing them is not thought desirable then at least to demand the inclusion of non-religious and humanist contributors.

As a result some local BBC radio stations are experimenting with non-religious reflections. Further, the case for keeping 'Thought for the Day' and the like is not helped, to my mind, by the fact that so often the quality of the 'thoughts' is so low. It would seem that opening up the contributions to those with a proven track record of thoughtfulness, as it were, and an ability to communicate, would both improve the content, deal with the issue of religious privilege and secure the 'thought for the day' element in future.

A note on contacts

The British Humanist Association has an accredited network of officiants for non-religious funerals, weddings, affirmations and naming ceremonies. For more information follow the click for Ceremonies on **www.humanism.org.uk**

For readers from other parts of the world similar resources can be found on various national humanist organisations' websites. The International and Ethical Humanist Union is a good place to start. See **www.iheu.org**

The National Secular Society offers what it calls 'de-baptism', a short rite that people may go through to show that they are not Christian though they may have been baptized as an infant. See **www.secularism.org.uk**

The Lesbian and Gay Christian Movement can advise on content appropriate for civil partnerships and gay blessings. It also has information about clergy who welcome gay relationships and conduct ceremonies. For more information follow the click for Blessings on **www.lgcm.org.uk**

For more information on green burials and natural death go to **www.naturaldeath.org.uk**

The Sea of Faith network is for humanists who believe religion is valuable but only as a human creation. It also offers advice on services and holds conferences. See **www.sofn.org.uk**

10 Mystery and wonderment

In a collection of essays, *Is Nothing Sacred?*, edited by Ben Rogers, the humanist, writer and Oxford philosophy professor Simon Blackburn has written: 'One of the challenges facing humanism is to convince people that things can be worthy of awe and reverence, without being holy and blessed.'

He identifies the problem as due to the fact that contemporary humanism is so often associated with words like utilitarian, materialistic, rationalistic and instrumental. This lends humanism a desiccated, grey character – which is in a way strange since clearly humanists do experience sublimity at nature, awe in music and reverence towards ancient things. Blackburn, for one, admits to sensing the sacredness of the medieval cathedral of Chartres, for all that some militant humanists might accuse him of a lapse of judgement for appearing to excuse the beliefs that inspired it.

Some of the colour returns when humanists admit that many, perhaps most, of the greatest works of art, literature, architecture and music are religious in character. For the atheistic humanist, this can be interpreted as a recognition of the human qualities of learning, skill, virtue, emotional sensibility and a desire to live life in all its fullness – to say nothing of the fact that religions have been around for a very long time.

The plot thickens

I wonder whether the problem goes deeper than this, though. In the essay that follows Blackburn's, Richard Dawkins also writes of how the scientist can appreciate some things as sacred. He puts it down to the capacity of the human brain to sense the geological ages of the Grand Canyon, or to create the resonant words of a poem. However, next, to my mind, he adds something very telling. His last paragraph concludes:

> Poetic imagination is one of the manifestations of human nature. As scientists, and biological scientists, it's up to us to explain that, and I expect that one day we shall.

He adds that such an explanation will in no way demean it. But is that right? The kind of wonder that Dawkins appears to have in mind is that of someone wondering how to do a puzzle. They will ponder it, perhaps be amazed at the ingenuity of the creator of the puzzle, but ultimately their wonder serves the compulsion to conquer it, to solve it. And like the science which Dawkins imagines will unpick the poetic imagination, they do not doubt that they will. This might be called instrumental wonder.

Instrumental wonder is arguably different in quality from that which is experienced in the face of a genuine mystery – let's call it contemplative wonder. For then, the wonder serves not to dissolve the mystery but to deepen it. It is perhaps a little like the pre-Socratic natural philosophers who saw science primarily as an occasion for mystery not manipulation. It is the confidence in the power of science – the belief that it has no explanatory limits – that undermines the capacity to experience contemplative wonder in the face of the unknown.

A question of limit

The difference might be considered in another way. The wonder which our ancestors experienced during a powerful thunderstorm was one of fear and perhaps foreboding for they had no ability to understand what caused the sky to split with light. Today, though, with modern meteorology, that sense of wonder is lost to us. We might feel in awe of the skies to a degree, but we can explain it, and so to a degree, explain it away.

Now, of course, modern science cannot explain everything. Personally, I suspect there are many things that it never will – natural things like consciousness, moral things like goodness, and metaphysical things like existence itself. However, the attitude that presumes science will one day ask all questions worth asking, and provide answers, seems to me to mitigate the capacity for contemplative wonder, reducing it to its instrumental cousin. It is this that I imagine people sense when they feel that humanism has the desiccated and dry character that Blackburn identifies.

The world as a gift

One final thought: when the religious person asks the question why there is something rather than nothing, they may well answer with the word God. Now, this is not a causal explanation, and so is in no way a substitute for science. However, what it does express is the sense that existence – the world in which we live – is something given. It is a gift. This is, in fact, the meaning of the doctrine of creation out of nothing, the traditional Christian belief.

The Yale professor of theology, Denys Turner, put it like this in a lecture entitled 'How to be an Atheist':

> What you mark by way of difference in saying that the world is created out of nothing is that it stands before us not in some brute, unmeaningful Russellian 'just thereness', in that sense as something just 'given' in which further questions are gratuitously ruled out, and that just at the point where they are beginning to get really interesting. Rather, in saying that the world is created out of nothing, you are beginning to say that the world comes to us, our existence comes to us, from an unknowable 'other'; that is to say, you are claiming that existence comes to us as pure gift, that for the world to exist just *is for it to be created*. As for why it exists, goodness only knows what the reason is.

Someone who does not believe in God cannot think of the universe as a gift. Rather, it is an accident, a delightfully fortuitous accident, but an accident nonetheless. An inability to see the world as a gift – because it does not make sense to think of it as 'coming to you' if you do not believe in a creator – strikes me, humanly speaking, as a drawback. The belief that science has no limits, that human intellect will one day master even the 'givenness' of the world, compounds the loss. Personally speaking, as an agnostic, it is one that I lament. Though therein, perhaps, lies another return for the deepest sense of mystery and wonder.

08

humanism as a way of life

In this chapter you will learn:
- about the resurgence of religion and what this means for humanism
- how in various ways humanists have found meaning
- about the state of humanism today, its strengths and the challenges it faces.

In this book we have tracked the history of humanism from its pre-history in Ancient Greece and Rome, to its emergence as a defining theme in the Renaissance, through the intellectual shifts of the Enlightenment, and into the modern world, where now many people call themselves humanists and look to the humanist tradition to make sense of things. Many great themes have kept recurring, from the importance of critique and reason, through the challenges of science and history, to the relationship between religious belief and humanist anthropocentrism – that being the one characteristic which draws the many humanisms we have encountered together. In this last chapter, let us review that story and ask ourselves where humanism is at now, how humanists are inspired by the tradition today, and what questions it faces for tomorrow.

Humanism in crisis?

It is possible to tell the story of humanism roughly as follows. Around 500 years ago, the medieval worldview – with its seamless integration of social, political and religious life – started to unravel. With the advent of the Renaissance, people began to develop a different sense of their worth; they sensed a dignity that was theirs without the necessity of making reference to God. At the same time, the old enchanted world – in which spirits abounded and physical objects like relics carried magical powers – was demythologized by early science. The earth was no longer the centre of the universe, and mechanical explanations for things showed astonishing power and promise.

The Reformation sealed and amplified these shifts. The hierarchies that were the fabric of medieval religious society were levelled in the experimental cities of reformers like Luther and Calvin: now everyone could aspire to the kind of human flourishing that previously had been the preserve of aristocrats and clergy. The process of disenchantment continued as the reformers declared the old system of relics, sacraments and indulgences superstitious nonsense – or worse, explicitly of the devil. From the sixteenth century onwards the conditions were optimal for the new science to prosper, which it did, for all that its greatest figures like Newton were obsessed with alchemy too.

The end of faith?

Then in the eighteenth century came the Enlightenment, when reason got to work on superstition, humankind's autonomy developed firmer foundations, the Church sustained a broadside that at least in terms of secular power fatally weakened it, and philosophers established the basic framework within which people could lead a secular life: they could be moral without religion and could find meaning and happiness without God.

In the nineteenth century, thinkers came to assume that religion would eventually disappear; faith was apparently retreating like the ebbing sea. One explanation of this change was provided by philosophers like Marx. They saw religion as the product of feudal discontent amongst the masses. As people's lives improved, they would no longer need the opiate. Coupled to this, the arguments that undermine religion – the rational demolition of the proofs for God and so on – would gradually persuade more and more people. When Darwin announced his theory of evolution, progress finally seemed indisputable and inevitable to many. Society itself could now become rational.

A post-secular society

During the twentieth century things grew more complicated again. Two world wars shocked human beings out of any easy assumptions about their dignity; as Freud commented, civilization is 'thin'. The totalitarianism of Stalin and Mao, and the development and use of nuclear weaponry, destroyed any automatic link between science and progress. And as the world became more globally connected, people came to feel more disconnected, with the result that, for many, religion seemed to provide increasingly attractive ways of belonging.

By the end of the century, an inevitable process of secularization was no longer plausible, let alone the conviction that today we can look forward to the end of faith. In America, Christianity is more powerful than it was when the Puritans first landed from Europe. In South America, South Asia, the Middle East and Africa religions are in rude health. Even in secular parts of the world – like China or Western Europe – belief is resilient and arguably resurgent. Though the figures are hotly contested, the 2001 census showed that 72 per cent of Britons called themselves Christian, even though only ten per cent regularly went to church. If you factor in the rise of New Age beliefs, then it seems

clear that the vast majority of people still think of themselves as
spiritual or religious in some way or other. This is why today
thinkers routinely talk of living in a 'post-secular' society.

The debate changed

However, this does not mean that humanism is in decline. In
fact, there is plenty of evidence that more individuals feel
themselves to be humanists too – in the sense that they look to
science for their understanding of the universe, make ethical
decisions without explicit reference to religious authorities, and
regard concern for their fellow human beings as a primary
consideration in politics. The number of humanists seems to be
between 15 and 30 per cent of the population. To put it another
way, humanism and religious sensibilities are not necessarily
incompatible; the relationship between them is not always a
zero sum game.

What has undoubtedly changed in the last 500 years is that
people have a choice. In a way that was inconceivable in the
centuries before the Renaissance, individuals now routinely rub
up against some people for whom religion determines their
sense of themselves, others for whom religion is entirely and
happily absent, and others again – perhaps a majority – for
whom belief is one factor amongst many that shapes their
world. Similarly, science did not win the war against religion, if
that metaphor of violent annihilation is the appropriate one to
deploy, but it did fundamentally change the terms of debate.

So today, it is perfectly possible to hold that only a thoroughgoing materialist rationalism makes sense, even as others assert
that the world never really lost its supernatural enchantment,
and others again sense that a scientific outlook alone is not
enough, and the lack must be made up by moral, aesthetic,
political and/or spiritual points of view.

Secular strength

The notion of a secular society is strong in the West, too, in the
sense of the separation of Church and state. Within the
European Union it is inconceivable that this could be
fundamentally undermined, for all that there are marginal
concerns over issues like creationism and faith schools. In the
US – where it is impossible to be president without declaring

yourself a Christian – the constitution has nonetheless withstood the rise of the religious right without difficulty, notwithstanding important battles over certain human rights that require protecting or remain to be won, say, in relation to gays.

What this all adds up to is not that humanism has failed because it has failed to rid the world of belief or at least forced religion into a wholly private and therefore hidden sphere. Such an exclusive humanism – humanism as an anti-religious worldview – was only ever one element within the full range of humanist opinion. Rather it is fair to say that humanism has succeeded because today we live in a pluralist, secular society – at least in the West, and not forgetting pressing dangers and flaws. What 500 years of human history have brought about is a taming of religious excesses on a scale that was common during the wars of religion; a widespread habit of respect for others of different positions and beliefs; the social and political institutions that enable people to coexist even when they radically disagree.

An uneasy pluralism

And yet, there is no room for complacency. The world never stands still and continual, universal progress towards a utopian tomorrow is, I believe, a delusion. Terrorism is a growing threat. War, poverty and exploitation do not cease. Consumerism – as secularism has shaped up in the West – seems humanly unsatisfying, if indicators such as rates of depression and social fragmentation are correct. It is quite easy to imagine that climate change, coupled with other political and economic factors, will radically destabilize the world. The President of the Royal Society – that venerable institution, the inspiration of which is the Renaissance humanist Francis Bacon – is Professor Martin Rees. He has calculated that human beings stand only a 50:50 chance of surviving the twenty-first century.

So the challenge to contemporary humanists is to carry forward this uneasy pluralism into the future. The hope that all people would share the same religious or humanist outlook was always a pipedream, though it is one some theists and atheists alike still maintain. Surely, though, the rich variety of human life is more desirable than oppressive, monochrome uniformity?

The search for meaning

So much for the political agenda that humanism faces. What of more personal issues and the question of meaning? In a world of co-existing and sometimes competing frames of understanding, the question of what gives life meaning can seem under threat for the very reason that there is, apparently, more than one answer. This can imply to some that meaning comes à la carte, which doesn't seem very meaningful, or that, inasmuch as the choices conflict, the modern quest for meaning is cursed by confusion.

Humanists have suggested that meaning comes in a variety of ways:

1 A scientific way of life

There is a scientific pursuit of meaning based on the following principles:

- Science and technology offer the best means of finding practical ways of increasing human well-being and therefore meaning – notably in terms of physical health but, as science progresses, in terms of psychological and even moral well-being too.
- Rational thought is able to sift the various questions that human beings have traditionally associated with meaning in order to discard those that make no sense, and promote those that are worthwhile. For example, life after death as a source of meaning can be discarded, not just because there is no such thing but because if life is not good now there is little sense in prolonging it indefinitely in eternity.
- Alternatively, the pursuit of happiness is a rational objective – be that found in sustainable pleasures or the love of life and others – since happiness is its own justification. Science and reason can tell us much about how to optimize our chances of success in this respect.

2 A narrative way of life

Alternatively – though in truth, these alternatives are not necessarily mutually exclusive – there is the use of stories to provide a sense of direction; in short, a narrative sense of meaning in life:

- Science is not enough for meaning or well-being. This is because science is objective and meaning is a subjective matter; science is about facts and meaning is about value; science seeks knowledge whereas meaning requires wisdom.

- What stories provide is a store of narratives about particular people and times that address the subjective matters of value and wisdom. Within these narratives individuals can associate and situate their own experiences to understand and interpret them better. Similarly, non-narrative art – like much music or visual art – is valuable.
- Narratives are not absolute in the sense that they do not apply to, or work for, everyone equally. Having said that, they do often contain strikingly similar themes and aspirations that enable us, through them, to connect with others in a way that is also meaningful.

3 A humanitarian way of life
Another source of meaning that is arguably more demanding, but perhaps ultimately more rewarding, too, is found in humanitarian action – humanism as practical charity, it might be said:

- Modern science and technology shows us that suffering through illness and poverty is widespread throughout the world. However, it also provides us with the means of alleviating this distress.
- Implicit in the concept of humanism is a call to care for others since we are like them. Moreover, justice demands it. This is meaningful activity because the suffering of another is alleviated, it is gratifying to have helped another, and because it suggests that for all the ills which exist in the world, good can prevail.
- A deeper sense of meaning comes about from helping others as well. It emerges from having empathy. Empathy takes us out of ourselves, and our personal petty worries, and enables us to see our lives in a wider context.

4 A religious way of life
Humanism does not necessarily exclude a religious sensibility. And there are grounds for a religious humanist's sense of meaning:

- Religious humanism recognizes that traditional conceptions of God often presented God as a kind of cosmic tyrant; similarly religion can appear to be a question of obeying rules; and religious authorities look morally oppressive.
- Instead, we need a more mature relationship to that which lies beyond us, that which can be called the divine. This is an attitude that does not seek absolute authority in moral matters but rather embraces the radical freedom to be

responsible for yourself. Such responsibility is in fact a much better notion of what it is to behave ethically. God comes to represent the ideals we have for the best way of life.

- Living a moral life is, therefore, to live life fully, to live life well, and to live life for others. Rather than trying to anchor a sense of meaning to some point outside of life, it finds meaning in saying an effusive 'Yes' to life, even in death. Religious practices, like prayer, church-going and 'good works', may often be couched in the old language but, ultimately, are aimed at orienting lives towards the highest ideals captured in the notion of God.

5 A wonderful way of life

There may be more options to consider, but finally here, let me suggest the sense of meaning that arises from the sceptical strand within the humanist tradition. This is wonderful in the literal sense, in that it finds life engaging because it is full of wonder.

- The sceptical humanist accepts that human capacities and knowledge are finite. Moreover, he or she believes that many of the ills that destroy human well-being result from hubris – the denial of fallibility and limit. 'Man is quite insane,' wrote Montaigne. 'He wouldn't know how to create a maggot, and he creates gods by the dozen.'
- Life is therefore something of an art. Like a painting, that is confined to the frame and constrained by the paint, life is lived well according to what we make of the limited means at our disposal, namely ourselves, those with us, and the society in which we live.
- This is, therefore, an examined life. It is worth living when individuals strive to know themselves and cultivate a fascination with the world around them. Such contemplative wonder results in the effort simply to see – both that which is becoming better known and that which remains ultimately unknowable. Mortals only have their allotted span. But the wonder is that in it they can touch the mystery of existence itself.

An old question revisited

Finally, then, let us return to the question with which we began: what is humanism?

From the start, we noted that humanism is not a specific doctrine or a unified system of thought. Rather it is a tradition that started in the Renaissance, gathered momentum during the Enlightenment, and became a key feature of the modern world. During this development it embraced a range of possible meanings, principles and practices. It is fundamentally an attitude or spirit that values learning, curiosity and imagination aimed at engaging with the questions of life – personal and political – that human beings face and indeed that make us human. There are therefore many flavours of humanism, many philosophers that can be used to underpin it. However, an anthropocentric view of things would be as good a candidate as any for the defining characteristic of humanism; as Pico put it, there is dignity in humankind and in the human individual's capacities.

The challenge of our times

Today, humanism is at something of a crossroads, though not in the sense that it is about to disappear; far from it. Rather, humanism as a philosophy is contested. This is largely as a result of concerns about the rise of fundamentalist religion and related challenges to secularism. In response, there are atheistic humanists who want to make the definitive characteristic of humanism as being against religion, though to my mind they distort the humanist tradition and caricature religious belief in so doing. Also, they perhaps unconsciously distract themselves from questions that humanism itself must face, many of which have been implicit in the pages of our exploration here.

It would be better to admit that the debate about humanism is open. It is open for the very good reason that the question of how people might live is also open, at least in a free society. As Kant pointed out when asking what Enlightenment might be, it is nothing without vibrant debate in the public sphere, encouraging people into maturity. To put it another way, the spirit of freethinking is crushed if humanists strive to assert fundamentals over and against other humanists, claiming that there are matters which any 'good' humanist should affirm.

Contemporary questions

Two things with which to end: First, it might be worth highlighting some of the questions that I have felt recurring as I have researched and written this book and, second, to state what humanism means to me.

The following questions are, I think, pressing for those who care
about humanism:

- Is humanism a doctrine or is it more like an attitude that
  shapes personal and political views?
- Is humanism essentialist, in the sense of celebrating some
  essence of human nature; or is it anti-essentialist, believing
  that the adulation of man leads to oppression and fascism?
- Is humanism for or against religion – or neither?
- Is humanist politics one that seeks primarily to prevent
  illiberality, such as curtailments to freedom of speech; or is it
  a politics that has a positive agenda and view of society too?
- Is humanism fundamentally tied up with an ideology of
  scientific progress and what does it make of the sceptical,
  fallibilist strands in the tradition?
- What is humanism to make of the evils that are done in the
  name of the scientific and rationalist worldview it might
  share?
- If humanism is diverse and not singular then in what ways
  does it make sense to talk of humanism? Might not
  'humanisms' be better?

There are no quick answers to these questions. I hope you will
be better able to address them as a result of this book. There is
much debate to be had.

Cosmic impiety and humility

If these are the questions, then what is humanism to me, having
written on and researched the subject?

The Renaissance is an inspiration, though not because it was a
period in which human beings supposedly awoke from a dark
age: the medieval period was one of extraordinary invention
and accomplishment. Rather, it is because the Renaissance
humanists were able to make something wonderful of their
times – in their joy of discovery and the embrace of the new,
their cultivation of character, political reform, critical
questioning, passion and potential. This still speaks to us, half a
millennium later.

Then came the Enlightenment, and it is the intellectual giants,
David Hume and Immanuel Kant, who impress me most. For
Hume, scepticism was the natural position for the
Enlightenment thinker – scepticism about religion for sure, but
scepticism about the fundamentals of science too. Hume was

also sceptical about what he called enthusiasm, defined as 'presumption arising from success'. That could apply to triumphalist rationalism and scientism as much as religion.

Kant found Hume's scepticism profoundly unsettling. He wanted to put things on a firmer foundation. And he did so, but only by writing *Critiques*. In these *Critiques*, the key issue was understanding the limits of human knowledge. When Kant said that Enlightenment was maturity he meant being able to live with this finitude and not reach out for false certainty. So we have Enlightenment humanism as scepticism and grappling with the reality of human knowledge and experience.

I would actually relate this to a tradition within religion, though one that is lamentably in decline today, called the 'apophatic', meaning 'negative way'. It stands in marked contrast to the 'cataphatic', meaning 'positive way'; the strident assertions of indisputable religious dogma and divine truth.

The apophatic is a way of approaching what is ultimately unknown by identifying what that unknown cannot be. In religion it says God is not mortal (immortal), not visible (invisible) – note, saying nothing positive about God. Its spirit is captured in the biblical story of Moses climbing the mountain. As he went up and symbolically got nearer to God, he did not ascend into greater light and clarity, but deeper cloud and unknowing. Thus, at its core is a sense of the sacred – that which is far greater than you and so takes you out of yourself and into the unknown.

In a way what the apophatic theologians explored was similar to what the sceptical Enlightenment philosophers like Hume and Kant articulated: both identify limits and seek intuitions of what lies beyond. It was called 'learned ignorance' by the first Renaissance humanist philosopher, Nicholas of Cusa, and he got the idea from Socrates. Socrates annoyed his fellow citizens in Ancient Athens because he showed that the key to wisdom is not how much you know but is understanding the limits of what you know. This dimension reaches back right to the antecedent origins of humanism. It runs right through any honest study of what it is to be human.

It is also this dimension that to my mind is needed to combat contemporary fundamentalisms – religious and scientific – particularly if you want to avoid becoming a humanist fundamentalist in response. It is a kind of committed agnosticism – a juxtaposition of words that only sounds strange, if it does, today.

Echoing the same spirit, the last word can come from a famous humanist and agnostic, the anti-Christian, though never quite atheist, Bertrand Russell. Towards the end of his *History of Western Philosophy*, he reflects on how human beings across the centuries have related to their potential and powers. Sometimes, he believes, they have been too humble. In other periods, too hubristic. And today? He worries that we are at risk of thinking of ourselves as gods.

> In all this I feel a grave danger, the danger of what might be called cosmic impiety. The concept of 'truth' as something dependent upon facts largely outside human control has been one of the ways in which philosophy hitherto has inculcated the necessary element of humility. When this check on pride is removed, a further step is taken on the road towards a certain kind of madness – the intoxication with power ... to which modern man, whether philosophers or not, are prone. I am persuaded that this intoxication is the greatest danger of our time, and that any philosophy which, however unintentionally, contributes to it is increasing the danger of vast social disaster.

This 'cosmic impiety', the greatest danger of his time, shows no sign of passing. Humanists must ensure that they help mitigate it.

glossary

agnosticism The view that God's existence, or not, cannot be proven because it is beyond the capability of human science.

altruism The selfless consideration of others.

atheism The view that there is no God, either because there is no evidence to warrant such a belief or because the traditional belief in God has been shown to be untenable.

alchemy The tradition that preceded modern science, particularly chemistry, that centred around transmuting base metals into gold, but also had a moral dimension in searching for the truth about life.

anthropocentrism The belief that humankind is the central and most important factor in the universe.

aporia The doubt that arises from the raising of philosophical puzzles for which there are no obvious solutions.

autonomy The doctrine that the human individual should be self-sufficient and subject only to their own will.

Byzantine Relating to the Byzantine Empire which continued the Roman Empire in the East.

civic That which relates to the city and the role of citizens.

cosmology The science of the universe.

deism The belief that God exists, as shown in nature, but does not directly interact with the world.

empiricism The theory of knowledge based upon sense experience.

Enlightenment The period in the history of ideas, around the eighteenth century, that stressed the importance of reason and critiquing existing human beliefs.

epistemology The part of philosophy concerned with knowledge and how we know things.

esotericism The study of natural or supernatural matters that are characterized by being mysterious.

essentialism The doctrine that there are fundamental properties of things or creatures that are necessary to understand to define the things or creatures.

existentialism The branch of philosophy that majors on the experience of what it is to be human, such as freedom.

fallibilism The view that no fact, rule or idea is ever certain.

fideism The belief that God exists but that nothing can be known about God except through faith in God.

freethinkers Individuals who think freely of traditional doctrines or beliefs, especially religious ones.

fundamentalism The religious attempt to take holy texts literally, and more broadly meant as a return to what are regarded as the fundamentals of a belief.

hedonism The doctrine that pleasure is the determining factor in the good life.

heliocentrism The view that the sun is at the centre of the universe.

hermeticism The study of the mystical writings that reach back to the semi-mythical character of Hermes Trismegistus.

humanities The collection of academic subjects that includes literature, philosophy and the arts.

idealism The doctrine that the world as we experience it is fundamentally a mental phenomenon.

ideology A set of beliefs or doctrines that someone uses to interpret the world.

institutions The established customs, laws, organizations or traditions that exist in a society.

instrumentalism The view that the value of things is determined by their usefulness.

materialism The view that the world consists only of physical things.

metaphysics The branch of philosophy concerned with everything that lies outside of the reach of science, not least the intellectual basis of science itself.

modernity The period in the history of ideas from the end of the Middle Ages to the present day.

morality The branch of philosophy concerned with values, ethics and how we live.

naturalism The doctrine that everything can be explained by natural causes and forces, and one that rejects any supernatural or teleological causes.

nihilism The belief that rejects all values, beliefs or existence.

noumenal world Used by Kant to express things as they are in themselves as opposed to things as we experience them, which he called the phenomenal world.

occult Experiences, events and influences that are put down to mystical or supernatural forces.

ontology The philosophy concerned with the nature of being.

pragmatism The doctrine that a practical applicability of a belief is what determines its value.

pre-Socratic The period of philosophy before the life of Socrates, roughly running up to the mid-fifth century BCE.

rationalism The theory that all knowledge is based upon reasoned thinking.

redaction The composing, drafting or editing of a document.

Renaissance The period of European history, starting roughly in the late-fourteenth century and extending to the sixteenth, that saw a flourishing of humanist concerns.

rhetoric The study of the use of language to communicate.

scepticism The doctrine that real knowledge of things is either impossible or elusive.

scholasticism The system of philosophy and teaching that dominated Europe in the Middle Ages based on the writings of Aristotle and Christian theologians.

scientific method A way of investigating things that proceeds by repeated observation and experiment to test hypotheses.

scientism The belief that only science can ask and answer questions worth pursuing.

sophism A pre-Socratic school of philosophy that majored on education and asked about what it is to be human.

teleology The view that some things are best explained by their purpose as opposed to their causes.

theism The doctrine that God exists.

transcendental That which lies beyond everyday experience though not necessarily outside of knowledge.

utilitarianism The school of ethics which believes that the moral course of action is that which brings the greatest happiness to the greatest number.

Further reading

The book list below is far from comprehensive. On areas like Renaissance humanism and the Enlightenment the bibliography is massive and always growing. However, in addition to the classic texts of the many big-hitters that we have met on the way – and others referred to in the text – these books will help readers to take things a step further.

General overview of philosophy

Kenny, A. (2005) *A New History of Western Philosophy,* (4 vols), OUP
(A new, authoritative history of western philosophy from arguably Britain's greatest living philosopher. Admirable for its clarity.)

Honderich, T. (ed.) (2005) *The Oxford Companion to Philosophy,* OUP
(The one volume encyclopedia of philosophy that no serious student of the subject can do without.)

Renaissance humanism

Burckhardt, J. (1990) *The Civilization of the Renaissance in Italy,* Penguin
(The classic history that defined the Renaissance.)

Katz, D. S. (2007) *The Occult Tradition,* Pimlico
(A fascinating and sane examination of the influence of occultism in its various shapes and forms from the Renaissance to the present day.)

Kekewich, L. (ed.) (2000) *The Renaissance in Europe: The Impact of Humanism*, Yale University Press
(An introductory text.)

Kraye, J. (ed.) (1996) *The Cambridge Companion to Renaissance Humanism*, CUP
(A collection of scholarly essays on various aspects of the Renaissance.)

Kraye, J. and Stone, M. W. F. (eds) (2000) *Humanism and Early Modern Philosophy*, Routledge
(Scholarly essays examining the philosophical contribution of Renaissance thinkers.)

MacCulloch, D. (2004) *Reformation*, Penguin
(An authoritative, comprehensive history of the Reformation, and a very good read to boot.)

Nauert Jr, Charles G. (1995) *Humanism and the Culture of Renaissance Europe*, CUP
(Another introductory text.)

The Enlightenment

Berlin, I. (1956) *The Age of Enlightenment*, Signet
(A collection of the famous philosopher's favourite Enlightenment thinkers.)

Gay, P. (1995) *The Enlightenment Vol 1: The Rise of Modern Paganism*, W. W. Norton

Gay, P. (1996) *The Enlightenment Vol 2: Science of Freedom*, W. W. Norton
(This two-volume history of ideas is one of the most authoritative around.)

Hampson, N. (1968) *The Enlightenment*, Penguin
(An introductory, narrative history.)

Kurtz, P. and Madigan, T. J. (eds) (1994) *Challenges to the Enlightenment: In Defense of Reason and Science*, Prometheus Books
(Looking at various contemporary challenges to Enlightenment thought.)

Rutherford, R. (ed.) (2006) *The Cambridge Companion to Early Modern Philosophy*, CUP
(A collection of scholarly essays on the period between the Renaissance and the Enlightenment.)

Modern humanism

Badmington, N. (ed.) (2000) *Posthumanism*, Palgrave
(A collection looking at the future of humanity, in terms of literature and technology.)

Baggini, J. (2003) *Atheism, A Very Short Introduction*, OUP
(Does what it says on the cover from a moderate atheist and good communicator of ideas.)

Blackham, H. J. (ed.) (1963) *Objections to Humanism*, Penguin Books
(A collection of answers to questions about humanism from one of the twentieth century's most well-known humanist campaigners.)

Brown, A. (1999) *The Darwin Wars: The Scientific Battle for the Soul of Man*, Simon and Schuster
(Informed, even-handed discussion of the implications for humanism of evolutionary theory.)

Cummings, D. (ed.) (2006) *Debating Humanism*, Societas
(A collection of short essays on questions facing contemporary humanism that has the great virtue of representing several different views.)

Davies, T. (1997) *Humanism*, Routledge
(A richly and passionately written challenge to humanism.)

Flew, A. (1993) *Atheistic Humanism*, Prometheus Books
(A defense of atheistic humanism from the philosopher who subsequently became a deist.)

Frayn, M. (2006) *The Human Touch*, Faber and Faber
(Erudite, accessible discussion of the latest developments in cosmology with a thoughtful eye to their implications for human self-understanding.)

Freeman, A. (2001) *God In Us: A Case for Christian Humanism*, Societas
(A naturalist account of Christianity, the original edition of which led to the author being sacked from his post as a clergyman in the Church of England.)

Grayling, A. C. (2003) *What is Good?*, Phoenix
(A lively history of the battle for rights from the fifteenth century, and an accessible philosophical history of ethics, from an evangelical atheistic humanist.)

Grayling, A. C. (2007) *Towards the Light: The Story of the Struggles for Liberty and Rights That Made the Modern West*, Bloomsbury

Herrick, J. (2005) *Humanism: An Introduction*, Prometheus Books
(An introduction from a sometime editor of the Rationalist Press Association and *New Humanist* magazine.)

Jacoby, S. (2004) *Freethinkers: A History of American Secularism*, Owl Books
(A well-written, narrative history of the story of humanism in the US.)

Joshi, S. T. (ed.) (2000) *Atheism: A Reader*, Prometheus Books
(A useful collection of some of the key texts in modern atheism and agnosticism.)

Kurtz, P. (ed.) (1973) *The Humanist Alternative: Some Definitions of Humanism*, Pemberton Books
(A very broad and engaging collection of essays on a variety of questions in humanism.)

Norman, R. (2004) *On Humanism*, Routledge
(A personal defence of an atheistic humanist position that advocates a narrative understanding of meaning.)

Russell, B. (1997) *Religion and Science*, OUP
(The eloquent twentieth-century humanist pursues the science and religion debate, still throwing fresh perspectives on various questions.)

Russell, B. (2004) *Sceptical Essays*, Routledge
(Some of the essays from the same man that show the limits as well as the strengths of his rationalist position.)

Said, E. W. (2004) *Humanism and Democratic Criticism*, Palgrave Macmillan
(An essay on humanism in universities.)

Taylor, C. (2007) *A Secular Age*, Harvard University Press
(A major study of secularism arguing that after the Renaissance religion didn't die but the world changed as people chose whether or not to believe in God.)

Vernon, M. (2007) *After Atheism: Science, Religion and the Meaning of Life*, Palgrave Macmillan
(An exploration of how to be an agnostic and why it matters.)

Walter, N. (1997) *Humanism: What's in the Word?*, Rationalist Press Association
(A detailed and authoritative history of modern humanism in all its shapes and forms.)

Websites

There are numerous websites dedicated to humanist thought, offering introductions and resources including book lists and materials for humanist ceremonies.

In addition to the websites of the organizations listed below, a number of the key texts from the history of humanism can be found online (from Google or another search engine), including:

Giovanni Pico della Mirandola's 'Oration on the Dignity of Man'

Karl Marx and Friedrich Engels' 'The German Ideology'

Jean-Paul Sartre's lecture 'Existentialism is a Humanism'

Bertrand Russell's lecture 'Why I am not a Christian'

Organizations

www.americanhumanist.org – the American Humanist Association site that has news, resources and details of *Humanist*, the association's magazine and over 110 local affiliated organizations.

www.humanism.ie – the site of the Humanist Associate of Ireland that offers ceremonies, courses and membership.

www.humanism.org.uk – the British Humanist Association site that offers an introduction, campaigns, histories, philosophical surveys, lists of famous humanists and more. You can join up too.

www.humanism-scotland.org.uk – the site of the Humanist Society of Scotland, campaigning on issues from a secular viewpoint in Scotland.

www.humaniststudies.org – the Institute for Humanist Studies site, a think tank that promotes public awareness of humanism.

www.iheu.org – this is the site of the International and Ethical Humanist Union which as well as having a lot of material of interest to humanists is also a good starting point from which to find national sites.

www.newhumanist.org.uk – the site of the New Humanist magazine, also linked to the Rationalist Press Association.

www.secularhumanism.org – the Council for Secular Humanism, chaired by the veteran campaigner Paul Kurtz, an organization for North American non-religious people.

www.secularism.org.uk – the UK's National Secular Society is another historical campaigning organization with resources and news.

www.sofn.org.uk – the Sea of Faith network for humanists who believe religion is of value as a human creation.

index

abandonment, and existentialism 110–11
Abbagnano, Nicola xiii
action, and existentialism 111–12
Adorno, Theodor 154
agnosticism xxii, 30, 197–8
  and ethics 68
  and organized humanism 142
  in Voltaire 62
Alberti, Leon Battista 42
alchemy 31
Alcoholics Anonymous 182
Alexander the Great 12
alienation 87–8
Al-Kindi 24
American Declaration of Independence
      79, 81
American Humanist Association 142
American pragmatism see pragmatism
American Revolution 80
Anaximander of Miletus 3, 4
Anaximenes of Miletus 3, 4
ancient Greece xv, xvi, 2–16
  Epicurus 3, 14–16, 17, 18
  pre-Socratic philosophers 2–9, 18
  and Renaissance humanism 3, 11, 20,
      26, 28, 30–1, 32, 42, 53
  scepticism 13–14, 50–1
  see also Aristotle; Plato; Socrates
ancient Rome xv, xvi, 16–17, 18
  and Renaissance humanism 26, 27,
      28, 29, 44, 53
animals
  animal welfare 95
  and climate change 161
  and language 131
anthropic principle 134
anthropocentrism 188
  and environmental ethics 161, 162

and Renaissance humanism 27–33, 38,
      43, 52
anti-essentialism 112–13, 196
anti-humanism 108, 115–23
  and evolutionary ethics 134
  and Foucault 115, 119–22
  and Freud 122
  and Nietzsche 115–18, 122
apophatic tradition in religion 197
Aquinas, Thomas 22–3, 147
Archimedes 24
Aristotle 3, 12–13, 18
  and Islamic humanism 23–4
  and medieval scholasticism 22–3
  Poetics 49
  and Renaissance humanism 13, 26,
      31, 32, 37, 43, 52
  and science 40
  and teleology 131
Arnold, Matthew 105, 149
art
  religious works of art 184
  and Renaissance humanism 41–2
  and socialism 91
atheism
  atheistic humanism xxi, 136–7, 142,
      144, 145–6, 147, 150, 156, 195
  and faith schools 158–9
  and religious works of art 184
  and wonderment 186
  and Enlightenment humanism 58–9,
      60, 62, 68, 83
  and existentialism 110, 113–14
  and the mind–body problem 177
  Nietzsche on the death of God 118–19
  and pragmatism 100
  of Stalin and Hitler 153–4
Augustine, St 43, 146–7

Auschwitz, humanism after 152–6
Averroes ('The Commentator') 24
Avicenna (Ibn Sinna) 24

Bacon, Francis 37–9, 162, 191
Badiou, Alain, *The Century* 176
Baggini, Julian 145
baptisms 179
Baron, Hans 27
Basel, Council of (1431) 30
BBC religious broadcasting 182–3
Belgium 182
Bellarmine, Cardinal Robert 40
Bentham, Jeremy 92, 93, 94, 174
Besant, Annie 137
BHA (British Humanist Association) xi, 183
birth control 140
Blackburn, Simon 183–4
Blackman, Harold, *Essentials of Humanism* 143
blasphemy 172–4
    and freedom of speech 173
    in secular law 173
Boethius, *The Consolations of Philosophy* 22
Bohr, Niels 126
Bonhoeffer, Dietrich xxi, 147–8
Bradlaugh, Charles 136–7
Braille, Louis 58
British Humanist Association xi, 183
Brotherhood of Common Love 30
Bruni, Leonardo 39–40
Bruno, Giordano 41
Bryan, William Jennings 127
the Buddha 114
Burke, Edmund, *Reflections on the Revolution in France* 80
Burkhardt, Jakob, *The Civilization of the Renaissance in Italy* 20–1, 25, 28, 41, 52
Byzantine Empire 25, 36

Calas, Jean 60
Calvin, John 45, 188
Cameron, Norman, *Hitler's Table Talk* 154
capitalism, and socialism 90–1, 92
Carolingian Renaissance 22
Central Secularist Society 136
ceremonies, humanist 179–82
Chardin, Teilhard de 141
Charlemagne 22
Chaucer, Geoffrey 105
children
    and faith schools 158–9, 160–1

Russell on religious teaching and 139, 140
Christian humanism xxi, 136, 146–9, 150
    and the Sea of Faith network 149, 183
    and sin 146–7
    and theological humanism 147–8
Christianity
    and blasphemy laws 172
    Calvinist theology 146
    Christian existentialists 113–14
    and Darwinism 127–8, 135
    dominion theology 38
    faith schools and religious education 156–61
    and gay ceremonies 181
    and Machiavelli 45
    and Nietzsche 116–17
    and pastoral care 182
    in post-secular society 189
    and the Reformation 45–7, 188
    and Renaissance humanism 22–3, 25–6, 31, 32, 33
    Roman Catholicism 82–3, 148
    Russell's objection to 138–40
    and suicide 180–1
    translations of the Bible 46, 48
    in the United States 189, 190–1
Chrysippus 17
Church of England 142
    schools 157
Cicero 9, 14, 18
    and Renaissance humanism 17, 20, 22, 28, 29, 43, 51, 53
Citizen's Advice Bureau 182
civic humanism 27
civil liberties, Rousseau on 63–4
civil partnerships 170, 182, 183
climate change 161–4, 191
Cola di Rienzo 29
communism
    and Marxist humanism xix, 87, 89–90
    and Russell 140
    and socialism 90, 91, 92
compassion, and religion 167–8
Comte, Auguste 81–3, 93
    and Sartre 112, 113
    and secularism 136, 137
Condorcet, Marquis de 174
Confucius 114
consciousness, and the mind–body problem 178
Constantinople 23, 25, 26
consumerism 191
contemplative wonder 185

contemporary diversity of humanism **xix**
Cornwall, John **153**
cosmic impiety **198**
cosmology, and Darwinism **134**
counselling services **182**
creationism **127–9, 130, 144, 145, 171**
  and faith schools **159**
critical attitude in Kant **77–0**
Cupitt, Don, *Taking Leave of God* **149**

d'Alembert, Jean **56–7, 58, 59, 62, 72**
Dante Alighieri, *Divine Comedy* **22**
Darrow, Clarence **127**
Darwin, Charles **83, 189**
  Origin of Species **125–6**
Darwinism **125–35**
  and cosmology **134**
  and creationism **127–9, 130**
  and evolutionary ethics **132–4**
  and God **125–6, 128, 134–5**
  and the origins of language **130–1**
  and the purpose of life **131–5**
  and science **125, 129–30**
Davies, Tony, *Humanism* **154**
Dawkins, Richard **184**
  The God Delusion **144, 153**
death, Lucretius on **14**
Declaration of the Rights of Man and of
  the Citizen **79**
deep ecology **161–4**
deism **59–61, 62, 144**
Democritus **16**
Descartes, René **36, 41, 108–9**
determinism, and evolutionary ethics **133**
Dewey, John **103**
d'Holbach, Baron **58–9, 61, 62**
Diderot, Denis **56–7, 59, 62, 72**
  Letter on the Blind **58**
  and Rousseau **63, 64**
diversity
  of humanism **xii, xviii–xxi**
    Enlightenment humanism **57–8**
    Renaissance humanism **52**
  and identity politics **169–71**
DNA, and Darwinism **126**
dominion theology **38**
Dostoevsky, F. **110**
  The Brothers Karamazov **164**
duty, Kant on **75–6**

ecology movement **161–4**
education
  faith schools and religious education
    156–61

and Renaissance humanism **34–7, 52**
Einstein, Albert **126**
Eliot, George **83**
empiricism, and Enlightenment humanism
  64–7
Encyclopédie **56–8, 59, 60, 63**
Engels, F. **89**
English Enlightenment **55–6**
enlightened self-interest **168**
Enlightenment humanism **54–84, 189,
  195, 196–6**
  and atheism **58–9, 60, 62, 68**
  and empiricism **64–7**
  in England **55–6**
  and Foucault **121**
  French *philosophes* **56–64**
  and the French Revolution **79–81, 84**
  and human nature **62–7**
  and human rights **81**
  and Nietzsche **119**
  and optimism **84**
  and positivist philosophy **81–3**
  and progress **62, 82, 83, 174**
  and Renaissance humanism **xxi, 55,
    62**
  scepticism in **66–7, 197**
  Scottish Enlightenment **56, 64**
environmental ethics **161–4**
Epicureanism **3, 14–16, 17, 18**
  and Renaissance humanism **39, 45**
Erasmus, Desiderius **30, 46, 47–9**
  Praise of Folly **48**
essentialism **63–4, 113, 196**
  and Foucault **119**
  Sartre and anti-essentialism **112–13**
ethical behaviour *see* morality
Euclid **24**
evolutionary psychology, and enlightened
    self-interest **168**
evolutionary theory *see* Darwinism
existentialism **xix–xxi, 108–14**
  and abandonment **110–11**
  and action **111–12**
  and anti-essentialism **112–13**
  and atheism **110, 113–14**
  and dignity as self-determination
    109–10
  and freedom **109, 110–11, 113–14, 123**
  and progress **114**
  and subjectivity **108, 114**

faith schools **156–61**
  and atheistic humanism **158–9**
  British tradition of **156–7**

case for 159–61
debate on 158
Russell's views on 157
fallibilism 103
feminism 105–6
Ferguson, Adam 56
Ficino, Marsilio 30–1, 33, 34
Flew, Anthony 136, 144
Florence, Council of (1439) 25–6
Forster, E.M. 143, 145
Foucault, Michel 115, 119–22
    and discourses 119–20
    The Order of Things 120
    and power-knowledge 120–1
    and sexuality 121–2, 170
Franklin, Benjamin 80
Frederick the Great 62
freedom
    and existentialism 109, 110–11,
        113–14, 123
    Kant on 74
    as a principle of humanism xiii, x
freedom of speech, and blasphemy 173
free will 48, 59
French language, and Renaissance
        humanism 36
French *philosophes* 56–64, 79
French Revolution 79–81, 84
Freud, Sigmund 122, 189
funerals xiii, 179, 181

Gaia hypothesis 162–3
Galen 24
Galileo Galilei 5, 36, 40–1
Gay News, blasphemy prosecution against
    172
gays *see* homosexuality
genes, and Darwinism 126
geometry 37
Germany *see* Nazi Germany
Gilligan, Carol 106
God, existence of
    argument from design 71–2, 125–6,
        134
    and Darwinism 125–6, 128, 134–5
    and existentialism 110
    Nietzsche on the death of God 118–19
    and pragmatism 100
    Russell on 138–40
    see also agnosticism; atheism;
        Christianity
Goethe, Johann von 78
Gorgias 3, 8
Greece *see* ancient Greece

Greek, and Renaissance humanism 34–5
green burials 181

Halliday, John 152
Hamlet (Shakespeare) 50
happiness
    and pragmatism 100
    pursuit of 192
    and secularism 137
    and utilitarianism 92, 93–5, 96
Hardy, Thomas 83
Harris, Sam, *The End of Faith* 156
Hayek, Friedrich von 175
hedonism, and Epicureanism 15–16
Hegel, G.W.F. 5
Heidegger, Martin 5
Heisenberg, Werner 126
heliocentrism 40–1
Henry VIII, King of England 47, 49
Heraclitus 3, 5–6, 18
hermeticism 31–2, 41, 44
Heydrich, Reinhard 152–3
Hippocrates 24
historical perspectivism, and Nietzsche
    117
history
    and evolutionary ethics 133
    historical diversity of humanism
        xviii–xix, 188–90
    and personhood xiv
Hitler, Adolf 152–3, 154
the Holocaust 78
Holyoake, George Jacob 136, 137
Homer 23
homosexuality
    Foucault on 121–2, 170
    gay ceremonies 181–2, 183
    gay marriage and civil partnerships
        170, 182
    gay rights 169–70
Howard League for Penal Reform 121
human dignity
    and existentialism 109–10
    and Nietzsche 117–18
    and progress 174
    and Renaissance humanism 42–5, 52,
        117
humanism
    contemporary questions on 195–6
    defining xi–xii, xiii, 194–5
    diversity of xii, xviii–xxi, 188–90, 196
    organized 135–40
    orienting principles of xii–xiv
    origins of the word xv

humanismus **xv**
humanist ceremonies **179–82**
humanist counselling services **182**
humanitarian way of life **193**
human nature
    and Christianity **146–7**
    and Enlightenment humanism **62–7**
    and Marxism **89–90**
human rights, and Enlightenment
        humanism **81**
Hume, David **56, 65–72, 84, 116, 196–7**
    and anti-humanism **115**
    death of **70–1, 72, 125**
    Dialogues Concerning Natural Religion
        71–2, 135
    and empiricism **64–7**
    and the ethics of sympathy **67–9**
    and Kant **73, 75, 78**
    on morality **67–9, 70–1, 167**
    on religion **71–2, 126**
    A Treatise of Human Nature **65, 66**
    on values and the naturalistic fallacy
        132
Huxley, Aldous **142**
Huxley, Julian **141–2**
Huxley, T.H. **xxii, 135, 141**

Ibn Sinna (Avicenna) **24**
identity politics **169–72**
individualism
    Kant on **77**
    and Renaissance humanism **28, 52**
    and socialism **91**
Innocent III, Pope **43**
Inquisition, and heliocentrism **40, 41**
instrumental wonder **184–5**
intelligent design, and creationism **128**
International and Ethical Humanist Union
        141, 183
Iraq war (2003), and utilitarianism **97**
Islam
    blasphemy in **172**
    Islamic humanism **23–4**
    women and the veil **106**
Is Nothing Sacred? (ed. Rogers) **183–4**
Italian language, and Renaissance
        humanism **36**
italic typeface **36**

James, William **xx, 98–102**
    The Varieties of Religious Experience
        102
Jaspers, Karl **114**
Jesuits **58, 59, 139**

Jesus Christ **114, 146**
    Russell's views on **139–40**
    and theological humanism **147–8**
Jews, in Nazi death camps **152–3, 155**
Jonson, Ben **49**
Julius Caesar (Shakespeare) **50**
Jung Chang **152**
justice, Hume on **69**
Justinian, Emperor **36**

Kabbalah **32, 44**
Kant, Immanuel **73–9, 84, 195, 196, 197**
    and anti-humanism **115**
    on critical attitude **77–0**
    and Foucault **121**
    on freedom **74**
    and immaturity **73–4, 77**
    and morality **75–9, 165, 166**
    on religion **74, 75–7, 78, 165, 166**
Kennan, George F. **152**
Kenny, Anthony **135**
Kierkegaard, S. **9, 108**
Knight, Margaret, *Morals Without Religion*
        143

language
    and Darwinism **130–1**
    and Renaissance humanism **34–7**
Latin, and Renaissance humanism **34–5,
        36, 48**
learned ignorance **197**
Lesbian and Gay Christian Movement
        173, 183
Levi, Primo, *If This Is a Man or Survival in
        Auschwitz* **155**
liberalism
    and Mill **93**
    and organized humanism **142**
    and progress **176**
liberty, limits of **83**
Lippi, Filippino **42**
Lisbon earthquake (1755) **60–1**
literary humanism **105**
Livy, *History of Rome* **29**
Locke, John **61–2, 81**
Lothar of Trasimund **43**
Lovelock, James **162–3**
Lucretius **14, 26**
    On the Nature of Things **45**
Luther, Martin **30, 33, 35, 45, 46, 48, 146,
        188**
Lynch, Gordon **145**

Machiavelli, Niccolò 34
  and anti-humanism 115
  Discourses 44–5
  The Prince 36, 45
Macmillan Encyclopaedia of Philosophy
  xiii–xiv
Maimonides, Moses 24–5
Malik, Kenan 171, 172
Manetti, Giannozzo 43
Maoism 78, 152, 153, 189
marriage, gay 170
Marxism xx, 86–90, 104–5, 108
  and alienation 87–8
  and feminism 105–6
  and homosexuality 169
  and human nature 89–90
  and organized humanism 142
  and religion 88, 189
  and totalitarianism 89
Marx, Karl xx, 83, 92, 189
  Communist Manifesto 89
  Economic and Political Manuscripts
    87, 88
materialism 61–2
mathematics
  and Enlightenment humanism 56
  and Islamic humanism 24
  and Protagoras 3, 5
meaning, search for 192–4
Medici, Cosimo de' 31
Mendel, Gregor 126
Meslier, Jean 59
metaphysical stage, and positive
    philosophy 82
Middle Ages, and Renaissance humanism
    20, 21–5, 29, 39, 188
Mill, John Stuart 83, 92–3, 105
  on Bradlaugh 136–7
  Utilitarianism 93, 94–5
  and women's rights 93, 106, 169
mind–body problem 177–9
Montaigne, Michel de 36, 38, 50–1
  and anti-humanism 115
  'Apology for Raimond Sebond' 51
  'On Experience' 51
morality
  and evolutionary theory 132–4
  and faith schools 158
  Hume on 67–9, 70–1, 167
  Kant on 75–9, 165, 166
  and progress 175
  and religion 69, 70–1, 164–8
  and religious humanism 193–4

Russell on religion and moral progress
    139–40
More, Thomas 35, 48–9
  Utopia 47–8, 87
multiculturalism 169–70, 171
mystery and wonderment 183–6

naming ceremonies 181
narrative way of life 192–3
National Secular Society 83, 137
naturalism 39–40
naturalistic fallacy 132, 133
natural law 81
natural philosophy 2
natural rights 92
natural world xiv, xv
Nazi Germany 113, 147
  and homosexuality 169
  humanism after Auschwitz 152–6
Netherlands 182
neuroscience, and the mind–body
    problem 177–8
New Humanism 105
New Humanist magazine 137
Newton, Isaac 56, 84, 116, 188
Nicholas V, Pope 33
Nicolas of Cusa 11, 26, 30, 33, 34, 197
Niethammer, Friedrich Immanuel xv
Nietzsche, Friedrich xxii, 115–18, 122
  and Christianity 116–17, 149
  on the death of God 118–19
  The Gay Science 117, 119
  and historical perspectivism 117
  and progress 116

occultism, and Renaissance humanism
    31–2, 41, 44
organized humanism 135–44
  publications 137
  and religion 142–5
  religious humanism 142
  and Russell 137–40
  scientific 141–2, 144
  and secularism 136–7

Paine, Thomas 79–81, 92, 169
pangenesis 126
panpsychism 178
Papacy, and Renaissance humanism 25,
    30, 32, 33, 36, 43
paradoxes of Zeno 7
Parmenides 3, 5, 6–7, 18
pastoral care 182

Peirce, C.S. xx
personhood xiv, xv
pessimistic humanism 142
Petrarch, Francesco 28–9, 30, 34, 35, 37
'Pico della Mirandola 32, 33, 34, 35, 47,
     50, 117, 174, 195
     Oration on the Dignity of Man 43–4,
        49–50, 125
Plato 3, 9, 10, 11, 12, 13, 18, 70
     Euthyphro's dilemma in 165–6
     and geometry 37
     and Marxism 87
     and More's *Utopia* 47–8
     and pragmatism 104
     and Renaissance humanism 23, 24,
        26, 30–1, 32
     Republic 87
     and Shakespeare 50
     Timaeus 43
Plethon, George Gemistos 25–6
pluralism 191
political correctness 171
politics
     humanist 196
     progress in 175
Pope, Alexander 56
Popper, Karl 129–30
positivist philosophy 81–3, 136, 137
post-secular society 189–90
power-knowledge, and Foucault 120–1
pragmatism xx, 98–104, 105, 108
     and humanism 102–4
     and religion 99–100, 101, 102
     Russell's rejection of 101
     and subject/object distinction 99
     and the will to believe 99–100
praise, Hume on 69
printing, and Renaissance humanism
        35–6
progress xiii, 174–7, 196
     and Enlightenment humanism 62, 82,
        83, 174
     and existentialism 114
     facts and statistics 175–6
     flaws in the ideology of 176–7
     Nietzsche's attack on scientific
        progress 116
     pillars of 175
     Russell on religion and moral progress
        139–40
Protagoras xx, 3, 7–8, 18
     On the Gods 7
punishment, morality and religion 166–7
Pythagoras 3, 5, 18, 37

quantum physics 126

Rahner, Karl 148
Raphael 42
     'The School of Athens' 13
rationalism, and organized humanism 142
Rationalist Press Association 83
rationality xiii
Rayner, Claire xi
reason
     and Christian humanism xxi
     and deep ecology 162
     and Enlightenment humanism 55
     Kant on 75–9
reductionism, and evolutionary ethics 133
Rees, Martin 191
the Reformation 45–7, 188
registry office weddings 180
Reid, Thomas 56
relativism 8
religion xi, xii–xiii, xiv
     apophatic tradition in 197
     and Aristotelian philosophy 25
     BBC religious broadcasting 182–3
     and blasphemy 172–4
     and compassion 167–8
     Comte on 82–3
     and Darwinism 125–9
     and deism 59–61, 62, 144
     and Enlightenment humanism 57, 58,
        59–62
        Hume on 71–2, 126
        Kant on 74, 75–7, 78, 165
        and morality 69, 70–1
        Paine on 80
     and existentialism 113–14
     and gay ceremonies 181–2
     and the history of humanism 188–90
     and Hitler 154
     and Islamic humanism 24
     and Marxism 88, 189
     and morality 69, 70–1, 164–8
     mystery and wonderment 183–6
     and organized humanism 142–5
     in post-secular society 189–90
     and pragmatism 99–100, 101, 102
     religious fundamentalism 127–8, 145,
        146, 156
     religious way of life 193–4
     and rites of passage 179–82
     and theological humanism 147–8
     see also Christianity; God, existence of
religious education (RE) 159
religious humanism 142, 193–4

religious tolerance 46–7, 61
Renaissance humanism xi, xv, xxi 19–53,
    55, 188, 195, 196
  and ancient Greece 3, 11, 20
  antecedents of 22–5
  and anthropocentrism 27–33, 38, 42,
    43
  and Aristotle 13, 26, 31, 32, 37, 43, 52
  and art 41–2
  and Cicero 17, 20, 22, 28, 29, 43, 51,
    53
  diversity of 52
  economic factors in 27
  end of the Renaissance 52
  and the Enlightenment xxi, 55, 62
  and hermeticism 31–2, 41, 44
  and human dignity 42–5, 52
  idea of the Renaissance 20–1
  language and education 34–7, 52
  origins of 25–7
  and personhood xiv
  printing and errors 35–6
  and the Reformation 45–7
  and religion xiv
  scepticism 50–1
  and science xii, 32, 37–41
  and Shakespeare 49–50, 52
RE (religious education) 159
responsibility, and existentialism 109–10,
    111
rhetoric, and Shakespeare 49–50
rights
  human rights 81
  natural rights 92
rites of passage 179–82
Robertson, Archibald 142–3
Roman Catholicism 82–3, 148
Romans see ancient Rome
Rorty, Richard 104
Rousseau, Jean-Jacques 57, 63–4, 72
  and Comte 83
  Discourse on the Origin of Inequality 64
  and Foucault 120
  and the French Revolution 79
  and Hume 65, 66
  and Marx 87
  on progress 175
  and Sartre 112
  The Social Contract 63, 64
Royal Society 38, 191
rule utilitarianism 97
Rushdie, Salman 172
Ruskin, John 83
Russell, Bertrand 7, 92, 137–40, 141

The Case for Socialism 90–1
  and Dewey 103
  History of Western Philosophy xii, 99,
    198
  rejection of pragmatism 101, 102
  views on faith schools 157
  What I Believe 138
  'Why I am not a Christian' 137

Saint-Simon, Comte 81
Samaritans 182
Sartre, Jean-Paul 108–12, 166
  Existentialism is a Humanism xix–xxi,
    108–9, 110, 113
Saussure, César de 56
scepticism
  in ancient Greece 13–14
  in Enlightenment humanism 66–7, 197
  and pragmatism 101
  in Renaissance humanism 50–1
  Russell and Christianity 138–40
  sceptical humanism 194
Schiller, F.C.S. xx, 102–3
Schleiermacher, Friedrich 148
'schools' of humanism xix
science xiv, xv, xxii, 55
  and ancient Greek philosophers 2, 12
  and climate change 162–3, 164
  and empiricism 65
  and Enlightenment humanism 56, 58,
    59
  and evolutionary theory 125, 129–30
  and materialism 61
  and the mind–body problem 177–9
  Nietzsche's attack on scientific
    progress 116
  and organized humanism 142
  and positive philosophy 82
  in post-secular society 190
  and the pursuit of meaning 192
  and Renaissance humanism 32, 37–41
  scientific progress 175, 196
  and wonderment 185, 186
scientific humanism 141–2, 144
Scopes trial 127–8
Scottish Enlightenment 56, 64
Sea of Faith network 149, 183
secularism 136–7, 189–91, 195
Sextus Empiricus 50–1
sexuality see homosexuality
Shakespeare, William 49–50, 52
sin, and Christian humanism 146–7
Singer, Peter 95, 105
slavery 169

Smith, Adam **56, 70–1**
Smoker, Barbara **143–4**
socialism **90–2**
  and Comte **83**
socialist humanism **90**
social market economics **92**
Socrates **xxii, 4, 9–12, 13, 14, 18, 20, 197**
  and existentialism **114**
  and Hume **70–1**
  and Renaissance humanism **51, 53**
Sophists **8–9, 18**
speech, freedom of speech, and
    blasphemy **173**
Stalin, Josef **78, 152, 153–4, 189**
Steiner, George **154**
Stoicism **16–17**
  and Shakespeare **50**
studia humanitatis **xv**
subjectivity
  and existentialism **108, 114**
  and the mind–body problem **177–8**
suicide, and Christian churches **180–1**
sympathy, ethics of **67–9, 78**

Taylor, Harriet **169**
teleology, and Darwinism **131, 134**
terrorism **145, 191**
Thales of Miletus **2–3, 4, 8, 18**
theological humanism, and Christian
    humanism **147–8**
theological stage, and positive philosophy
    82
Thinkers' Library **137**
torture **96**
totalitarianism **89, 176, 189**
transcendental idealism **73**
truth
  and existentialism **108**
  and pragmatism **103, 104**
Turner, Denys, 'How to be an Atheist' **186**
Twain, Mark **137**
Tyndale, William **48**

UNESCO **141**
United Nations Convention on the Rights
    of the Child **159**
United States, and Christianity **189,
    190–1**
Universal Declaration of Human Rights
    (1948) **81**
the universe
  and the anthropic principle **134**
  and the 'first cause' **138**
Urban III, Pope **41**

utilitarianism **92–8, 105, 108**
  and climate change **161, 163**
  contemporary **95**
  core elements of **97–8**
  critics of **96–7**
  and felicific calculus **93–4**
  and progress **174**
  rule utilitarianism **97**
Valla, Lorenzo **33, 34, 39**
values, and the naturalistic fallacy **132,
    133**
Vanini, Lucilio **41**
Vasari, Giorgio **41–2**
Virgil, *Opera* **36**
Voigt, George **xv**
Voltaire, François-Marie Arouet de **57,
    59–61, 62, 70, 72**
  Candide **61**
  and materialism **61**
  and Rousseau **64, 65**
  and science **116**

Walter, Nicolas **144**
Watts, Charles **137**
wealth, inequalities of **176**
weddings **179**
  registry office **180**
Wells, H.G. **137**
Whitehead, A.N. **9**
Whitehouse, Mary **172, 173**
Wilberforce, Bishop Samuel **135**
Wilberforce, William **169**
Wilde, Oscar **83, 91**
Williams, Bernard **97**
will to believe, and pragmatism **99–100**
women's rights, and Mill **93, 106, 169**
wonderment **183–6**

Zeno **6, 7**
Zola, Emile **83**